Famous Leaders among Men

Sarah Knowles Bolton

Famous Leaders among Men

ISBN: 978-1-64799-246-0

PREFACE

Napoleon said, "My maxim has always been, a career open to talent without distinction of birth." It will be seen in these pages that most of these men rose to leadership by their own efforts. Napoleon was poor, and often without employment in early life, but his industry, good judgment, will, and ambition carried him to the heights of power.

Nelson was the son of a minister, whose salary did not support his numerous family, but his boy had the energy and force that won success.

Bunyan, a travelling tinker, twelve years a prisoner in Bedford jail, could, while poor and in prison, write a book that is read more than any other in the world, save the Bible.

Arnold, through love for his work, and his untiring energy and good sense, became the ideal teacher.

Phillips and Beecher, both eloquent, the latter beginning his labors on a salary of $200 a year, were led into their great careers through a great motive,—their hatred of slavery.

Kingsley, the Christian socialist, knowing that the pulpit must help in the solution of the labor problem, lived and preached the brotherhood of man.

Sherman, the son of a widow, adopted by his father'sPg vi friend, had early failures, and won his place of distinction with Grant and Sheridan by his own ability.

Spurgeon, whose work was marvellous, was poor, and without a college education.

Phillips Brooks, whose death was an irreparable loss, made his way even more by his sincerity and unselfishness than by his eloquence.

Napoleon, who was especially fond of biography and history, was always eager to learn what qualities produced greatness or success. Perhaps some will find it interesting to trace in these pages what enabled these men to be leaders in various fields.

CONTENTS

Preface iii

Napoleon Bonaparte 1

Horatio Nelson 52

John Bunyan 73

Thomas Arnold 88

Wendell Phillips 103

Henry Ward Beecher 127

Charles Kingsley 153

General William Tecumseh Sherman 169

Charles Haddon Spurgeon 196

Phillips Brooks 216

NAPOLEON BONAPARTE

"The series of Napoleon's successes is absolutely the most marvellous in history. No one can question that he leaves far behind the Turennes, Marlboroughs, and Fredericks; but when we bring him up for comparison an Alexander, a Hannibal, a Cæsar, a Charles, we find in the single point of marvellousness Napoleon surpassing them all....

"Every one of those heroes was born to a position of exceptional advantage. Two of them inherited thrones; Hannibal inherited a position royal in all but the name; Cæsar inherited an eminent position in a great empire. But Napoleon, who rose as high as any of them, began life as an obscure provincial, almost as a man without a country. It is this marvellousness which paralyzes our judgment. We seem to see at once a genius beyond all estimate, a unique character, and a fortune utterly unaccountable."

Thus wrote John Robert Seeley, Professor of Modern History in the University of Cambridge, of the man whom he regarded as the greatest enemy England has ever known.

Napoleon has been more praised and villified, probably, than any man in history. Lanfrey, though careful as to facts, and Taine, are bitter, always ready to impute sinister motives. John S. C. Abbott is adulatory; Walter Scott cannot be impartial; and Bourrienne, the discarded private secretary, Madame de Rémusat, and the Duchess d'Abrantès, must be read with allowance for prejudice. Thiers, in his twenty volumes on "The Consulate and the Empire," gives a most valuable picture of the times, friendly to the great leader; John Codman Ropes's "First Napoleon" is able; and the life by William O'Connor Morris of Oxford is generally fair and interesting.

Napoleon Bonaparte was born at Ajaccio, in the Island of Corsica, Aug. 15, 1769. This date has been disputed by some authors, who claim that Napoleon was born Jan, 7, 1768. Colonel Jung, in "Bonaparte et son Temps," thinks the dates of birth of Napoleon and his brother Joseph were exchanged by the parents, who wished, in 1778, to send Napoleon to a military school at Brienne supported by the State, and he must needs be under ten years of age.

As Corsica became subject to France in June, 1769, some persons believe that Napoleon himself changed the date of his birth from 1768 to 1769, that he might appear to the French nation as a French subject; but the date, Aug. 15, 1769, is usually accepted as correct.

The Bonaparte family were originally from the nobility of Florence, where they had taken a somewhat prominent part in politics and literature. They had lost their fortune; and Charles Bonaparte, the father of Napoleon, earned his living by the law. He was an eloquent

1

man, and an adjutant under Pasquale Paoli, a patriot of Corsica. This island, in the fourteenth century, was under Genoa. When it gained its independence under Paoli, such rights as Genoa still possessed she sold to France. As a result, in 1769 a French army of twenty-two thousand subjugated the island, and Paoli fled to England, where he lived for twenty years.

Charles Bonaparte, at eighteen, married a girl not yet fifteen, Letizia Ramolini, descended from a noble family of Naples, a person of unusual beauty and strength of character. Although so young, she entered heartily into the warfare for Corsican independence, and shared the perils of her husband at the front.

Napoleon was the fourth of her thirteen children, the eldest, a son, and the second, a daughter, both dying young. He was born in the midst of war. He wrote Paoli, in 1789, when he was twenty years old, "I was born when my country was sinking; the cries of the dying, the groans of the oppressed, and the tears of despair surrounded my cradle from my birth."

The Duchess d'Abrantès tells this story of Napoleon's boyhood. When he was seven years old, being accused by one of his sisters of eating a basket of grapes and figs, although he denied the offence, he was whipped and kept on bread and cheese for three days.

On the fourth day a little friend of the family arrived at the home, and confessed that she and Napoleon's sister, Marianna (afterward Elisa) had eaten the fruit. The lad was asked why he had not accused his sister, and replied that he suspected that she was guilty, but said nothing out of consideration for the friend.

After the submission of Corsica to France in 1769, Count Marbœuf was appointed viceroy of the island. He became a friend of the Bonapartes; and Charles, the father, was made king's assessor to the Judicial Court for Ajaccio. Through Marbœuf's influence three of the Bonaparte children were placed in fine schools,—Joseph, Marianna, and Napoleon, the last at the military school of Brienne, near Paris. Here he remained for five years. He was a quiet, studious lad, devoted to Plutarch's Lives and Cæsar's Commentaries. He was always trying to find out what made certain men great. He was easily at the head of his class in mathematics. His industry and perseverance were astonishing.

"During play-hours," says Bourrienne, "he used to withdraw to the library, where he read works of history, particularly Polybius and Plutarch. I often went off to play with my comrades, and left him by himself in the library."

He was cold in manner, talked very little with his classmates, and felt keenly his poverty and the submission of his country to France.

Most of the boys at the school were rich, and they often ridiculed Napoleon and his country. And yet he bore them no ill-will; and, says Bourrienne, "when he had the supervision of any duty which they infringed, he would rather go to prison than denounce the criminals." During the winter of 1783-84, when the fall of snow was unusually heavy, Napoleon, then fourteen, suggested to his mates that they build a snow fort, "divide ourselves into sections, form a siege, and I will undertake to direct the attacks." This sham war was carried on with great enthusiasm for a fortnight.

Three of the best scholars were sent every year from each of the twelve provincial military schools of France to the Military College of Paris. Napoleon was one of the three sent from Brienne.

Here the young men lived so expensively that the youth of fifteen wrote a letter of protest to the Vice-Principal Berton of Brienne. He urged that, instead of so many attendants, and two-course dinners, they should wait upon themselves, clean their own boots, and eat the coarse bread made for soldiers. Temperance and activity would fit them, he said, for the hardships of war.

Napoleon won the admiration of his teachers. The professor in history, M. de l'Eguille, said: "A Corsican by birth and character, he will do something great if circumstances favor him."

After a year at this school, he was made second lieutenant of artillery in the regiment of La Fère, in 1785. The next five years he passed at different military stations in France. He was always studying. He pored over maps and plans of fortresses. He read with avidity books on law, philosophy, theology, political economy, and various forms of government. He wrote an essay on the question, "What are the institutions most likely to contribute to human happiness?" He also wrote a history of Corsica and her wrongs.

Abbott relates that on a day of public festivity at Marseilles, Napoleon was criticised because he did not join in the amusements. He replied, "It is not by playing and dancing that a man is to be formed."

At Auxonne, Napoleon and some other officers boarded with a plain barber. The wife of the barber did not like the taciturn young Napoleon, who stayed in his room and devoured his books, while the other officers pleased her from their social ways, and enjoyment of the gossip of the town.

Years after, Napoleon, who had won several victories, passed that way. He asked the barber's wife if she remembered an officer by the name of Bonaparte in her home. "Indeed I do," was the reply, "and a very disagreeable inmate he was. He was always either shut up in his room, or, if he walked out, he never condescended to speak to any one."

"Ah, my good woman," said Napoleon, "had I passed my time as you wished to have me, I should not now have been in command of the army of Italy."

Napoleon was at this time very slight in physique, five feet six and a half inches tall, with a very large head, pale face, piercing eyes of grayish blue, brown hair, a smile that could be sweet and captivating, and beautiful hands.

3

In 1791, when he was twenty-two years old, Napoleon, now first lieutenant, visited Corsica on furlough. Remaining too long, his name was struck off the army lists. He returned to Paris, and anxiously looked about for some way to earn a living. He met his schoolmate, Bourrienne, who usually paid for any meal they took together at a restaurant, as, although poor, he was richer than Napoleon. Each day they had projects for earning money. They found some houses building, and desired to rent them, and then underlet them, but the owners asked too much to realize any profit. Napoleon solicited employment at the war office. "Everything failed," says Bourrienne.

Bonaparte's mother, left a widow with eight children in 1785, was, of course, powerless to help Napoleon. Her husband had gone on business to Montpellier in the south of France, and died of a cancerous ulcer in the stomach in the thirty-ninth year of his age. His wife was only thirty-five. Madame Bonaparte was possessed of wonderful energy, great strength of will, and excellent judgment. These her son Napoleon inherited in a marked degree.

She proved equal to the care of her fatherless children. "She managed everything," said Napoleon, "provided for everything with a prudence which could neither have been expected from her sex nor from her age. Ah, what a woman! Where shall we look for her equal? She watched over us with a solicitude unexampled. Every low sentiment, every ungenerous affection, was discouraged and discarded. She suffered nothing but that which was grand and elevated to take root in our youthful understandings. She abhorred falsehood, and would not tolerate the slightest act of disobedience. None of our faults were overlooked. Losses, privations, fatigue, had no effect upon her. She endured all, braved all. She had the energy of a man, combined with the gentleness and delicacy of a woman."

When Bonaparte was waiting in Paris for some position to open, the French Revolution had begun. On June 20, 1792, a ragged mob of five or six thousand men surrounded the Tuileries, put a red cap on the head of Louis XVI., and made him show himself at the windows to the crowd in the garden. Napoleon was indignant, and said to Bourrienne, "Why have they let in all that rabble? They should sweep off four or five hundred of them with the cannon; the rest would then set off fast enough."

Napoleon also witnessed the storming of the Tuileries on Aug. 10, when the Swiss guards were massacred. Although a Republican in sentiment, he had no sympathy with the extreme democracy of the Jacobins, and said: "If I were compelled to choose between the old monarchy and Jacobin misrule, I should infinitely prefer the former."

Years later, when Napoleon was Emperor, when asked to allow a person to return to France who had been prominent in the downfall of the Bourbon dynasty, he said, "Let him know that I am not powerful

4

enough to protect the wretches who voted for the death of Louis XVI. from the contempt and indignation of the public."

Corsica and Paoli (who had returned and become her governor) were shocked at the excesses of the French Revolution, and hoped and planned once more for independence. Finding themselves unable to achieve it alone, they sought the aid of England. Bonaparte and his family favored adherence to France, and were banished from the island, their home plundered, and they made their escape at midnight to Marseilles. Here they were for some time in extreme poverty. Joseph, the eldest son, found employment as a clerk in an office, and in August, 1794, married Julia Clari, the daughter of one of the richest merchants of Marseilles. This was a great pecuniary benefit to the whole family.

Napoleon had finally been reinstated in the army; for with the Reign of Terror at home, and wars with monarchies abroad, all fearful of the growth of republican sentiments and consequent revolutions, the French army was in need of all its able young men.

Napoleon's first important work was at the siege of Toulon. This was the great naval depot and arsenal of France. The Royalists, or followers of the Bourbon king, Louis XVI., had centred here, and, opposed to the republic, had surrendered the city, with its forts and ships, to England.

The place must be retaken; and the Republic sent out an army under Carteaux, a portrait painter. For some months the siege was carried on, but almost nothing was accomplished. Sixty thousand men were needed, and Carteaux had but twenty-five thousand.

Napoleon, on his way from Avignon to Nice, passed through Toulon, stopping to see a friend who introduced him to Carteaux. The young officer saw at once the mistakes of the campaign. "Instead of attacking the town," said Napoleon, "try and establish batteries which shall sweep the harbor and the roadstead. If you can only drive away the ships, the troops will not remain."

Cape l'Eguillette separates the two harbors, and here batteries were placed to sweep the sea; for Napoleon had said, putting his finger on the map, at the cape, "Toulon is there!"

As he predicted, the English ships were driven off after a terrible bombardment; fifteen thousand of the inhabitants of Toulon in dismay fled to the ships of the allies; the plan of Napoleon had proved a great success.

He was not responsible for the horrors which followed. The Royalists set fire to the arsenal and ships before their departure; while the town was in flames, cannon from the shore sunk boat-loads of fugitives, and hundreds in the city who could not escape were deliberately shot in the streets and in their homes, so desperate had become the hate between Royalists and Republicans, or really Jacobins.

Fouché, afterwards prominent under the Empire, wrote to a friend, Dec. 23: "We have only one way of celebrating victory. This evening we shoot two hundred and thirteen rebels. Adieu, my friend; tears of joy run down my cheeks, and my heart is overflowing."

"It was," says Walter Scott, concerning this taking of Toulon, Dec. 17, 1793, "upon this night of terror, conflagration, tears, and blood, that the star of Napoleon first ascended the horizon; and, though it gleamed over many a scene of horror ere it set, it may be doubted whether its light was ever blended with that of one more dreadful."

For this brilliant undertaking Napoleon was made General of Artillery. General Dugommier, who commanded at Toulon, said, "Promote this young officer, or he will promote himself." Napoleon was wounded in his thigh by a bayonet thrust in one of the charges. He was at this time but twenty-four years of age, poor, ambitious, and with little prospect of his future wonderful career.

He was sent to defend the coast of Provence, and was denounced by the Jacobins, who said he was building a bastile at Marseilles to enslave the people. In March, 1794, he rejoined the army of Italy at Nice, and was so useful that the commander-in-chief wrote: "I am indebted to the comprehensive talents of General Bonaparte for the plans which have insured our victory."

In July, 1794, he was sent on a mission to Genoa, to examine the fortresses and the neighboring country. Meantime, one set of French leaders had been superseded by a set equally bad. Through jealousy, and as a friend of the younger Robespierre, Napoleon was arrested as a "suspected person," was two weeks in prison, and nearly lost his life. He seems to have been spared for the selfish reason, "the possible utility of the military and local knowledge of the said Bonaparte." He addressed an eloquent letter to his accusers, quoted by Lanfrey, in which he says: "Remove the oppression which surrounds me; give me back the esteem of patriots. An hour afterwards, if bad men wish for my life, I care so little for it, I have so often counted it for nothing.... Yes, nothing but the idea that it may be of use to the country gives me courage to bear its weight."

Soon after this, to scatter such officers as himself, who were supposed to be Jacobin in tendency, Napoleon was ordered to La Vendée to put down civil dissensions. He rebelled against being separated from the army of Italy. "You are too young," said Aubrey, the Girondist deputy, "to be commander-in-chief of artillery."

"Men age fast on a field of battle," said Napoleon, "and I am no exception."

For refusing to proceed to his post, Napoleon's name was struck off the army lists, and again he was in Paris, out of employment. When he and Bourrienne took a stroll at evening on the Boulevards, and saw the rich young men on horseback, apparently living a life of ease and luxury, "dandies with their whiskers," says Madame Junot (Duchess

6

d'Abrantès), Napoleon would exclaim bitterly, "And it is on such beings as these that Fortune confers her favors. How contemptible is human nature!"

He told Count Montholon, when in exile at St. Helena, that at this time he came near committing suicide by throwing himself into the river. With head down, and meditating upon his determination, he ran against a plainly dressed man, who proved to be Démasis, a former comrade in the artillery.

"What is the matter?" he said to Napoleon. "You do not listen to me! You do not seem glad to see me! What misfortune threatens you? You look to me like a madman about to kill himself."

Napoleon told him his needs, and his mother's poverty. "Is that all?" said Démasis. "Here are six thousand dollars in gold, which I can spare without any inconvenience. Take them, and relieve your mother."

Hardly aware of what he was doing, Napoleon grasped the money, and sent it to his mother. Afterwards he could find nothing of Démasis. Fifteen years later, when the Empire was near its fall, Napoleon met him, made him accept sixty thousand dollars to repay the loan of six thousand, and appointed him director-general of the crown gardens, at a salary of six thousand dollars a year, and the honors of an officer in the household. He also provided a good situation for Démasis' brother.

He never forgot a kindness. A humble shoemaker, who worked for him in these days of poverty, and waited for his pay, was always employed by Napoleon after he became Emperor, though he was urged to go to some one more fashionable. A jeweller, who once trusted him, was remembered in Napoleon's days of prosperity, and thus made his fortune. To a lady, a stranger to him, who once was kind to him in sickness in these early years, he sent two thousand dollars, hearing that her circumstances had changed. To an old man in Jersey, who had once loaned his father twenty-five louis, he sent ten times that sum.

Reverses began to attend the army of Italy. Whenever it was convenient to use his services, it seemed always to be remembered that he had knowledge and sagacity. Napoleon was asked by the director of military affairs to draw up a plan of operations for the army. It was sent to Kellermann, commander-in-chief of the army of Italy, who rejected it, saying, "The author is a fit inmate for a lunatic asylum." Lanfrey and other historians consider the plan altogether brilliant and admirable.

Napoleon, by years of study, had made himself a master in the science of war, as well as along other lines. He had made himself ready for a great opportunity, and a great opportunity came to him.

France, in her struggle for self-government, had adopted a new constitution, under a Directory of five persons, with a Council of two hundred and fifty Ancients, and a Council of Five Hundred, somewhat like our House of Representatives. The new government, though acceptable to the provinces, did not please either the Royalists or

Jacobins of Paris, and the people, now so used to bloodshed, resorted to force to destroy the Directory.

Barras, one of the Directors, who knew Napoleon, immediately thought of him as a young man who could quell a mob. "It is that little Corsican officer," he said, "who will not stand upon ceremony!" The Directory had but about eight thousand soldiers; the National Guard numbered forty thousand. Napoleon spent the whole night in turning the Louvre and the Tuileries into a sort of camp, with artillery posted at all the outlets. He armed all the members of the government, that they might defend themselves if the necessity arose, and he took care to leave a way of retreat open to St. Cloud.

The National Guards appeared on the morning of Oct. 5, 1795 (13th Vendémiaire, as the month was called by the Revolutionary Calendar), in front of Napoleon's troops. All day the two armies were within fifteen paces of each other. At four o'clock in the afternoon, General Danican of the National Guards gave the signal for attack. Napoleon mounted his horse, and the fight began at several places.

The cannon swept them down at every point. At six o'clock the battle was over, and order was restored in Paris. About eighty only were killed, and three or four hundred wounded, as the guns were loaded with powder after two discharges. Napoleon was, as he deserved to be, the hero of the hour. With the utmost self-possession, with a clear brain and never-failing courage, he had been equal to the emergency.

Napoleon was made General of the Interior, with the command of Paris. The days of poverty were over. He found places for several of his family, and was much sought after by those in high position. He was especially good to the poor, and the Duchess d'Abrantès tells how he climbed to attics and went down into cellars to feed the hungry. As he was stepping out of his carriage one day at the home of the Duchess, a woman held her dead child before him. It had died from want. She had come to ask him to save her other children. "If nobody will give me anything," she said, "I must even take them all five and drown myself with them." Napoleon remembered how near he had been to drowning himself only a little time before. He obtained the wages due to her husband, who had been killed while at work on the roof of the Tuileries, and a pension was granted her.

Soon after this an attractive boy about fourteen years of age came to Napoleon and asked for the sword of his father, who was a general of the Republic, and had been put to death by the Jacobins, because he was a Girondist, or moderate Republican.

"I was so touched by this affectionate request," said Napoleon, "that I ordered it to be given to him. This boy was Eugène Beauharnais. On seeing the sword he burst into tears. I felt so affected by his conduct, that I noticed and praised him much. A few days afterwards his mother came to return me a visit of thanks. I was struck with her appearance, and still more with her esprit."

The young general of twenty-six became thoroughly in love with the graceful and lovable widow of thirty-two. Josephine Tascher, the only child of French parents, had been born in the Island of Martinique, Jan. 24, 1763. She was married when sixteen to Viscount de Beauharnais, a major in the army, who introduced her to the court of Marie Antoinette, but who, with all his wealth and position, did not make her life a happy one. After four years of marriage and the birth of two children, Hortense and Eugène, to whom she was most tenderly attached, she and Beauharnais separated, and she returned to Martinique, but at his persistent request she came back to him after three years.

On his imprisonment during the Reign of Terror she attempted to save him and was thrown into prison, where she narrowly escaped the guillotine. He was beheaded July 23, 1794.

"Josephine," says Meneval, the secretary of Napoleon after Bourrienne, "was irresistibly attractive.... Her temper was always the same. She was gentle and kind, affable and indulgent with every one, without difference of persons. She had neither a superior mind nor much learning; but her exquisite politeness, her full acquaintance with society, with the court, and with their innocent artifices, made her always know the best things to say or do."

Napoleon found at the home of Madame de Beauharnais the most noted persons in Paris, and, what was more important for his happiness, the one woman whom he ever after loved.

Years later he said, "Josephine was truly a most lovely woman, refined, affable, and charming.... She was so kind, so humane—she was the most graceful lady and the best woman in France. I never saw her act inelegantly during the whole time we lived together. She possessed a perfect knowledge of the different shades of my character, and evinced the most exquisite tact in turning this knowledge to the best account....

"I was the object of her deepest attachment. If I went into my carriage at midnight for a long journey, there, to my surprise, I found her, seated before me and awaiting my arrival. If I attempted to dissuade her from accompanying me, she had so many good and affectionate reasons to urge, that it was almost always necessary to yield. In a word, she always proved to me a happy and affectionate wife, and I have preserved the tenderest recollections of her."

Barras, the ardent friend of Josephine, urged her marriage with Napoleon, and her children favored it. She admired him, but hesitated. She wrote a friend, "Barras assures me that if I marry the general, he will obtain for him the appointment of commander-in-chief of the army of Italy. Yesterday Bonaparte, speaking to me of this favor, which has already caused some jealousy among his companions in arms, although it is not yet granted, said, 'Do they think I need patronage to insure my success? Some day they will be only too happy if I grant them mine. My sword is at my side, and that will carry me a long way.'"

They were married March 9, 1796, Napoleon having been appointed to the command of the army of Italy on the preceding 23d of February. He remained in Paris but a few days, and then hastened to his army, reaching Nice towards the last of March.

He found an army of about thirty thousand men, "without pay, without provisions, without shoes," opposed to about twice their number of Austrians and Sardinians. He issued an address to them: "Soldiers, you are poorly fed and half-naked. The government owes you much, but can do nothing for you. Your patience, your courage, do you honor, but they bring you no advantage, no glory. I am about to lead you into the most fertile plains in the world; there you will find larger cities and rich provinces; there you will find honor, glory, and wealth. Soldiers of Italy, shall you lack courage?"

His soldiers, who till his death idolized him and would die for him, were soon to prove on scores of battle-fields that they never lacked courage.

This slight, boyish-looking general of twenty-six said to his veteran officers, "We must hurl ourselves on the foe like a thunderbolt, and smite like it."

And this was done. The first battle was on April 12, at Montenotte. The Austrians were routed, leaving their colors and cannon with the French, and three thousand dead and wounded. Napoleon afterwards said to the Emperor of Austria, "My title of nobility dates from the battle of Montenotte."

The battles of Millesimo and Mondovi quickly followed. On the heights of Monte Zemolo, Napoleon looked out upon the fertile plains of Italy, and exclaimed, "Hannibal crossed the Alps, but we have turned them!"

Then he addressed his enthusiastic soldiers: "In fifteen days," he said, "you have won six victories; captured twenty-one flags, fifty cannon, many fortified places; conquered the richest part of Piedmont; you have captured fifteen thousand prisoners, and killed and wounded ten thousand men. You lacked everything; you have gained battles without cannon; crossed rivers without bridges; made forced marches without shoes; often bivouacked without bread; the Republican phalanxes were alone capable of such extraordinary deeds. Soldiers, receive your due of thanks!"

Murat, his aide-de-camp, who afterwards married Napoleon's sister Caroline, and became King of Naples, was sent to Paris with the armistice proposed by the King of Sardinia, and Junot with the flags, which caused the greatest rejoicing. Fêtes were celebrated at the Champ de Mars, and Napoleon's name was honored as the conqueror of Italy.

Napoleon writes to his bride: "Your letters are the delight of my days, and my happy days are not very many. Junot is carrying twenty-two flags to Paris. You must come back with him; do you understand? It would be hopeless misery, an inconsolable grief, continual agony, if I should have the misfortune of seeing him come back alone, my adorable one.... You will be here, by my side, on my heart, in my arms! Take wings, come, come! But travel slowly; the way is long, bad, and tiresome."

Almost daily he writes to his wife: "My only Josephine, away from you, there is no happiness; away from you, the world is a desert, in which I stand alone, with no chance of tasting the delicious joy of pouring out my heart. You have robbed me of more than my soul; you are the sole thought of my life. If I am worn out by all the torment of events, and fear the issue; if men disgust me; if I am ready to curse life, I place my hand on my heart,—your image is beating there."

She is not well, and does not come to him, and again he writes: "My dear, do remember to tell me that you are certain that I love you more than can be imagined; ... that no hour passes that I do not think of you; that it has never entered my mind to think of any other woman; ... that you, as I see you, as you are, can please me and absorb my whole soul; that you have wholly filled it; that my heart has no corner that you do not see, no thoughts that are not subordinate to you; that my strength, my arms, my intelligence, are all yours; ... and that the day when you shall have changed, or shall have ceased to live, will be the day of my death; that nature, the earth, is beautiful, in my eyes, only because you live on it."

General Marmont says in his memoirs: "Bonaparte, however occupied he may have been with his greatness, the interests intrusted to him, and with his future, had, nevertheless, time to devote to feelings of another sort; he was continually thinking of his wife.... He often spoke to me of her, and of his love, with all the frankness, fire, and illusion of a very young man.... During a trip we made together at this time, to inspect the places in Piedmont that had fallen into our hands, one morning, at Tortona, the glass in front of his wife's portrait, which he always carried with him, broke in his hands. He grew frightfully pale, and suffered the keenest alarm."

Again he says, "Never did a purer, truer, or more exclusive love fill a man's heart, or the heart of so extraordinary a man."

Lanfrey says, "In this love, which has been said to be the only one that touched his heart, all the fire and flame of his masterful nature showed itself."

Napoleon pushed on his troops to conquer the Austrian Beaulieu, crossed the river Po at Piacenza, and overtook the enemy at the town of Lodi on the Adda River. The town was taken by the French; nut, to cross the Adda and reach Beaulieu, it was necessary to storm a narrow wooden bridge, which was defended by artillery and by from twelve to sixteen thousand Austrians. Napoleon immediately placed a battery on his own side of the river, sent a detachment of cavalry to ford the river and attack the enemy's rear, and then, at the head of several thousand men, bade them force a passage across the bridge.

The French were mowed down by the Austrian cannon. They wavered, when Napoleon seized a standard, and, with Lannes and one or two other officers, rushed among the troops and inspired them to gain a complete victory. Lannes was the first to cross the bridge and reach the Austrian gunners, who were sabred at their guns, and Napoleon the second. Lannes was promoted on the spot for his valor. So proud were the troops that their general should fight in the ranks, that they ever after called him their "Little Corporal." The conflict was a bloody one. The Austrian loss was much heavier than the French.

Napoleon said, "It was not till after the terrible passage of the bridge of Lodi that the idea shot across my mind that I might become a decisive actor in the political arena. Then arose, for the first time, the spark of great ambition."

He said to his aide-de-camp, Marmont, "In our time, no one has devised anything great; I must set an example."

On May 15, 1796, Napoleon entered Milan in triumph. The people hated the rule of Austria, and hoped for liberty under the French Republic. A triumphal arch was erected in the city, and flowers were scattered in the path of the French. To his soldiers, "who had rushed," he said, "like a torrent from the height of the Apennines," Napoleon gave all the glory.

In accordance with the wishes of the Directory in France, he levied twenty million francs on Milan, and took some of her best art works to Paris. The army was supported by the countries through which it passed, as was Sherman's in our Civil War.

Late in June, Josephine reached Milan, and for a brief period they were happy; but Napoleon was obliged very soon to be at the front. The war now centred about Mantua, which was strongly fortified. Seven or eight thousand French troops were besieging it, when it was ascertained that Würmser, the Austrian general, was marching against the French with seventy thousand men, in three armies, while Napoleon had but about forty-five thousand.

At once the siege of Mantua was raised, the gun-carriages burned, the powder thrown into the river, the cannon spiked, and the French forces were led against Würmser.

Napoleon, with his usual celerity and tact,—he used to say, "War, like government, is mainly decided by tact,"—managed to defeat each of the three Austrian armies in turn.

At Lonato the Austrians lost ten thousand in killed, wounded, and prisoners. The day after the battle, one of the Austrian divisions, reduced to four thousand men, wandered into Lonato, and demanded the surrender of the garrison of twelve hundred. Napoleon called his

12

staff together; and when the bandage was removed from the eyes of the officer, he said with authority, "Go and tell your general that I give him eight minutes to lay down his arms!" The Austrians surrendered, and were soon chagrined to find that four thousand had succumbed to twelve hundred Frenchmen.

Napoleon said at Lonato, "I was at ease; the Thirty-second was there!" So rejoiced were the men at these words that they had them embroidered on their regimental flag.

In this short campaign twenty thousand Austrians had been killed and wounded, fifteen thousand taken prisoners, with seventy pieces of artillery, and twenty-two stands of colors. The latter were sent to Paris.

Early in September, Napoleon again defeated Würmser at Bassano. After the battle, at midnight Napoleon rode over the battle-field by moonlight, the quiet broken only by the moans of the wounded and dying. Suddenly a dog sprang from beneath the cloak of his dead master, rushed to Napoleon as though asking aid, and then back to the body, licking the face and hands of the dead, and howling piteously.

Napoleon was strongly moved, and said years afterward, "I know not how it was, but no incident upon any field of battle ever produced so deep an impression upon my feelings. 'This man,' thought I, 'must have had among his comrades friends, and yet here he lies forsaken by all except his faithful dog.' ... Certainly, in that moment, I should have been unable to refuse any request to a suppliant enemy."

When at St. Helena, Madame Montholon, seeming to be afraid of a dog, Napoleon said, "He who does not love a dog has never known what real fidelity means."

Austria soon put another general in the field with over sixty thousand men. She was determined not to lose Italy. At first the French army lost some battles, the general-in-chief not being with them. When he came to his army, he said to some regiments, "Soldiers, I am not satisfied with you. You have shown neither discipline, constancy, nor courage.... Let it be written on the colors, 'They are not of the army of Italy.'"

The men seemed heart-broken. "Place us in the van of the army," they said, "and you shall then judge whether we do not belong to the army of Italy."

They were soon put to the test. Napoleon marched out of Verona on the night of Nov. 14, descended the Adige river, and fell upon the rear of Alvinzi, the Austrian general, at Arcola. The village is surrounded by marshes, crossed by causeways or bridges.

When the French rushed upon the bridges, they were repulsed by the guns of the Austrians. Napoleon sprang from his horse, seized a standard, and shouted, "Follow your general!" but he was borne by the struggling soldiers off the bridge into the marsh.

Frenzied at the probable loss of their general, the French fought desperately. Muiron, who had saved Napoleon at Toulon when he was wounded in the thigh, covered his general with his own body, and received his death wound from a shell. Lannes received three wounds in endeavoring to protect Napoleon, who was finally extricated, and was again at the head of the column. After three days of battle, the French were victorious. It is estimated that twenty thousand men perished in the swamps of Arcola.

Napoleon wrote a letter of sympathy to the young widow of Muiron, who in a few weeks died at the birth of a lifeless child.

To the Directory he wrote: "Never was a field of battle more valiantly disputed than the conflict at Arcola. I have scarcely any generals left. Their bravery and their patriotic enthusiasm are without example."

In the midst of this toil and carnage, Napoleon could find time to write to Josephine. She had followed him for a while after coming to Milan, but her dangers were so great that it was soon found to be impossible.

After Arcola he writes her: "At length, my adored Josephine, I live again. Death is no longer before me, and glory and honor are still in my breast.... Soon Mantua will be ours, and then thy husband will fold thee in his arms, and give thee a thousand proofs of his ardent affection. I shall proceed to Milan as soon as I can; I am a little fatigued. I have received letters from Eugène and Hortense. I am delighted with the children.... Adieu, my adorable Josephine. Think of me often. Death alone can break the union which sympathy, love, and sentiment have formed. Let me have news of your health. A thousand and a thousand kisses."

If she does not write often he is distressed; "Three days without a word from you," he writes, "and I have written you several times. This absence is horrible; the nights are long, tiresome, dull; the days are monotonous.... I don't really live away from you; my life's happiness is only to be with my sweet Josephine. Think of me! write to me often, very often; it is the only balm in absence which is cruel, but I hope will be short.... Day before yesterday I was in the field all day. Yesterday I stayed in bed. A fever and a raging headache prevented me from writing to my dear one; but I received her letters. I pressed them to my heart and my lips; and the pang of absence, a hundred miles apart, vanished."

Yet, with all this intensity of feeling, Napoleon had wonderful self-command. He said, "Nature seems to have calculated that I should endure great reverses. She has given me a mind of marble. Thunder cannot ruffle it. The shaft merely glides along."

Austria made another desperate effort to overcome Napoleon and save Würmser, shut up in Mantua. At four o'clock in the morning, Jan. 14, 1797, the battle of Rivoli began. For twelve hours Napoleon was in the hottest of the fight. Three horses were shot under him.

After a desperate but victorious battle, the troops marched all night, conquered Provera before Mantua the next day, and La Favorita on the third day. The Austrian army had lost thirty thousand men in three days, of whom twenty thousand were taken prisoners. Napoleon, in his report of the battle of Favorita, spoke of the terrible Fifty-seventh. Thereafter the Fifty-seventh adopted the name of "The Terrible," proud of this distinction of their chief.

Massena's men had marched and fought incessantly for four days and nights. No wonder the Austrians said, "The French do not march, they fly." Napoleon wrote, "The Roman legions used to make twenty-four miles a day; our men make thirty, and fight in the intervals." ...

Würmser surrendered Mantua Feb. 3, 1797. Twenty-seven thousand men had died of wounds or sickness since the commencement of the siege. The horses had all been eaten, and the city could sustain itself no longer. Würmser had declared that he could hold out for a year. But Napoleon knew that so brave a marshal as Würmser would not surrender unless reduced to the last extremity.

He therefore allowed Würmser to retire with all his staff and two thousand cavalry. He surrendered to France eighteen thousand prisoners. Würmser wished to salute the young conqueror of twenty-seven; but Napoleon had gone to Bologna, not liking to subject the marshal of seventy to humiliation. Lanfrey thinks this was done for effect, but there seems no good reason for always imputing bad motives to Napoleon. A man so worshipped by his soldiers, and, indeed, by the nation, had much that was noble and refined in his nature.

Würmser, out of gratitude to Napoleon, saved his life at Bologna, by making known to him a plot to poison him.

Napoleon now turned his attention towards the Papal States. The Pope had no love for the "godless Republic." Thousands of priests had fled from France to Rome. Austria and Rome were closely allied, and both ready to sustain war against France whenever an opportunity offered.

The Directory had written to Napoleon "that the Roman Catholic religion would always be the irreconcilable enemy of the Republic," but Napoleon bore no ill-will towards his mother's faith and the faith in which he himself died.

He issued a proclamation in which he said, "The French soldier carries in one hand the bayonet, the guaranty of victory, and in the other an olive branch, the symbol of peace and pledge of his protection."

When within three days' march of Rome, the Pope sued for peace, and the treaty of Tolentino was signed Feb. 19, 1797.

Napoleon writes to Josephine on the same day: "Peace has just been signed with Rome. Bologna, Ferrara, the Romagna, are ceded to the Republic. The Pope gives us shortly thirty million francs and many works of art....

15

"My dear, I beg of you think of me often, and write me every day.... You, to whom nature has given intelligence, gentleness, and beauty, you, who rule alone over my heart, you, who doubtless know only too well the absolute power you exercise over my heart, write to me, think of me, and love me. Ever yours."

Austria was not yet humbled. Napoleon determined to march against Vienna. The young Archduke Charles, brother of the ruler of Austria, was in command of the Austrian army. "He is a man," said Napoleon, "whose conduct can never attract blame.... More than all, he is a good man, and that includes everything when said of a prince."

Charles had beaten Napoleon's generals on the Rhine, but he could not beat the "Little Corporal." His fifty thousand men melted away as they fled, wounded and distracted, over the Alps.

When within sight of Vienna, Napoleon proposed peace; and Austria, tired of war for a time at least, accepted the conditions.

Early in May, France declared war against the Venetian Republic. The latter had been neutral, although both Austrians and French had crossed her territory. Her aristocracy had no sympathy with the French Republic, and preferred Austria. Perhaps to guard herself from both nations, she raised an army of sixty thousand men, and put herself in the attitude of armed neutrality. She refused to ally herself to France. "Be neutral, then," said Napoleon; "but remember, if you violate your neutrality, if you harass my troops, if you cut off my supplies, I will take ample vengeance.... The hour that witnesses the treachery of Venice shall terminate her independence."

Whether or not her government desired to keep the peace, insurrections arose among the people in Verona and elsewhere, French soldiers were killed, Napoleon took "ample vengeance," and in the treaty of Campo Formio, Oct. 17, 1797, Venice was handed over to Austria. The Republic ceased to exist. In taking the hated oath of allegiance to Austria, the ex-Doge of Venice became insensible, and died soon after.

Napoleon now returned to Milan, and for a time lived in peace and happiness at the Serbelloni Palace. Josephine won every heart by her grace and her kindness. Napoleon said, "I conquer provinces, but Josephine wins hearts."

Madame de Rémusat wrote: "Love seemed to come every day to place at her feet a new conquest over a people entranced with its conqueror."

The people waited to see Napoleon pass in and out of his palace. They did him honor as though he were a king. He had sent for his mother, his brothers Joseph and Louis, and his beautiful sister Pauline, sixteen years of age, of whom Arnault, the poet, said, "if she was the prettiest person in the world, she was also the most frivolous."

Imbert de Saint-Amand, in his "Citizeness Bonaparte," quotes this incident to show Josephine's power over her husband. "He was absolutely faithful to her," says Saint-Amand, "and this at a time when there was not a beauty in Milan who was not setting her cap for him."

Josephine owned a pug dog, Fortuné, which, when she was imprisoned in the Reign of Terror, was brought to her cell with a letter concealed in his collar. Ever since she had been extremely fond of him. They were all at the Castle of Montebello, a few leagues from Milan, during the warm weather. "You see that fellow there?" said Napoleon to Arnault, pointing to the dog who lay on the sofa beside his mistress, "he is my rival. When I married I wanted to put him out of my wife's room, but I was given to understand that I might go away myself or share it with him. I was annoyed; but it was to take or to leave, and I yielded. The favorite was not so accommodating, and he left his mark on my leg."

Fortuné barked at everything, and used to bite other dogs. The cook's dog, a mastiff, returned the bite one day, and killed Fortuné. Josephine was in despair; but the mischief was done, and there was no help for it.

Nov. 17 Napoleon left Milan, and, after a continued ovation along the route, reached Paris Dec. 5, where, a change having taken place in the government, he thought it wise to be for a time. Though the Directory was jealous of the rising power of Napoleon, the people demanded a magnificent reception for him, which was prepared in the Luxembourg.

Napoleon made an address which was eagerly listened to, and the people were wild with enthusiasm. Thiers says, "All heads were overcome with the intoxication." Talleyrand gave a great ball costing over twelve thousand francs. Bourrienne, his secretary, remarked that it must be agreeable to "see his fellow-citizens so eagerly running after him."

"Bah! the people would crowd as fast to see me if I were going to the scaffold," was Napoleon's reply. So well did he understand human nature.

He said to Bourrienne, "Were I to remain in Paris long, doing nothing, I should be lost. In this great Babylon one reputation displaces another. Let me be seen but three times at the theatre and I shall no longer excite attention; so I shall go there but seldom."

Napoleon was made a member of the Institute, in the class of the Sciences and Arts. This honor he greatly valued, writing to the president of the class, "I feel well assured that, before I can be their equal, I must long be their scholar.... True conquests—the only ones which leave no regret behind them—are those which are made over ignorance. The most honorable, as well as the most useful, occupation for nations is the contributing to the extension of human knowledge."

"He had," says Bourrienne, "an extreme aversion to mediocrity," or to people who are too indolent to read and improve themselves.

"Mankind," he said, "are, in the end, always governed by superiority of intellectual qualities."

The Directory were anxious for an attack upon England, which had joined the Coalition against France in 1793, and was her most formidable enemy. "Go there," said Barras, "and capture the giant Corsair that infests the seas; go punish in London outrages that have too long gone unpunished."

Arnault said to Napoleon, "The Directory wishes to get you away; France wishes to keep you."

"I am perfectly willing to make a tour of the coast," said Napoleon to Bourrienne. "Should the expedition to Britain prove too hazardous, as I much fear that it will, the army of England will become the army of the East, and we will go to Egypt." He spent a week in looking over the ground, and said, "I will not hazard it. I would not thus sport with the fate of France."

He determined to colonize Egypt. He would take with him men of science, artists, and artisans. He said to Montholon at St. Helena, "Were the French once established in Egypt, it would be impossible for the English to maintain themselves long in India. Squadrons constructed on the shores of the Red Sea, provisioned with the products of the country, and equipped and manned by the French troops stationed in Egypt, would infallibly make us masters of India, and at a moment when England least expected it."

The fleet set sail from Toulon May 19, 1798, with forty thousand men besides ten thousand sailors. Josephine came to Toulon to say good-by, and wished to go with her husband, but this would have been most unwise.

The fleet arrived off Malta June 10, which, with almost no opposition, surrendered to the French its twelve hundred pieces of cannon, its ten thousand pounds of powder, its ships, and its forty thousand muskets.

On June 30 the fleet appeared before Alexandria, which was soon captured. Then the army set out to cross the desert towards Cairo.

The heat was intense, they suffered for lack of water, and murmured at the Directory. Napoleon bivouacked in their midst, and dined on lentils.

On July 21 they came in sight of the Pyramids. The whole army halted. "Soldiers," said Napoleon, "from the summit of those pyramids forty centuries look down upon you!"

Before them lay the intrenched camp of Embabeh, with ten thousand Mameluke horsemen under Mourad Bey. These charged upon the immovable squares of the French only to be cut to pieces by bayonets.

They fought desperately, but were routed, and many of them driven into the Nile. Over two thousand perished, while the French did not lose over one hundred and fifty in killed and wounded. "The banks of the Nile," says Bourrienne, "were strewed with heaps of bodies, which the waves were every moment washing into the sea." The soldiers bent their bayonets into hooks, and for days fished up the bodies of the Mamelukes, on each of which they found from five to six hundred louis in gold.

Ten days after this battle of the Pyramids, the French fleet was destroyed by Nelson in the terrible battle of the Nile. Admiral Brueys was killed, and the bodies of his men seemed to fill the Bay of Aboukir.

Napoleon was virtually a prisoner in Egypt. The blow was irreparable. The army was despondent, but Napoleon was calm. "Unfortunate Brueys," he said, "what have you done!"

It was evident that he must organize Egypt as soon as possible. He established in Cairo an Institute of Arts and Sciences, he built factories, and he planned two canals, one uniting the Red Sea with the Mediterranean across the Isthmus of Suez, and the other connecting the Red Sea with the Nile at Cairo.

Meantime France was threatened with war on every side. Russia and Turkey had joined hands with England and Austria. They were sweeping over Italy. Turkey had raised an army in Syria, and Napoleon hastened thither with thirteen thousand men over a desert of seventy-five leagues.

He took El Arish Feb. 20, 1799, then Gaza; then Jaffa was taken by assault, as the garrison refused to yield, and beheaded the messenger sent to them, putting his head on a pole. The massacre which followed was horrible. Some two thousand prisoners were taken to the seashore and shot by Napoleon's order. Bourrienne says, Napoleon "yielded only in the last extremity, and was one of those, perhaps, who beheld the massacre with the deepest pain."

Napoleon has been greatly blamed for this act. These men would, of course, have gone back to the enemy, and the Turks themselves give no quarter; and yet, for humanity's sake, one wishes that they could have been spared.

After the battle at Jaffa the French began the siege of St. Jean d'Acre, where Djezzar, which name signifies butcher, the head of the army, resided. The siege lasted sixty days. Sir Sidney Smith of England, with two ships of war, assisted the fort, and Phélippeaux, an old schoolmate of Napoleon at Brienne, directed the artillery. Napoleon's battering train, sent forward by sea, had been taken by the English. The siege had to be raised, four thousand of the French being disabled, and the army retreated to Jaffa. The plague was decimating the ranks; and Napoleon, to inspire his men, went among the plague-stricken soldiers and often touched them. The wounded and sick were carried on horses, while Napoleon and all his officers went on foot. Napoleon said, "Sir Sidney Smith made me miss my destiny."

Napoleon defeated the Turks at Aboukir, July 25, with a loss to them of ten thousand men, and then, learning of the perilous condition of France in her wars with the allied powers, hastened to Paris, leaving General Kléber in charge in Egypt. Napoleon narrowly missed being captured by the English cruisers.

France was overjoyed at his return. Bells were rung and bonfires kindled. He reached Paris Oct. 16, 1799. Josephine had gone to Lyons to meet him. He had started for Paris by a different route, and she missed him.

When she returned Napoleon refused to see her. While in Egypt Junot had foolishly told him some gossip about Josephine, who was obliged to be courteous to everybody, which had made him jealous. It probably came from Napoleon's brothers, who disliked her great influence over him.

Josephine was nearly heart-broken. She had not seen Napoleon for a year and a half. Both Eugène and Hortense begged that Napoleon would take their mother back into his heart.

Finally he opened his door, and with a stern look at Josephine, said to Eugène, then eighteen, who had just returned with him from Egypt, "As for you, you shall not suffer for your mother's misdeeds; I shall keep you with me."

With commendable spirit, the boy, who idolized his mother, replied, "No, General; I bid you farewell on the spot."

Seeing his mistake, he pressed Eugène to his heart, folded Josephine in his arms, and sent for his brother Lucien, to show him how thoroughly he and Josephine were reconciled to each other.

Napoleon had reached Paris at an opportune moment. The Directory were disliked, and he had made up his mind to overturn the government. A dinner was given to Napoleon at the Temple of Victory by five or six hundred members of the two Councils, the Ancients, and the Five Hundred. In the evening Josephine did the honors of the drawing-room at their own house. "She fascinated every one who came near her," says Saint-Amand, "by her exquisite grace and charming courtesy. All the brusqueness and violence of Bonaparte's manners were tempered by the soothing and insinuating gentleness of his amiable and kindly wife."

Only a few persons were in Napoleon's secret. By a provision of the Constitution, the Council of the Ancients, in case of peril to the Republic, could convoke the Legislative Body (the two Councils) outside the capital to avoid the influence of the multitude, and choose a general to command the troops to defend the legislature.

The 18th Brumaire (Nov. 9) was the day set for this Council at the Tuileries to vote to change the place of meeting to St. Cloud. It was given out that he was to take a journey, so his officers and some cavalry were to be at his house at six o'clock in the morning to go with him to the Tuileries, that he might review the troops, to be gathered there at seven.

At six o'clock, Lefebvre, the commander of the military division, had arrived. Napoleon said to him, "Here is the Turkish sabre which I carried at the battle of the Pyramids. Do you, who are one of the most valiant defenders of the country, accept it? Will you let our country perish in the hands of the pettifoggers who are ruining it?" It was gladly accepted.

All rode to the Tuileries. The Ancients voted to meet at St. Cloud on the morrow, and gave Napoleon the command of the troops.

On the 19th Brumaire the way to St. Cloud was crowded with troops and carriages. All was excitement and confusion. Napoleon's friends said, "You are marching to the guillotine." "We shall see," was his cool reply. When Napoleon arrived at St. Cloud he entered the hall of the Council of the Ancients and made a brief address. Then he went to the Council of the Five Hundred. It was five in the afternoon. At the sight of him they shouted, "Down with the Dictator! Down with the tyrant!" They brandished daggers and threatened his life. His soldiers hastened to his aid; and one grenadier, Thomé, had his clothes cut by a dagger. Bourrienne says they were simply torn. Lucien Bonaparte, the president of the Five Hundred, left his seat in disgust at the tumult. He called upon the general and the soldiers "to execute the vote of the Ancients." The drums were beaten, the soldiers entered the hall, the deputies fled in every direction, and the old government was a thing of the past. Three consuls were elected, of whom Napoleon was the First Consul. He rode home at three in the morning. At thirty he had conquered France as well as Italy.

There is no doubt that a large majority of the people of France were rejoiced at the change in government. "Napoleon," says Alison in his History of Europe, "rivalled Cæsar in the clemency with which he used his victory. No proscriptions or massacres, few arrests or imprisonments, followed the triumph of order over revolution. On the contrary, numerous acts of mercy, as wise as they were magnanimous, illustrated the rise of the consular throne. The elevation of Napoleon was not only unstained by blood, but not even a single captive long lamented the ear of the victor."

On the 19th of February, 1800, Napoleon took up his residence in the Tuileries. His salary was five hundred thousand francs a year. Ten days before his removal to the Tuileries, Feb. 9, when the seventy-two flags taken from the Turks at Aboukir were placed in the Hôtel des Invalides, a funeral oration was pronounced on Washington, who had died Dec. 14, 1799. Napoleon issued this order to his army: "Washington is dead! That great man fought against tyranny. He established the liberty of his country. His memory will be ever dear to the freemen of both hemispheres, and especially to the French soldiers, who, like him and the American troops, have fought for liberty and equality. As a mark of respect, the First Consul orders that, for ten days, black crape be suspended from all the standards and banners of the Republic."

21

Feb. 20 he received a letter from Louis XVIII., in which the Bourbon King said, "Save France from her own violence, and you will fulfil the first wish of my heart. Restore her king to her, and future generations will bless your memory." But Napoleon knew that the French did not want the House of Bourbon. They had put Louis XVI. to death, and still celebrated that anniversary.

Napoleon devoted all his time to the improvement of the state. He drew around him the ablest persons. "The men whom he most disliked," says Bourrienne, "were those whom he called babblers, who are continually prating of everything and on everything." He often said, "I want more head and less tongue."

He gave France a new constitution, which was accepted by the votes of the people almost unanimously, over 3,000,000 in the affirmative, and a few hundreds in the negative. He abolished the annual festival celebrating the death of Louis XVI. He opened the prisons where those opposed to the state were confined; hundreds of exiles returned to France. The country was bankrupt; but now that confidence was restored, with the help of the best financiers, the Bank of France was established, a sinking fund provided, judicious taxation adopted, and an era of prosperity began. Napoleon built canals, roads, and bridges, and splendid monuments. He restored Sunday as a day of rest, which had been set aside when the Goddess of Reason was worshipped during the Revolution.

A little later, duly 15, 1801,—by the Concordat,—he recognized the Roman Catholic religion as the religion of France. He said, "I am convinced that a part of France would become Protestant, were I to favor that disposition. I am also certain that the much greater portion would continue Catholic, and that they would oppose, with the greatest zeal, the division among their fellow-citizens. We should then have the Huguenot wars over again, and interminable conflicts. But by reviving a religion which has always prevailed in the country, and by giving perfect liberty of conscience to the minority, all will be satisfied."

He did not like numerous festival days. "A saint's day," he said, "is a day of idleness, and I do not wish for that. People must labor in order to live."

Nobody labored harder than Napoleon. He kept several secretaries busy. Writing fatigued him, and he wrote so hurriedly that the last half of the word was usually a dash, or omitted. He could go without sleep, snatching a few minutes in his chair, or in his saddle before a battle. He seldom took over twenty minutes for dinner, even when he was Emperor, and rose from the table as soon as he had finished. His time was too precious to wait long for others. He was very prompt, and required others to be so.

He said, "Occupation is my element.... I have seen the extent to which I could use my eyes, but I have never known any bounds to my capacity for application."

Lanfrey says he "had a prodigious power of work," and "a rapidity of conception that no other man has probably ever possessed to the same extent." He used often to say, "Succeed! I judge men only by results."

Nobody knew better the value of time. "I worked all day," said a person to him, in apology for not having completed some duty. "But had you not the night also?" was the reply.

"Ask me for whatever you please except time," he said to another; "that is the only thing which is beyond my power."

While taking his bath, Bourrienne read to him. While being shaved, he read, or somebody read to him. He ate fast, and was irregular at his meals, sometimes passing a whole day without eating. He always walked up and down the room, with his arms folded behind him, when dictating to his secretaries. "He was exceedingly temperate," says Bourrienne, "and averse to all excess."

"The institutions of modern France date not, as is often said, from the Revolution, but from the Consulate," says Professor Seeley. "The work of reconstruction which distinguishes the Consulate, though it was continued under the Empire, is the most enduring of all the achievements of Napoleon."

"The institutions now created," says Seeley, "and which form the organization of modern France, are, 1. The Restored Church, resting on the Concordat; 2. the University; 3. the judicial system; 4. the Codes: Code Civil, called Code Napoléon Sept. 3, 1807, Code de Commerce, Code Pénal, Code d'Instruction Criminelle; 5. the system of local government; 6. the Bank of France; 7. the Legion of Honor."

"My code will outlive my victories," said Napoleon, truly. He put the best minds of France upon the codification and improvement of her laws, and he carefully watched every detail.

"Bourrienne," Napoleon used to say, "it is for France I am doing all this! All I wish, all I desire, the end of all my labors, is, that my name should be indissolubly connected with that of France!"

Now that France was prosperous and settled, Napoleon wrote to George III., King of England, proposing peace. Lord Grenville, for his nation, which had grown more confident since the battle of the Nile and the successes in Egypt, declined to treat with the Consular Government of France. Canning spoke of this "new usurper, who, like a spectre, wears on his head a something that has a phantom resemblance to a crown." Who would have prophesied then that young Napoleon IV would have died fighting the battles of England in Zululand?

He proposed peace to Austria, but she decided like her ally, England. Napoleon said bitterly, "England wants war. She shall have it. Yes! yes! war to the death."

He immediately sent General Moreau with one hundred and

thirty thousand men against the Austrian army on the Rhine, and took forty thousand himself to Italy, crossing the Alps over the Great St. Bernard. The carriages and wheels were slung on poles; the ammunition boxes were borne on mules; the cannon were carried in trees hollowed out, each dragged up the heights by a hundred men; the soldiers crept up the icy steeps each with sixty or seventy pounds upon his back. At the well-known Hospice kept by the monks, Napoleon had sent forward supplies for his men, who, cold and exhausted, were overjoyed at the repast.

The story is told that the young guide who led Napoleon's mule over the Alps confided to the sympathetic stranger his poverty, his desire to marry the girl of his choice, and his inability to provide her a home. The small man in a gray overcoat gave him a note to the head of the convent. To his astonishment, it provided him with a house and a piece of ground.

The army then swept down upon Italy. The First Consul entered Milan June 2; Lannes was victorious at Montebello June 9, and on the morning of June 14 forty thousand Austrians were opposed to a much smaller number of French on the plain of Marengo. The battle was hotly contested for twelve hours. At first the Austrians seemed victorious, till Desaix, who had just come back from Egypt, rushed upon the field with his reserves. He was shot dead, but his columns were soon avenged.

Six thousand Austrians threw down their arms, a panic spread through their troops, the cavalry plunged over the infantry to be first in crossing the Bormida, and thousands perished in the dreadful confusion. Marengo is regarded by many as Napoleon's most masterful battle.

Desaix's death was a sad blow to Napoleon. Savary found his body stripped of clothing, wrapped it in a cloak, laid it across a horse, and Napoleon had it carried to Milan to be embalmed. He said, "Victory at such a price is dear." Kléber was killed in Egypt on the same day. At St. Helena, Napoleon said, "Of all the generals I ever had under my command, Desaix and Kléber possessed the greatest talent—in particular Desaix.... Kléber and Desaix were irreparable losses to France."

Napoleon returned to Milan and went in state to the Cathedral to the Te Deum, four days after the battle of Marengo. The people everywhere gave him an ovation. "Bourrienne," he said, "do you hear the acclamations still resounding? That noise is as sweet to me as the sound of Josephine's voice." Napoleon reached Paris late in June.

Dec. 3 of this same year, 1800, Moreau fought the famous battle of Hohenlinden, in the black forests of Germany, at midnight. In the blinding snowstorm both armies got entangled in the forests. The Austrians left ten thousand in dead and wounded on the field, with seven thousand prisoners. The poem of Campbell is well known:—

"On Linden, when the sun was low,
All bloodless lay the untrodden snow,
And dark as winter was the flow
Of Iser rolling rapidly."

Finally a treaty of peace between France and Austria was signed at Lunéville, Feb. 9, 1801, followed March 27, 1802, by the treaty of Amiens, between France and England.

Both countries rejoiced in the cessation of hostilities. Fox came over from England and was received with great cordiality. Napoleon said, "I considered him an ornament to mankind, and was very much attached to him."

Four months later, Aug. 4, 1802, by an overwhelming majority of the votes of the people, over three and a half millions in favor to about eight thousand against it, Napoleon was declared Consul for life. La Fayette could not conscientiously favor it, unless liberty of the press were guaranteed. He said to Napoleon, "A free government, and you at its head—that comprehends all my desires."

Napoleon said, "He thinks he is still in the United States—as if the French were Americans. He has no conception of what is required for this country." Napoleon felt, no doubt sincerely, that France was more stable under an Emperor than a President. And yet since the fall of Napoleon III France has shown that she can live and prosper as a republic.

All through these years the Royalists were plotting to return to the throne; for when did ever a king reign who did not think it was by "Divine right"?

Louis XVIII wrote another letter to Napoleon: "You must have long since been convinced, General, that you possess my esteem.... We may insure the glory of France. I say we, because I require the aid of Bonaparte, and he can do nothing without me. General, Europe observes you; glory awaits you; I am impatient to restore peace to my people." In answer to this letter, Napoleon wrote, "You must not seek to return to France. To do so, you must trample over a hundred thousand dead bodies."

Several attempts were made to assassinate Napoleon. Possibly some of these were the work of Jacobins, who feared that the republic was slipping into an empire; but they were for the most part traced to Royalists, the leaders of whom lived in England, and were receiving yearly pensions, because they had aided her in former wars.

On the evening of Dec. 24, 1800, as Napoleon was going to the opera to hear Haydn's Oratorio of "The Creation," he was obliged to pass through the Rue Saint-Nicaise, where an upturned cart covered a barrel of gunpowder, grape-shot, and pieces of iron. The "infernal machine" exploded two seconds after he had passed in his carriage. The carriage was uplifted from the ground, four persons were killed, sixty wounded, of whom several died, and forty-six houses were badly damaged. One of the horses of Napoleon's escort was wounded.

Other plans were soon discovered, concocted by Georges Cadoudal, General Pichegru, and others, all in the confidence of the Comte d'Artois, afterwards Charles X, the brother of Louis XVIII He lived in or near London.

Cadoudal, or Georges as he is usually called, was to meet Napoleon in the streets, and, with a band of thirty or forty followers, kill him and his staff. When all was ready, the Bourbon princes were to be near at hand to head the revolt of the people. Georges was arrested and executed with eleven of his companions.

The Duke d'Enghien, Louis Antoine, Henri de Bourbon, son of the Duke of Bourbon, and a descendant of the great Condé who had done so much for France in her wars, was living at Ettenheim, under the protection of the Margrave of Baden, to be near the lady whom he loved, the Princess Charlotte de Rohan, and "to be ready," says Walter Scott, "to put himself at the head of the royalists in the east of France," if opportunity offered.

It was reported to Napoleon that the duke came over into France probably on political errands, and that he was corresponding with disaffected persons in France.

Napoleon sent some officers to seize the duke on the night of March 15, 1804; he was carried to Strasburg, and thence to the Castle of Vincennes, near Paris, arriving on the afternoon of Tuesday, March 20. He was aroused from sleep a little before six on the morning of the 21st, and innocently asked if he were to be imprisoned. He was conducted outside the castle; by the light of a lantern5 his sentence was read to him. He denied any complicity in the conspiracy against the life of the First Consul, which was doubtless true; requested to see Napoleon, which was refused; asked an officer to take a ring, a lock of hair, and a letter to his beloved, and was shot at six in the morning, by his open grave, his devoted dog by his side. Bourrienne says, "This faithful animal returned incessantly to the fatal spot.... The fidelity of the poor dog excited so much interest that the police prevented any one from visiting the fatal spot, and the dog was no longer heard to howl over his master's grave."

Josephine had heard of Napoleon's intention to send terror among the Bourbon conspirators, and had begged him, on her knees and with tears, to save the life of the young prince. It would have been well for him had he listened to her entreaties.

France, and Europe as well, were shocked at this death. The Russian court went into mourning for the Bourbon prince. No doubt Napoleon was incensed by the Bourbon plots, and after this death these ceased; but Las Cases, at St. Helena, said Napoleon always regretted it, saying, "Undoubtedly, if I had been informed in time of certain circumstances respecting the opinions of the prince, and his disposition, if, above all, I had seen the letter which he wrote to me, and which, God knows for what reason, was only delivered to me after his death, I should certainly have forgiven him."

Napoleon has been blamed for another matter,—the taking of Saint Domingo, and the imprisonment of Toussaint L'Ouverture. This remarkable colored man, who had been a slave, had acquired the control of the island by driving the French and Spanish troops out, and making it a republic, with a nominal dependence upon France. Napoleon, with a desire unfortunately shown and carried out by other nations, wished to enlarge his colonies and also to settle some dissensions in the island, and sent Dec. 14, 1801, General Leclerc, who had married his pretty sister Pauline, with 25,000 men to Saint Domingo to re-establish French sovereignty. He was to send back to France any who rebelled. Toussaint L'Ouverture, who was among them, was imprisoned in the fortress of Joux, near Besançon, in Normandy, and died in ten months, away from his own people, the victim of the spirit of conquest, which is not dead even in the nineteenth century. The climate destroyed the French army. Only two or three thousand ever returned. General Leclerc died, like the rest, of yellow fever.

Napoleon said at St. Helena, "I ought to have been satisfied with governing it Saint Domingo through the medium of Toussaint.... The design of reducing it by force was a great error."

Only a year after the treaty of Amiens was concluded, it became evident that it would not last. It was said that Napoleon's power was becoming too great for the security of Europe. England had determined not to give up Malta to the Knights as she had promised. Under Pitt's guidance she was arming and making herself ready for a great combat. The Royalists were using their pens in their English homes, to abuse the head of the French nation, held there by the votes of the French people. It was, of course, exasperating, and tended to produce revolt. Napoleon called attention to the terms of the treaty, which stipulated that neither of the two nations should give any protection to those who were injuring the other. Commercial tariffs bred dislike. English pride was stirred because Napoleon said, "England, single-handed, is unable to cope with France."

Finally in May, 1803, the war began. Alison says, and Scott agrees with him, "Upon coolly reviewing the circumstances under which the contest was renewed, it is impossible to deny that the British government manifested a feverish desire to come to a rupture, and that, as far as the transactions between the two countries are concerned, they are the aggressors."

Napoleon was determined to invade England,—Bourrienne thinks it was only a feint, and that his real motive "was to invade Germany and repulse the Russian troops,"—and he gathered an army of 150,000 in and around Boulogne, and an immense flotilla which

27

should be able to transport these men ten leagues across the channel to the English coast.

While these preparations were going on, the French Senate, undoubtedly in accord with the views of the First Consul, suggested publicly the idea of an empire over which Napoleon should be the hereditary ruler. The people were tired of Bourbon plottings, and, if Napoleon were killed, the scenes of the Revolution might again be witnessed in the streets of Paris. Napoleon was declared Emperor of the French, May 18, 1804, and publicly crowned by Pope Pius VII., at Notre Dame, Dec. 2 of the same year.

Paris was thronged with people on the day of the coronation. At half-past ten in the morning Napoleon and Josephine drove to the cathedral in a carriage largely of glass, surmounted by a golden crown upheld by four eagles with outstretched wings, drawn by eight superb horses. Twenty squadrons of cavalry led the procession, Marshal Murat at the head. Eighteen carriages, each drawn by six horses, followed.

Napoleon wore a coat of crimson velvet faced with white velvet, white velvet boots, a short cloak of crimson lined with white satin, and a black velvet cap with two aigrettes and several diamonds.

At the Archbishop's Palace, Napoleon put on his coronation robes. These were a tight-fitting gown of white satin, a crimson mantle covered with golden bees, having an embroidered border with the letter N, and a crown above each letter, the lining and cape of ermine, the whole weighing eighty pounds, and held up by four persons. His crown was of golden laurel; his sword at his left side was in a scabbard of blue enamel, covered with eagles and bees.

Josephine wore a white satin gown, with a train of silver brocade covered with bees, a girdle of very expensive diamonds, necklace, bracelets, and earrings of precious stones and antique cameos, and a diadem of four rows of pearls with clusters of diamonds. The Emperor was much struck with Josephine's beauty, and said to his brother Joseph, "If father could see us!"

As Napoleon entered the cathedral, which was draped in crimson and gold, twenty thousand spectators shouted, "Long live the Emperor!"

The Emperor and Empress knelt on blue velvet cushions before the Pope, who anointed Napoleon on the head and hands, and the Empress in the same way. Then high mass began with three hundred performers. When the moment came for the Pope to crown the Emperor, Napoleon took the crown from his hands and placed it upon his own head, and then crowned Josephine. Her crown was formed of eight branches set in diamonds, emeralds, and amethysts, under a gold globe surmounted by a cross. Then they proceeded to the great throne reached by twenty-four steps, Josephine sitting one step lower than her husband. France had placed her all in the hands of one man; and Lanfrey justly remarks, "A nation that carries love of ease so far as to thrust the whole burden of duties and responsibility on a single man is always punished for it."

After the gorgeous ceremony was over, Napoleon and the Empress dined alone, and were happy. He said to David, who had painted the coronation scene at the moment when Napoleon was placing the crown upon the head of the lovely Josephine, "I thank you for transmitting to ages to come the proof of affection I wanted to give to her who shares with me the pains of government." Then he raised his hat to the artist, and said, "David, I salute you." Josephine had opposed Napoleon's becoming Emperor, because it meant hereditary succession, and she had no child by Napoleon. His brothers had for some years urged a divorce, so that Josephine's life had been one of much sorrow.

Napoleon had said to Bourrienne, "It is the torment of my life not to have a child. I plainly perceive that my power will never be firmly established until I have one. If I die without an heir, not one of my brothers is capable of supplying my place. All is begun, but nothing is ended. God knows what will happen!"

Josephine had urged her young daughter Hortense into a marriage with Louis, the brother of Napoleon, Jan. 2, 1802, with the hope that their child might be the heir to the empire. Each loved another person before marriage, and their married life was one of constant misery.

Their first child, Charles Napoleon, born Oct. 10, 1802, whom Napoleon would have adopted, a beautiful and most intelligent boy, died when he was four years and ao half old, of croup, May 5, 1807. "Sometimes when his parents were quarrelling," says Saint-Amand, "he succeeded in reconciling them. He used to take his father by the hand, who gladly let himself be led by this little angel, and then he would say in a caressing tone: 'Kiss her, papa, I beg of you;' then he was perfectly happy when his father and mother exchanged a kiss of peace."

Hortense, the mother, was so prostrated with grief, that it was feared she would lose her reason. Madame de Rémusat says of her, "The Queen has but one thought, the loss she has suffered; she speaks of only one thing, of him. Not a tear, but a cold, calm, and almost absolute silence about everything, and when she speaks she wrings every one's heart. If she sees any one whom she has ever seen with her son, she looks at him with kindliness and interest, and says, 'You know he is dead.' When she first saw her mother, she said to her, 'It's not long since he was here with me. I held him on my knees thus.' ... She heard ten o'clock strike; she turned to one of the ladies and said, 'You know it was at ten that he died.' That is the only way she breaks her almost continual silence."

Josephine was doubly crushed by the blow. She saw her hopes for the future blighted. The Emperor wrote to her from the seat of war; "I can well imagine the grief which Napoleon's death must cause. You can understand what I suffer. I should like to be with you, that you might be moderate and discreet in your grief.... Let me hear that you are calm and well! Do you want to add to my regret? Good-by, my dear."

Napoleon was not cold-hearted, but believed that only those accomplish much in life who have self-control. Two of his soldiers having committed suicide on account of love affairs, Napoleon caused it to be inserted in the order-book of the guard, that "there is as much true courage in bearing up against mental sufferings with constancy as in remaining firm on the wall of a battery."

Nearly six months after the crowning in Notre Dame, the Emperor was crowned King of Italy in the cathedral of Milan, May 26, 1805, with the iron crown of Charlemagne. This crown of gold and precious stones covers an iron ring said to have been made from a spike which pierced the Saviour's hand at the crucifixion. Napoleon and the Empress were both gorgeously arrayed. He placed the crown upon his own head, repeating the words used in ancient times: "God has given it to me—woe to him that touches it."

Everywhere Napoleon and Josephine were adored by the people. They went into the cabin of a poor woman, who was anxious and needy because her husband could not get work. "How much money would make you perfectly happy?" asked Napoleon. "Ah, sir, a great deal! As much as eighty dollars."

The Emperor gave her several hundreds, and told her to rent a piece of ground and buy some goats.

"Josephine," says Saint-Amand, "had all the qualities that are attractive in a sovereign,—affability, gentleness, kindliness, generosity. She had a way of convincing every one of her personal interest. She had an excellent memory, and surprised those with whom she talked by the exactness with which she recalled the past, even to details they had themselves nearly forgotten. The sound of her gentle, penetrating, and sympathetic voice added to the courtesy and charm of her words. Every one listened to her with pleasure; she spoke with grace and listened courteously. She always appeared to be doing a kindness, and thus inspired affection and gratitude."

"Her only fault," says Saint-Amand, "was extravagance." But it must be remembered that Napoleon wished her to dress elegantly. It seemed as though everybody came to ask her to buy, and she bought, says Saint-Amand, "simply to oblige the dealers. There was no limit to her liberality. She would have liked to own all the treasures of the earth in order to give them all away." ... Napoleon, economical by nature, scolded and forgave. "He could refuse Josephine nothing," says the same writer, "and she was really the only woman who had any influence over him."

Napoleon made Josephine's son, Eugène, Viceroy of Italy,—he often said, "Eugène may serve as a model to all the young men of the

30

age,"—returned to Paris, and then started for his troops at Boulogne. There he waited for some days for his feet under Villeneuve, who, having been watched by the English, and in part crippled by them, failed to appear. He dared not proceed to Brest, which the English blockaded, and so repaired to Cadiz, to be crushed soon after by that Napoleon of the sea, Horatio Nelson, at the battle of Trafalgar. Villeneuve afterwards committed suicide, stabbing himself to the heart. He left a letter for his wife in which he said, "What a blessing that I have no children to reap my horrible heritage and bear the weight of my name!"

Meantime, Russia, Austria, and Sweden had joined themselves to England to defeat Napoleon. The Emperor, with that quickness of decision and rapidity of execution for which he was phenomenal, managed to separate the armies of his foes, and beat them in turn. At Ulm, Oct. 20, 1805, over thirty thousand Austrians under General Mack, led by sixteen generals, surrendered, laid down their arms, and retired to the rear of the French army. More than twenty thousand Austrians had been taken prisoners in the few days preceding, and the Austrian army of eighty thousand was well-nigh destroyed.

Napoleon wrote to Josephine Oct. 21: "I am very well, my dear. I have made an army of thirty-three thousand men surrender. I have taken from sixty to seventy thousand prisoners, more than ninety flags, and more than two hundred cannon. In the military annals there is no such defeat."

Napoleon pushed on to Vienna, which he entered Nov. 14, and went to the palace of Schönbrunn. The Emperor Francis had fled, and joined the Tsar and the Russian army at Brunn. Thither Napoleon marched at once. On the night of Dec. 1, 1805, he mounted his horse to reconnoitre the enemy's lines. As he returned, going on foot from one watch-fire to another, he fell to the ground over the stump of a tree. A grenadier lighted a torch of straw, then the whole line did the same and cheered the Emperor. They remembered that the next day, Dec. 2, was the anniversary of the coronation. The Russians thought the French were retreating. Then all slept for a few hours, and awoke to the battle of Austerlitz.

At daybreak there was a heavy mist, then the sun shone out full and clear, and the French believed they would win a glorious victory. They were not disappointed. During the terrible conflict the Russians and Austrians lost over thirty thousand in killed and wounded, treble the number of the French. The enemy fled across the lakes, the ice of which being broken by the French batteries, thousands were ingulfed. Their cries and groans, says Lanfrey, were heard on the following day.

Napoleon said, "I have fought thirty battles like that, but I have never seen so decisive a victory, or one where the chances were so unevenly balanced." The Russian and Austrian forces greatly

31

outnumbered the French. To his soldiers Napoleon said, "I am satisfied with you; you have covered your eagles with undying glory."

To Josephine he wrote: "The battle of Austerlitz is the greatest I have won; forty-five flags, more than one hundred and fifty cannon, the standards of the Russian guards, twenty generals, more than twenty thousand killed,—a horrid sight! The Emperor Alexander is in despair, and is leaving for Russia. Yesterday I saw the Emperor of Germany in my bivouac; we talked for two hours, and agreed on a speedy peace.... I shall see with pleasure the time that will restore me to you."

The defeat of the allies at Austerlitz hastened the death of William Pitt of England. He looked long on the map of Europe, and said, "Henceforth we may close that map for half a century." He died Jan. 23, 1806.

On Napoleon's return to Paris he erected a column in the Place Vendôme to the Grand Army. It was constructed of cannon taken from the enemy, and has illustrations upon it of the campaigns of Ulm and Austerlitz. W. O'Connor Morris calls Austerlitz "the most perfect of battles on land, as the Nile was the most perfect on sea." Seeley thinks, in its historical results, Austerlitz "ranks among the great events of the world."

The peace of Pressburg was effected between France and Austria, Dec. 26, 1805. Charles James Fox, who had succeeded Pitt in England, was favorable to peace5 between the nations, but the war party in England was strong. Fox soon died, and the peace negotiations failed.

Napoleon said at St. Helena, "The death of Fox was one of the fatalities of my career. Had his life been prolonged, affairs would have taken a totally different turn. The cause of the people would have triumphed, and we should have established a new order of things in Europe."

Meantime Napoleon had placed his brother Joseph on the throne of Naples, Louis on the throne of Holland, and had formed a Confederation of the Rhine out of several states in the valley of the Rhine, which had fourteen million people. Napoleon was elected Protector of the Confederation.

Russia now became an ally of Prussia, and war was declared against France Oct. 14, 1806. The double battle of Jena and Auerstädt was fought, and the Prussians were completely defeated. Alison says, "The loss of the Prussians was prodigious; on the two fields there fell nearly twenty thousand killed and wounded, besides nearly as many prisoners.... Ten thousand of the killed and wounded fell at Auerstädt."

Napoleon entered Berlin in triumph Oct. 27, 1806, and established himself in the king's palace. He did not like the beautiful Queen Louise, because he felt that she had inspired the soldiers by her presence, and urged her husband to make war. He was unjust to her in his bulletins, and Josephine reproached him for "speaking ill of women."

Napoleon visited the palace of Sans Souci to see the room where Frederick the Great died, still preserved as he left it, and then went to the church where he is buried. At the tomb, says General de Ségur, "Napoleon paused at the entrance in a grave and respectful attitude. He gazed into the shadow enclosing the hero's ashes, and stood thus for nearly ten minutes, motionless, silent, as if buried in deep thought." The sword of Frederick he took with him, and gave it to the Hotel des Invalides in Paris, with the flags carried by his guard in the Seven Years' War.

Early in November, Prince Hohenlohe surrendered twenty thousand Prussians to the French; and Blücher, whom Napoleon was to meet again at Waterloo, surrendered twenty thousand men and over five hundred officers.

With all this victory, Josephine was not happy. Napoleon wrote her Nov. 1: "Talleyrand has come, and tells me you do nothing but cry." She wrote to Hortense, more miserable than herself, that she could not be happy so far from the Emperor.

Napoleon, while at Berlin, issued, Nov. 21, 1806, his famous "Berlin Decree," wherein he declared the British Islands blockaded. All commerce with England and her colonies was prohibited; all property belonging to an English subject confiscated; every native of England found in a country occupied by French troops to be made prisoner of war.

Napoleon declared that this was a retaliatory measure against England. Every French port was, in fact, blockaded by English vessels from the Elbe to Brest, by a decree of the British Government, passed in May, 1806, according to Alison. Some months after the Berlin Decree, England issued further prohibitory acts, called Orders in Council. The consequence of all this was that hate between the two nations was increased.

After the humiliation of Prussia, the war went on with Russia. After some minor battles, both armies met on the bloody field of Eylau, Feb. 7, 1807. Jomini thinks the forces about equal, though some historians place the number at eighty thousand Russians, and sixty thousand French. Part of Feb. 7 and all of Feb. 8, the armies were in deadly conflict. A blinding snowstorm part of the time prevented the armies from seeing each other. The snow and ice were so thick that men fought on ponds and did not know it.

Fifty thousand dead and wounded lay on the snow. Marshal Augereau's corps was almost destroyed; three thousand only remained out of fifteen thousand. Napoleon wrote in his bulletins: "Imagine, on a space a league square, nine or ten thousand corpses; four or five thousand dead horses; lines of Russian knapsacks; fragments of guns and sabres; the earth covered with bullets, shells, supplies; twenty-four cannon surrounded by their artillerymen, slain just as they were trying to take their guns away; and all that in plainest relief on the stretch of snow."

He said, as he looked upon the ghastly field, "This sight is one to fill rulers with a love of peace and a horror of war." At three o'clock in the morning of Feb. 9, he wrote to Josephine: "We had a great battle yesterday. I was victorious, but our loss was heavy; that of the enemy, which was even greater, is no consolation for me. I write you these few lines myself, though I am very tired, to tell you that I am well and love you.

Ever yours."

Baron de Marbot, in his most interesting memoirs, tells of his thrilling experiences in this battle. He was at that time an officer under Augereau. His horse, Lisette, of whom he was extremely fond, was addicted to biting, but valued for her speed. At great risk, Marbot carried a message to the Fourteenth. "I see no means of saving the regiment," said the major; "return to the Emperor, bid him farewell from the Fourteenth of the line, which has faithfully executed his orders, and bear him the eagle which he gave us, and which we can no longer defend; it would add too much to the pain of death to see it fall into the hands of the enemy."

Marbot took the eagle, when a cannon ball went through the hinder part of his hat, forcing, by the shock, the blood from his nose, ears, and even eyes. His limbs were almost paralyzed. A hand to hand combat raged around him. Several Frenchmen, not to be struck from behind, set their backs against the sides of Lisette, who stood quite still. One of the Russians thrust his bayonet into Marbot's left arm, and then into Lisette's thigh.

"Her ferocious instincts being restored by the pain," says Marbot, "she sprang at the Russian, and at one mouthful tore off his nose, lips, eyebrows, and all the skin of his face, making of him a living death's-head, dripping with blood. Then, hurling herself with fury among the combatants, kicking and biting, Lisette upset everything that she met on the road."

She seized another Russian who had tried to hit Marbot, "tore out his entrails, and mashed his body under her feet, leaving him dying on the snow."

When Lisette and her rider reached the cemetery of Eylau, where the battle was hottest, the poor creature fell exhausted. The young Marbot, supposed to be dead amid the piles of dead and wounded, was stripped of his clothing. He was marvellously rescued by a servant, who cut up the shirt of a dead soldier and bandaged the leg of Lisette, by which she also was saved. Lisette, after doing service just before Friedland by galloping twelve leagues on a hot day to carry a message of warning to the Emperor, was cared for by the wife of an officer, and died of old age.

Napoleon shared with his soldiers all the dangers and privations of war. He wrote to his brother Joseph: "The staff-officers have not taken off their clothes for two months, and some not for four. I have myself been a fortnight without taking off my boots. We are deep in the snow and mud.... The wounded have to be carried in open sleighs for fifty leagues."

Josephine wished to come to him. He wrote: "You couldn't be racing through inns and camps. I am as anxious as you can be to see you and be quiet.... All my life I have sacrificed everything—peace, interest, happiness—to my destiny."

The next great battle was at Friedland, when eighty thousand French met seventy-five thousand Russians. "This is the anniversary of Marengo," said Napoleon, June 14, 1800, "and to-day fortune is with me."

And so it proved. The Russians fought desperately, but they were overpowered. They retreated towards the river, and thousands who were not captured were drowned. They lost twenty-six thousand, says Marbot, in dead and wounded, and the French about half that number.

The conquered were glad to make peace, which was concluded at Tilsit, July 7, 1807, between Alexander I. of Russia, Frederick William III of Prussia, and Napoleon. By this treaty, among other articles, some provinces west of the Elbe were made into the kingdom of Westphalia, and another brother of Napoleon, Jerome, was placed upon a throne. He had married, when nineteen, Miss Elizabeth Patterson of Baltimore; but througho Napoleon's influence the union was annulled, and he married, at twenty-three, Aug. 23, 1807, the daughter of the king of Würtemberg. She proved a noble woman. When her husband was dethroned in 1814, she refused to obtain a divorce, writing to her father: "Having been forced, by reasons of state, to marry the king, my husband, it has been granted me by fate to be the happiest woman in the world."

Napoleon said of her at Saint Helena, "Princess Catherine of Würtemberg has, with her own hands, written her name in history."

Napoleon returned to Paris after the peace of Tilsit, and was received with unbounded love and honor. He made Paris more beautiful with arches and churches, he developed her industries, and he established schools and colleges. He said, "We must not pass through this world without leaving traces which may commend our memory to posterity."

England was still the bitter enemy of Napoleon. The decrees of both regarding commerce were soon to plunge nearly all Europe into war. By agreement of Alexander and Napoleon, if England did not consent to peace, they were to summon Denmark, Sweden, Portugal, and perhaps Austria, to close their ports against her. Denmark wished to be neutral. While she hesitated, England, having heard of this project, sent a fleet against Copenhagen and bombarded it.

Napoleon sent an army under Junot into Portugal to compel her assent, and Murat into Spain, which at that time was friendly with France, though distracted by royal dissensions. Napoleon placed his brother Joseph on the throne. Mr. Ropes thinks, and probably correctly, that Napoleon supposed "the population of the Spanish peninsula was ready for the great reforms in government in which France had led the way, and in which Holland, Western Germany, and Italy were then cheerfully and hopefully marching, and that the better and more enlightened part of the Spanish people would be thankful to see a liberal, intelligent, and conscientious man like Joseph take the place of the bigoted and profligate Charles IV."

Napoleon said at St. Helena: "It was the subject of my perpetual dreams to render Paris the real capital of Europe.... My ambition was of the highest and noblest kind that ever existed,—that of establishing and consecrating the empire of reason, and the full exercise and complete enjoyment of all the human faculties."

A dreadful insurrection took place in Spain against the rule of Joseph, and Napoleon sent a large army to quell it. He succeeded in reinstating Joseph on the throne for a time. He abolished the Inquisition and began several reforms.

The insurrection in Spain gave great joy in England. "The general rapture knew no bounds," says Alison. England sent her armies into Spain and Portugal, and the Peninsular War resulted, which Napier has described so vividly. To restore Ferdinand, the son of Charles IV., to Spain, England spent, says Napier, one hundred millions sterling, about five hundred million dollars, "and the bones of forty thousand British soldiers lie scattered on the plains and mountains of the Peninsula." The heroic Sir John Moore fell at Corunna, and was buried in his bloody cloak at night by torchlight.

> "Not a drum was heard, not a funeral note,
> As his corse to the ramparts we hurried;
> Not a soldier discharged his farewell shot
> O'er the grave where our hero we buried."

His last words were, "I hope the people of England will be satisfied. I hope my country will do me justice." After his death, Sir Arthur Wellesley, the Duke of Wellington, was made commander-in-chief of all the English troops in the Spanish peninsula. Austria considered this an opportune time to make war on Napoleon. The latter raised another immense army,—Lanfrey says with much truth, "France was bleeding to death,"—marched against Austria, and several bloody battles resulted.

At Eckmühl the Austrians, says Marbot, admitted a loss of five thousand killed, and fifteen thousand prisoners. Napoleon said at St. Helena, "The greatest military manœuvres I ever made, and those for which I give myself most credit, were performed at Eckmühl."

At Ratisbon the Emperor was wounded in the foot, just before the retaking. So wild were the soldiers at the news, that as soon as his wound was dressed he rode in front of the whole line to appease their anxiety.

After some other successes, Napoleon reached Vienna, May 10, the Emperor Francis having fled, as before, to a place of safety. Napoleon went at once to the royal palace of Schönbrunn.

The enemy were now on the left bank of the Danube. The spring rains had swollen the great river, and the crossing was most hazardous. In the midst of the thousand yards of water was the huge Island of Lobau, four and a half miles long. Here the troops of Napoleon intrenched themselves, and built a bridge of boats to either side of the Danube. As soon as a portion of the French troops had crossed the river, and reached the towns of Aspern and Essling, the Austrians fell upon them with great slaughter, compelling the French to retreat to the Island of Lobau, in the middle of the river. In these battles the heroic Lannes had both legs crushed by a cannon-ball. One leg was amputated. The Emperor knelt beside the stretcher and wept as he embraced Lannes, whose blood stained Napoleon's white kerseymere waistcoat.

"You will live, my friend, you will live," said the Emperor.

"I trust I may, if I can still be of use to France and your Majesty," was the reply.

After his death, said Marbot, "Napoleon embraced the marshal's body, bathing it with tears, and saying repeatedly, 'What a loss for France and for me!'"

The losses at this double battle are variously estimated from twenty to fifty thousand; Lanfrey accepts the latter number. Seeley calls it "one of the most terrible and bloody battles of the period." Napoleon at once began to build substantial bridges on piles across the Danube, one of them eight hundred yards long, broad enough for three carriages to pass abreast. These bridges were finished in twenty days, and compelled great admiration.

To the astonishment of the Austrians, he crossed most of his army of 150,000 men during the night of July 4, and on July 6 fought the dreadful battle of Wagram. About 300,000 were in the battle. Fifty thousand on both sides were killed and wounded, probably about an equal number in each army.

The weather was extremely hot, and the corn on the battle-field caught fire from the shells. "The movements of both armies were hampered by the necessity of avoiding it," says Marbot; "for if once troops were overtaken by it, pouches and wagons exploded, carrying destruction through the ranks.... Of the soldiers who were severely wounded, great numbers perished in the flames; and of those whom the fire did not reach, many lay for days hidden by the tall corn, living during that time on the ears. The Emperor had the plains searched by bands of cavalry, and vehicles were brought from Vienna to remove the wounded, friends and foes alike. But few of those even whom the fire had passed recovered, and the soldiers had a saying that straw-fire had killed nearly as many as gun-fire."

"After the battle," says General Savary, "the Emperor sent sixty francs in crown pieces to each wounded soldier, and more than this to each officer."

Oct. 14, 1809, the peace of Vienna was signed at Schönbrunn, between France and Austria. "I committed a great fault after the battle of Wagram," said Napoleon at St. Helena, "in not reducing the power of Austria still more. She remained too strong for our safety, and to her we must attribute our ruin."

On Napoleon's return to France he had made up his mind to an act which will always tarnish his fame, and from which the decadence of his empire may be dated. He would divorce Josephine, and marry another, with the hope that he might have an heir to the throne. Undoubtedly he believed he was doing the best thing for France; and Thiers says the French people, while they loved Josephine, wished for the divorce.

On Nov. 30, 1809, as he and Josephine were dining together at Fontainebleau, not a word having been uttered except Napoleon asked one of the servants what time it was, he communicated to her his decision. After dismissing the servants, he came to her, took her hand, pressed it to his heart, and said, "Josephine! my dear Josephine! You know how I have loved you.... To you, to you alone, I owe the only moments of happiness I have tasted in this world. But, Josephine, my destiny is not to be controlled by my will. My dearest affections must yield to the interests of France."

"I expected this," said poor Josephine, "but the blow is none the less mortal."

She became at once insensible; and Napoleon, alarmed, hastily called assistance and bore her to her room. He came to see her in the evening, and wept.

Eugène determined at once to resign his position as Viceroy of Italy, but his mother begged him to remain the friend of Napoleon.

On Dec. 15, at the Tuileries, before the officers of the Empire, the divorce was announced. Josephine was almost overcome by her sobs. "The Emperor will always find in me his best friend," she said, and so it proved.

The next day the divorce was consummated before the Senate. Eugène announced the divorce, saying, "The tears of the Emperor do honor to my mother." Josephine, in a simple white muslin dress, leaning on the arm of Hortense, entered and signed the fatal decree. Both mother and daughter were in tears, as well as many of those present. Eugène, who idolized his mother, fell fainting to the floor. That evening when Josephine thought her husband had retired, she came to his room, her eyes swollen with weeping, and tottering towards the bed fell upon his neck, and sobbed as though her heart would break. They wept together, and talked for an hour. The next day Napoleon came to see her, accompanied by his secretary, Meneval. "He pressed her to his bosom with the most ardent embraces," says Meneval. "In the excess of her emotion she fainted."

At eleven o'clock the same day, veiled from head to foot, Josephine entered a close carriage drawn by six horses, said good-by to the Tuileries forever, and was driven to Malmaison. She retained the title of Empress, with $600,000 a year for her support. Napoleon passed eight days in retirement at Trianon. On his return to the Tuileries, he wrote to her, "I have been very lonely.... This great palace appears to me empty, and I find myself in solitude. Adieu, my love."

He frequently visited Malmaison. One day he found Josephine painting a violet. She says, "He threw himself with transport into the arms of his old friend.... It seemed impossible for him to cease gazing upon me, and his look was that of the most tender affection. At length he said, 'My dear Josephine, I have always loved you. I love you still. Do you still love me?"

Three months later, Mar. 11, 1810, Napoleon was married by proxy at Vienna, Archduke Charles representing him at the wedding, to Marie Louise, the daughter of Emperor Francis I. of Austria. He met her with his suite at the palace of Compiègne. She was eighteen, with light hair, and blue eyes, and gentle in manner. Napoleon was forty.

The civil marriage was celebrated at St. Cloud, April 1; and the next day they made their triumphal entry into Paris, by the Arc de l'Étoile, to the Tuileries, amid the cheers of three hundred thousand people. The world must have been amazed at such a union of France and Austria,—nations which had been at war for years. No wonder Napoleon, at St. Helena, spoke of it as "an abyss covered with a bed of flowers."

Two weeks later Josephine wrote him, "Your majesty shall never be troubled in his happiness by an expression of my grief. I offer incessant prayers that your majesty may be happy."

A year after his marriage, Mar. 20, 1811, a son, Napoleon Francis, was born to Napoleon, called the King of Rome, as the Roman States had been annexed to the Empire. All France rejoiced when the firing of one hundred guns announced the event.

Josephine wrote at once, telling Napoleon, "More than any one in the world do I rejoice in your joy." Of Marie Louise she wrote, "She cannot be more tenderly devoted to you than I am, but she has been enabled to contribute more toward your happiness, by securing that of France.... Not till you have ceased to watch by her bed, not till you are weary of embracing your son, will you take your pen to converse with your best friend. I will wait."

Napoleon brought his child to Josephine. "The moment I saw

you enter," she wrote him, "bearing the young Napoleon in your hands, was unquestionably one of the happiest of my life."

He said at St. Helena: "Josephine would willingly have seen Marie Louise. She frequently spoke of her with great interest.... Marie Louise manifested the utmost dislike, and even jealousy, of Josephine. I wished one day to take her to Malmaison, but she burst into tears when I made the proposal. She said she did not object to my visiting Josephine, only she did not wish to know it. But whenever she suspected my intention of going to Malmaison, there was no stratagem which she did not employ for the sake of annoying me."

The emperor was devoted to his son, and always considerate and tender to Marie Louise. The boy developed into a very beautiful and bright child, winning the love of everybody.

A little more than a year after the birth of the King of Rome, Russia and France were again at war. Whatever Alexander's personal feelings toward Napoleon, his nobles were opposed to him; they disliked his restrictions on commerce, and feared his growing power. Russia and England became allies, though Napoleon offered to make peace with the latter, which offers she always declined. Probably the real truth was they all wished to humble Napoleon.

Russia and France each raised a great army, the latter about a half million men.

Napoleon left Paris for Dresden, May 9, taking Marie Louise with him. He left her at Prague. Before he started from Paris he spent two hours in earnest conversation with Josephine at Malmaison.

This Grand Army must have made an imposing appearance, with their twenty thousand carriages, one hundred and eighty thousand horses employed in the artillery, besides thousands of provision wagons and baggage.

He began to cross the river Niemen, which empties into the Baltic, on the night of June 23, 1812. The policy of the Russians was to retreat, burning the towns through which they passed, and destroying all produce, that the French might find no support in the desolated country.

The first terrible battle was at Borodino, Sept. 7, where the French lost about thirty thousand, and the Russians fifty thousand, in killed and wounded.

On Sept. 14, Napoleon and his weary army—many thousands had been stationed at various places along the route—entered Moscow. Here they hoped for food and rest. They found the great city deserted. Powder had been placed under the Kremlin, and shells under the larger palaces, where Napoleon and his officers would be apt to lodge; water-pipes had been cut, fountains destroyed; and, the day after Napoleon's arrival, the whole city was set on fire by Russians detailed for that purpose. No wonder Napoleon said, years later, of this terrible destruction of a great city, "It was the most grand, the most sublime, the most terrific sight the world ever beheld!"

Napoleon wrote to the Tsar proposing peace; but no answer was ever returned, though he waited some weeks in Moscow, hoping to hear favorably. The more intelligent serfs offered to rise against their masters, and aid Napoleon, but he did not desire civil war.

On Oct. 19, 1812, the Grand Army of France, one hundred thousand strong, commenced its heart-breaking retreat. Deep snow had already come, earlier than usual. Kutusof, the Russian general, moved his army parallel to the French, and fought them at every available point. Marshal Ney covered the rear, and made for himself an immortal record. Napoleon rightly called him "The Bravest of the Brave." When they reached Borodino they sadly turned their heads away from the battle-fields where the bodies of thirty thousand men were half devoured by wolves. The cold became intense. Horses slipped and fell on the icy ground. Artillery and baggage were abandoned. There was no food in the devastated country. Where Napoleon had left provisions on his way to Moscow the enemy had destroyed them. Men ate their horses for food. They lay down at night on the snow to sleep, and never rose. "Every morning," says Marbot, "we left thousands of dead in our bivouacs.... So intense was the cold that we could see a kind of vapor rising from men's ears and eyes. Condensing,o on contact with the air, this vapor fell back on our persons with a rattle such as grains of millet might have made. We had often to halt and clear away from the horses' bits the icicles formed by their frozen breath.... Many soldiers of all ranks blew out their brains to put an end to their misery.... All ranks were confounded; there were no arms, no military bearings; soldiers, officers, generals, were clad in rags, and for boots had nothing but strips of leather or cloth, hardly fastened together with a string." The Emperor himself was grave, calm, and self-controlled, with no diminution of courage.

The soldiers of the allies of Napoleon, Austria, Prussia, Spain, and others, deserted by the thousands, the Russians having sent proclamations in various languages into the camps, telling them they should be returned to their homes.

Finally they reached the river Beresina, the bridge over which had been destroyed by the Russians. Tearing down the hovels in the village, the French built two bridges at night, the men standing for six or seven hours in the water. Then the troops surged upon them, and one bridge broke under the weight of guns and men. In rushing upon the other, great crowds were forced into the river and drowned. The Russians meantime swept them with cannon. From twenty to twenty-five thousand men perished in this dreadful crossing of the Beresina.

On Dec. 5, 1812, they were within the borders of Poland; and Napoleon, having learned that his death had been proclaimed in Paris, and that a man had tried to usurp the power, left his army in charge of

Murat, and, with two officers, hastened by sledges to Paris, which he reached Dec. 18.

The loss of the French army and its allies in the Russian campaign Thiers estimates as 300,000 men; other authorities make it 350,000; 100,000 were killed in the advance and retreat from Moscow; 150,000 died of hunger, fatigue, and cold; 100,000 were taken prisoners. The Russian losses were also heavy.

Prussia now joined herself to Russia, and declared war against France. Napoleon at once raised another army of nearly two hundred thousand by conscription, and defeated the enemy at Lützen, or Gross-Beeren, and Bautzen. His young conscripts fought heroically. His beloved Marshal Duroc was killed just after the latter battle. Napoleon wept as he left him dying, saying, "Duroc, there is another life.... We shall one day meet again."

Austria offered to be a mediator, but failing, hastened to join Prussia and Russia. The marriage with Marie Louise had not won Napoleon friends, as he had fondly hoped.

The allies now had five hundred thousand men, the Prussians under Blücher, the Austrians under Schwarzenberg. Upon Aug. 27, 1813, Napoleon defeated them at Dresden, where they left forty thousand on the field, half of whom were prisoners, but was himself defeated in the dreadful battle of Leipsic, Oct. 16-19.

Bavaria and Westphalia had been compelled to join the allies, whose forces thrice outnumbered the French. The Swedes, under Bernadotte, had now turned against France. "In the three days' battle," says Alison, "the French lost 60,000 men, and the allies nearly as many."

In the retreat of the French from Leipsic they were obliged to cross the Elster river. The bridge had been mined, and by a mistake was exploded before all the French had passed over. Marbot says, of those who were left in Leipsic, about 13,000 were killed, and 25,000 made prisoners.

Meantime the English had been victorious over the French in Spain and Portugal, and Joseph Bonaparte had been driven from the throne. He came to the United States and lived at Bordentown, New Jersey, for some years, dying at Florence, Italy, July 28, 1844, at the age of seventy-six.

The allies now pushed into France, determined to enter Paris and dethrone Napoleon. The Emperor raised a new army, and with prodigious energy and courage fought against the coalition of Europe. Often with his forces greatly inferior in number to the allies, he defeated them, but finally he was overborne. Marie Louise fled to Blois. The young King of Rome refused to go. "They are betraying my papa," he said, "and I will not go away. I do not wish to leave the palace." He wept as he was taken to the carriage. His governess promised that he should come back, but she was never able to keep her promise.

Paris capitulated March 30, 1814; and the Senate, through the lead of Talleyrand, declared that Napoleon and his family had forfeited the throne.

Napoleon arrived at Paris a few hours after the capitulation, stunned at the news. Fearless as ever, he wished to attack the allies, but was persuaded by his marshals to desist.

With agony of soul, but calmness of demeanor, he signed his abdication at Fontainebleau, April 6, 1814: "The Emperor Napoleon declares that he renounces, for himself and his heirs, the throne of France and Italy; and that there is no personal sacrifice, not even that of life itself, which he is not willing to make for the interests of France."

By the will of the allies, Louis XVIII was recalled, and Napoleon was banished to the Island of Elba, east of Corsica, with an annual income from France of $500,000. He bade the Old Guard an affectionate good-by. "Adieu, my children," he said. "I would that I could press you all to my heart. Let me at least embrace your general and your eagle." He put his arms around General Petit, and kissed the eagle on its silver beak. Amid the tears and sobs of his brave soldiers, on April 20, Napoleon drove away from Fontainebleau to Fréjus, and in the British frigate, The Undaunted, set sail for Elba, April 27, 1814.

He had frequently written to Josephine through these melancholy months. Once he wrote: "To me death would now be a blessing. But I would once more see Josephine," and he saw her before his departure.

Four days before he left Fontainebleau for Elba, he wrote, "Adieu, my dear Josephine. Be resigned, as I am, and never forget him who never forgot, and who never will forget you. Farewell, Josephine."

She longed to follow him to Elba, but waited to see if Marie Louise would join him. At first Marie Louise desired to go to him, but was prevailed upon by her father, the Emperor Francis, to return to Austria, where she and her son became virtually prisoners. She finally retired to the Duchy of Parma, which the allies had given her, and later married her chamberlain, Count de Neipperg, an Austrian general.

Josephine wrote to Napoleon: "I have been on the point of quitting France to follow your footsteps, and to consecrate to you the remainder of an existence which you so long embellished. A single motive restrains me, and that you may divine.... Say but the word, and I depart."

As soon as Napoleon went to Elba, Josephine's health rapidly declined. She caught cold in driving in the park at Malmaison. When near death she said to Hortense, "I can say with truth, in this, my dying hour, that the first wife of Napoleon never caused a single tear to flow."

Napoleon landed at Elba, May 4, 1814. A month later, May 29, Josephine died, uttering, with her last breath, "Napoleon! Elba!"

"I have seen," said Mademoiselle Avrillon, the first lady of her bedchamber, "the Empress Josephine's sleeplessness and her terrible dreams. I have known her to pass whole days buried in the gloomiest thought. I know what I have seen and heard, and I am sure that grief killed her!"

Napoleon's mother, a woman of sixty-four, and his sister Pauline, joined him at Elba. The latter had married Prince Borghese in 1803, but they soon separated. After several years they were reconciled to each other. She died at Florence in 1825.

Napoleon remained at Elba ten months, when he escaped, landed at Cannes, Mar. 1, 1815, raised an army in France as if by magic, and entered Paris at its head, Mar. 20.

The people seemed glad to be rid of Louis XVIII., who fled at midnight, Mar. 19. Napoleon said, with much truth, "The Bourbons, during their exile, had learned nothing, and forgotten nothing." The Grand Army joyously received their leader. The people shouted themselves hoarse. They wept, and sang songs of thanksgiving. Paris was brilliant with illuminations. When he reached the Tuileries, he was seized and borne aloft above the heads of the throng. The ladies of the court, says Alison, "received him with transports, and imprinted fervent kisses on his cheeks, his hands, and even his dress. Never was such a scene witnessed in history." Hortense and her two children were at the Tuileries to welcome Napoleon.

The allies cared little whom France wished to rule her. They preferred the conservative Bourbons or indeed anybody who would not disturb the so-called balance of power in Europe. They at once banded themselves together, England, Austria, Russia, Prussia, Portugal, Spain, and Sweden, to crush this "enemy and disturber of the world."

A million men were soon raised by the allies, and Napoleon brought together over 200,000. He decided at once to take the offensive rather than let the allies invade France. He left Paris for Belgium, June 12, 1815, taking with him about 120,000 men. He drove the Prussians out of Charleroi, and on June 16 gained a victory over the Prussian marshal, Blücher, at Ligny. Jomini, who is usually authentic, says Napoleon had 72,000 in the battle, and Blücher from 80,000 to 90,000. It was a hotly contested battle-field in which the Prussians lost from 12,000 to 20,000 men. Thiers says 30,000.

Blücher had his gray charger, given him by the Prince Regent of England, shot under him, and was nearly killed in the retreat.

The same day occurred the desperate battle of Quatre-Bras, in which Marshal Ney was defeated.

On June 18, 1815, the decisive battle of Waterloo was fought, nine miles south-east of Brussels. Napoleon's forces, according to Jomini and Thiers, were 70,000 in number; Seeley and Ropes say 72,000. Wellington had about 68,000.

The ground was so drenched by rains that the battle was not begun till a little past eleven. Both sides fought desperately. Blücher, a few miles to the right of Wellington, at Wavre, had promised to join him. Napoleon had told Marshal Grouchy to follow the Prussians and thus prevent their union with the English. He started too late for Wavre; he did not take the advice of some of his officers to hasten to Napoleon when they heard the sound of battle, and his 33,000 men failed to help at Waterloo. Ropes gives an interesting account of this in the Atlantic Monthly, June, 1881, "Who lost Waterloo?"

All day long the battle raged. Hand to hand combats were constant. The battle seemed in favor of the French. Meantime Blücher was coming from Wavre, with his guns sinking axle-deep in the mud. "We shall never get on," was heard on all sides. "We must get on," said the bluff Blücher; "I have given my word to Wellington."

Napoleon kept watching for Grouchy. Early in the afternoon about 30,000 Prussians under Bulow had come to Wellington's assistance. Night came on and the firing of musketry was heard. "There's Grouchy!" said the Emperor. His aide-de-camp, Labédoyère, rushed to announce it to the army. "Marshal Grouchy is arriving, the Guard is going to charge. Courage! courage! 'tis all over with the English."

"One last shout of hope burst from every rank," says M. Fleury de Chaboulon, ex-secretary of the Emperor; "the wounded who were still capable of taking a few steps returned to the combat, and thousands of voices eagerly repeated, Forward! forward!"

It was not Grouchy, but Blücher with thirty or forty thousand fresh troops. The Imperial Guard did indeed charge with all their wonted impetuosity. They were mowed down like grain. Ney, with five horses shot under him, marched on foot with his drawn sword. Napoleon watched them, pale, yet calm. "All is lost!" said he, "the Guard recoils!"

The Emperor was everywhere in the battle. "Death shuns you. You will be made a prisoner," said his generals, and an officer seized the bridle of his horse and dragged him away.

The French were completely overcome, and the Prussians pursued them with great vigor. It is estimated that the French lost thirty thousand on the field of Waterloo, and the loss of the allies was probably not much less. It was one of the most bloody battles of modern times.

Napoleon returned to Paris, and then retired to Malmaison. He abdicated in favor of his son, Napoleon II.; but the allies, when they captured Paris a second time, July 7, 1815, placed Louis XVIII. again on the throne.

Napoleon repaired to Rochefort with the hope that he might embark for America, but the coast was so blockaded by the English steamers that this was impossible. He surrendered himself to go on board the English ship, Bellerophon, July 15, with the hope that he should find a generous foe. He soon learned, to his inexpressible grief, that he was destined for St. Helena. On Aug. 7 he was transferred to the

Northumberland, and sailed for his lonely place of exile, which he reached Oct. 16, 1815.

The Island of St. Helena, ten miles broad and seven long, is in the Atlantic Ocean, fourteen hundred miles west of the west coast of South Africa. It is composed of rugged mountains of volcanic origin, with littlevegetation. Wherever a vessel could approach a fort was planted, so that the island formed a complete prison.

Lieutenant John R. Glover, who accompanied the British admiral who took Napoleon to St. Helena, said of the island (Century, for November, 1893): "Nothing can possibly be less prepossessing, nay, more horribly forbidding, than the first appearance of this isolated and apparently burnt up barren rock, which promises neither refreshment nor pleasure.... During our eight months' residence we experienced little variation, and had continued rains. The climate is by no means healthy, ... the children being sickly, and the adults suffering from the liver, of which complaint many of our men died."

Here Napoleon lived for six years, till his death, May 5, 1821, at the age of fifty-two, of a cancer in the stomach, the same disease which had killed his father. He was allowed to take with him to St. Helena three of his generals and their families, and a secretary, Las Cases.

His jailer, Sir Hudson Lowe, seems to have been a most unfortunate choice in the surveillance of a high-spirited and remarkable man.

Napoleon was allowed to walk or ride only within certain limits, with a British officer near at hand. His accommodations were poor and plain. "The rats," says Dr. O'Meara, "are in numbers almost incredible. I have frequently seen them assemble like broods of chickens round the offal thrown out of the kitchen." Besides he says, through the roof "the rain entered in torrents." Napoleon's letters were all opened, both those sent or received. He was never addressed as Emperor, England ungenerously insisting that he be called simply General Bonaparte. Books addressed to "The Emperor" were not delivered to him. William O'Connor Morris says: "His humiliation was degrading and needless.... Admitting that the allies had a right to deprive him of liberty, they had no right to subject him to insult and wrong; and St. Helena is a blot on the fair fame of England." From his idolized son he was not permitted to hear.

He said to Countess Montholon, at St. Helena, "On receiving into my arms that infant, so many times fervently implored of Heaven, could I have believed that one day he would have become the source of my greatest anguish? Yes, madame, every day he costs me tears of blood. I imagine to myself the most horrid events, which I cannot remove from my mind. I see either the potion or the empoisoned fruit which is about to terminate the days of that young innocent by the most cruel sufferings."

The boy worshipped his father. "Tell him," said the little King of

Rome, then four years old, when Meneval, Napoleon's former secretary, left Marie Louise in Austria, "that I love him dearly." He looked like his father, had his ambition, and, as he grew to manhood, longed to return to France. When Charles X. was overthrown in 1830, he said, "Why was I not there to take my chance?" He was then nineteen. Napoleon had foreseen the fall of the Bourbons, as he said at St. Helena, "They will not maintain their position after my death; a reaction in my favor will take place everywhere, even in England."

Napoleon II. died at Vienna, July 22, 1832, at the age of twenty-one, of consumption, at Schönbrunn, the summer home of the Emperor. He expired upon the same narrow bed on which his father slept when he came as the conqueror of Austria. General Hartmann said,o "Having passed my life on battle-fields, I have often seen death, but I never saw a soldier die more bravely."

When near death, Napoleon II said, "So young, and is there no remedy? My birth and my death will be the only points of remembrance." He lies buried in the plain Church of the Capucines, beside his mother. His heart is in a small silver urn in St. Augustine's Church.

For six years Napoleon lived in this prison at St. Helena, dictating his memoirs and commentaries to Count Montholon, Baron Gourgaud, and Count Las Cases. His health failed rapidly after the first year. Not taking exercise, on account of the constant espionage, he was finally prevailed upon by the physician to work a little in a garden, which he found a relief.

At the end of a year, Las Cases was banished with his son to England, because he had forwarded a letter to Lady Clavering, telling how badly the Emperor was treated, and it had not passed through the hands of Sir Hudson Lowe. This was a great blow to Napoleon, as he was the only one who could read, speak, and understand English. Dr. O'Meara was also obliged to leave St. Helena on account of Sir Hudson Lowe's treatment of him.

After some months of illness, the friends of Napoleon were permitted to send Dr. Antommarchi, a Corsican, to him. In the spring of 1821, Napoleon grew feeble and emaciated. He made his will, remembering his friends most generously. April 22, from perspiration on account of his great pain, Count Montholon writes, "On this night I changed the Emperor's linen seven times." April 25, as Montholon watched by his bedside, at four o'clock in the morning, Napoleon exclaimed, "I have just seen my good Josephine, but she would not embrace me. She disappeared at the moment when I was about to take her in my arms. She was seated there.... She is not changed. She is still the same, full of devotion to me. She told me that we were about to see each other again, never more to part. Did you see her?"

Three days later he gave directions about his death, asking that his heart might be put in spirits of wine, and carried to Parma, to Marie

Louise. "You will tell her that I tenderly loved her," he said, "that I never ceased to love her."

Five days before his death he dictated for two hours his desires about the Palace of Versailles, and the organization of the National Guard for the defence of Paris. To the last he carried out his chosen motto, "Everything for the French people."

He remembered his servants, and wished to see them and say good-by. One of them exclaimed excitedly, "I will die for him."

May 2 the Emperor was delirious, and, thinking he was with his army, shouted, "Desaix! Massena! Ah! victory is declaring. Run! hasten! press the charge! They are ours!" He sprang from the bed and fell prostrate upon the floor.

On the night of May 4 a tornado swept the island, uprooting the trees which the Emperor had planted. During the night, says Count Montholon, "Twice I thought I distinguished the unconnected words, 'France—armée, tête d'armée (head of the army)—Josephine.'"

During the whole of May 5 he lay quiet and peaceful, conscious, his right hand out of bed, seemingly absorbed in deep meditation. At eleven minutes before six o'clock he died.

England would not permit his body to be embalmed or to be carried to France, as he had requested, or his heart to be given to Marie Louise; so, at half-past twelve, on May 8, he was buried under some willows at St. Helena. The English garrison, two thousand five hundred strong, which had been on the island to keep Napoleon from escaping, now followed his body to the grave. Three volleys of fifteen guns each were fired over it. The soldiers had unbounded admiration for the unrivalled leader, and begged to kiss the blue cloak which he wore at Marengo, and which was thrown over the coffin.

"We were not allowed," says Dr. Antommarchi, "to place over the grave either a stone or a modest inscription, the governor Sir Hudson Lowe opposing this pious wish."

The Emperor had written in his will, "It is my wish that my ashes may repose on the banks of the Seine, in the midst of the French people, whom I have loved so well."

On May 5, 1840, nineteen years after Napoleon's death, the French, now that Louis Philippe had become king, asked England that his body might be removed to France. Consent being given, Prince de Joinville, the son of the king, with Gourgaud, Bertrand, and the son of Las Cases, with two armed ships, proceeded on their sad errand, bearing an ebony coffin, with the one word, "Napoleon," on it in gold letters. Within was a coffin of lead. The funeral pall was of purple velvet, embroidered with bees, and bordered with ermine.

At midnight, Oct. 5, 1840, the work of exhuming the body of the Emperor was begun. At ten o'clock in the forenoon the coffin was reached, so difficult had it been to remove the heavy stones and cement which covered the vault. The first coffin of mahogany was opened, then the leaden one, then one of mahogany, then one of tin. The body was found wonderfully preserved, and seemed as though recently interred. The hands were perfect, with the smooth skin as if in life. The clothes retained their color,—the dark green coat faced with red, the white pantaloons, and the hat, resting on the thigh. The body was exposed to the air only two minutes; the coffins were re-sealed and placed in those brought from France.

The ships reached France early in December. Never was there such a funeral in Paris. One hundred and fifty thousand soldiers and more than a million citizens assisted at the magnificent obsequies. The funeral car, its cenotaph rising fifty feet from the ground, was drawn by sixteen black horses, four abreast, covered with cloth of gold. The Emperor's war-horse was draped with a veil of purple crape, embroidered with bees. The remnants of the Old Guard were there— the hosts who idolized Napoleon and would have died for him; but the son, the King of Rome, was sleeping in a coffin in Austria, and Josephine was resting in the church at Rueil, two miles from Malmaison.

At the funeral service three hundred musicians played Mozart's Requiem in the Church of the Invalides, where now the great hero rests. The seemingly countless throng of people were moved to tears. Could he who was its object have looked forward to all this love and homage, when he lay dying among the rocks of St. Helena, the agony might have been lessened. Could he have foreseen how tens of thousands, every year, from all the world, would stand by that tomb, under the dome of the Invalides, and do honor to the wonderful soldier and statesman, that bitter exile and death might not have been quite so desolate and pathetic.

"Posterity," as he said, "will do him justice." Already the harshness of his critics is giving place to a correct estimate of his extraordinary genius.

"I have formed and carried into effect," he said to Dr. O'Meara, "a code of laws that will bear my name to the most distant posterity. From nothing I raised myself to be the most powerful monarch of the world."

Napier thought Napoleon "the greatest man of whom history makes mention." "Never," says Alison, "were talents of the highest, genius of the most exalted kind, more profusely bestowed upon a human being."

Napoleon worked incessantly. He saved every moment. He believed in himself. He had great courage, will, and energy. He said to Las Cases that he liked two-o'clock-in-the-morning courage, which he had rarely met. "I mean," he said, "unprepared courage; that which is necessary on an unexpected occasion, and which, in spite of the most unforeseen events, leaves full freedom of judgment and decision."

Napoleon had this courage. Three horses were killed under him at Toulon, several in Italy, and three or four at the siege of Saint Jean d'Acre. When his body was prepared for burial, it was found that there were several scars upon it, some slight, and three very distinct.

He hated selfishness. Madame la Générale Durant, first lady to the Empress Marie Louise, relates in her book, "Napoleon and Marie Louise," that once, when Marie Louise said everybody was selfish, and that she was also, he replied, "Don't say, my Louise, that you are selfish; I know no more hideous vice."

He had great dignity combined with kindliness. After a ball, during which he conversed with Goethe, he wrote Josephine: "I have attended a ball in Weimar. The Emperor Alexander danced. But I? No! Forty years are forty years."

"He had a directness of action," says Emerson, "never before combined with so much comprehension.... Here was a man who, in each moment and emergency, knew what to do next.... Few men have any next; they live from hand to mouth, without plan, and are ever at the end of their line, and, after each action, wait for an impulse from abroad. Napoleon had been the first man of the world, if his ends had been purely public....

"We cannot, in the universal imbecility, indecision, and indolence of men, sufficiently congratulate ourselves on this strong and ready actor, who took occasion by the beard, and showed us how much may be accomplished by the mere force of such virtues as all men possess in less degrees; namely, by punctuality, by personal attention, by courage and thoroughness."

While indomitable in battle, he was, says General Gourgaud, "of all generals, whether ancient or modern, the one who has paid the greatest attention to the wounded. The intoxication of victory never could make him forget them. His first thought after every battle was always of them."

Count Segur relates that, after the battle of Borodino, when Napoleon and his escort were going over the field, a horse stepped on a dying man, who expired with a groan. Napoleon uttered a shriek of pain. Some one, to soothe him, said, "It was only a Russian." With much warmth, Napoleon replied, "After victory there are no enemies, but only men."

His despatch was marvellous. He was generous, and never forgot the poorest who needed his kindness. He was ambitious; but Europe, fearing him, forced him into many of his wars. He knew how to govern himself as well as others. He said of Lannes, one of his generals who lost his temper, that a man could not be great who permitted himself to get angry. The officer heard of this remark, and ever after controlled his temper.

Napoleon was more moral than his age. He loved children and nature. "How many times," says Bourrienne, as they walked toward Rueil from Malmaison, "has the bell of the village church interrupted our most serious conversations! He would stop, lest the noise of our footsteps should drown any portion of the delightful sound."

He believed, in an age of unbelief. He said to Bertrand at St. Helena, "I know men, and I tell you that Jesus Christ is not a man.... Everything in him astonishes me. His spirit overawes me, and his will confounds me. Between him and whoever else in the world there is no possible term of comparison."

Napoleon compared the reign of Christ with that of Cæsar, Alexander, Hannibal, and of himself; "My armies have forgotten me, even while living, as the Carthaginian army forgot Hannibal. Such is our power! A single battle lost crushes us, and adversity scatters our friends.... What an abyss between my deep misery and the eternal reign of Christ, which is proclaimed, loved, adored, and which is extended over all the earth! Is this to die? Is it not rather to live? The death of Christ! It is the death of God."

The life of Napoleon, truly called "the Great," is more interesting and pathetic than any novel. It will always remain one of the marvels of the world.

HORATIO NELSON

It is a significant fact that the life of a leader is never an easy one. Nelson's life was one of struggle from beginning to end; a battle with poverty, lack of appreciation ofttimes by his country, much ill-health, domestic disquietude, and many hardships. He died at forty-seven, the greatest naval hero of the age.

Horatio Nelson, the son of a country rector, the Rev. Edmund Nelson, was born Sept. 29, 1758, at Burnham Thorpe, Norfolk, England. The mother, Catherine, was descended from a good family, her grandmother being an elder sister of Sir Robert Walpole, Earl of Oxford. Catherine died when her little son, Horatio, was nine years old, leaving eight out of eleven children to mourn their capable mother. Nelson said of her later, just a short time before he died, "The thought of former days brings all my mother into my heart, which shows itself in my eyes."

The boy Nelson was fearless and ambitious. It is related of him that, straying away from the house when a mere child, his grandmother thought he had been carried off by gypsies. When found sitting beside a brook which he could not cross, the old lady said, "I wonder, child, that hunger and fear did not drive you home."

"Fear," said the boy, "I never saw fear; what is it?"

At another time, some pears were wanted from the schoolmaster's garden. Without debating the question of the sin of stealing, nobody dared venture for fear of the consequences. Horatio volunteered to get them, was lowered at night by a sheet from his window, gathered the pears, and gave them to his mates, keeping none for himself. "I only took them," he said, "because every other boy was afraid."

His father was poor, always in frail health, and apparently unable to do much for his numerous progeny. Horatio determined to do something for himself. Seeing in the newspaper that his uncle on his mother's side, Captain Maurice Suckling, had been appointed in the navy to the ship Raisonnable, of sixty-four guns, Horatio said to his brother, a year and a half older than himself, "Do, William, write to my father, and tell him that I should like to go to sea with Uncle Maurice."

Mr. Nelson was at Bath for his health. He at once wrote to the captain about his twelve-year-old son, who was as sickly in body as himself. The uncle wrote back, "What has poor Horatio done, who is so weak, that he, above all the rest, should be sent to rough it out at sea? But let him come, and the first time we go into action, a cannon-ball may knock off his head, and provide for him at once."

His father took him to London, from whence he found his way to Chatham, where the ship was lying. His uncle was absent at the time, and the first few days were lonely in the extreme. The sailors were rough, their treatment by officers often harsh, not to say cruel, and the lad who had so yearned for the sea soon came to despise the Royal Navy.

He soon went on a West Indian voyage, in a small merchant ship commanded by Mr. John Rathbone, who had served as master's mate under Captain Suckling. Here, with keen observation, and a constant desire to rise in his profession, he learned rapidly.

Later, young Nelson went as coxswain under Captain Lutwidge in the Carcass on a Polar voyage. They were beset by the ice; left their ships, expecting they would be crushed, and dragged their boats by hand; had the usual fights with walruses and bears, Nelson exposing himself in an encounter with the latter, that he might carry a skin home to his father.

Nelson's next voyage, at fifteen, was in the Seahorse, of twenty guns, to the East Indies in a squadron under Sir Edward Hughes. He was stationed at the foretop at watch and watch, where his attention to duty soon made him a midshipman.

After eighteen months in this debilitating climate, he became dangerously ill, and was sent home in the Dolphin in 1776. The youth of sixteen became very despondent. "I felt impressed," he says, "with an idea that I should never rise in my profession. My mind was staggered with a view of the difficulties I had to surmount, and the little interest I possessed. I could discover no means of reaching the object of my ambition. After a long and gloomy revery, in which I almost wished myself overboard, a sudden flow of patriotism was kindled within me and presented my king and country as my patrons. My mind exulted in the idea. 'Well, then,' I exclaimed, 'I will be a hero, and, confiding in Providence, I will brave every danger.'"

From that time he often told his friend Hardy, "a radiant orb was suspended in his mind's eye, which urged him onward to renown."

Captain Suckling had now become comptroller of the navy; and as soon as Nelson was recovered, through his uncle's influence, he was made fourth lieutenant of the Worcester, a ship of sixty-four guns, commanded by Mark Robinson, going out to Gibraltar. At nineteen he passed an excellent examination in naval matters, and was made second lieutenant on the Lowestoffe, of thirty-two guns, under Captain William Locker, then fitting out for the West Indies. The vessel arrived at Carlisle Bay, Barbadoes, July 4, 1777.

Nelson soon showed his usual bravery. An American letter-of-marque was captured. The first lieutenant was ordered to board her; but, unable to reach her by reason of the high sea, Nelson volunteered, and though his boat swept over the deck of the American privateer, he finally got aboard, and made her his prize.

Soon after Nelson was appointed third lieutenant of the flag-ship Bristol, and in 1779 commander of the Badger, protecting the Mosquito

Coast and the Bay of Honduras from the privateers. Many French merchantmen were captured.

During these years from 1777 to 1780, the skirmishes with the Spaniards and French, though marked with great energy and bravery on the part of Nelson, were ruinous to him and his men. Hundreds of the latter died from the malaria of the climate, or were poisoned by the bites of serpents. Nelson himself, more dead than alive, was carried back to England, and for many months remained at Bath, endeavoring to regain his health.

Fretting at his inactive life, he applied for a position which was not granted for some months; and then he was sent, much against his will, to the bleak North Sea to protect the home trade. Here he spent a winter in discomfort, but he learned many things which were of inestimable value in one of his great battles afterwards.

In 1782 he sailed in his ship, the Albemarle, for Newfoundland and Quebec, and while cruising along the coast, captured the Harmony, a schooner which belonged to a fisherman by the name of Carver. Nelson employed him as a pilot in Boston Harbor, and then restored him the schooner and cargo, giving him a certificate so that no other vessel should capture him. This certificate was framed, and hung in the house of Isaac Davis of Boston. Carver was so grateful to Nelson that he came afterwards to the Albemarle, at the hazard of his life, bringing a present of sheep, poultry, and fresh provisions. The scurvy was raging on board, and the ship's company had not enjoyed a fresh meal for five months, so that Carver's present was most acceptable.

While at Quebec in 1782, when he was twenty-four, Nelson fell in love with an American lady, whom he much desired to marry, but was prevented by the decision of his friend Alexander Davison, who hurried him off to sea.

In October of this same year, 1782, Nelson sailed for New York, where he found the Barfleur with twelve sail-of-the-line under command of Lord Hood. The latter introduced him to Prince William Henry, Duke of Clarence, afterwards William IV. The duke was greatly pleased with the boyish-looking captain, dressed in his full laced uniform, with his hair tied in a stiff Hessian tail of an extraordinary length. The duke says of his quaint figure, "I had never seen anything like it before, nor could I imagine who he was nor what he came about. But his address and conversation were irresistibly pleasing; and when he spoke on professional subjects, it was with an enthusiasm that showed me he was no common being."

Under Lord Hood, Nelson sailed to the West Indies, and remained there till January, 1783, when peace with France was concluded.

"I have closed the war," said Nelson, "without a fortune; but there is not a speck in my character. True honor, I hope, predominates in my mind far above riches."

54

On July 11 Nelson was presented at court, and received much attention from the king, perhaps on account of the good words of Prince William, his son, for the sailor. The young man of twenty-five had not particularly distinguished himself as yet, but he had improved every opportunity of making himself familiar with naval matters. He would be ready for the great opportunity if it ever came.

As he was now on half-pay, he determined to go to France for a time to study the French language. Here he fell in love with Miss Andrews, one of the three daughters of an English clergyman. As his income was only £130 a year, he wrote his uncle, William Suckling, asking that he might be allowed £100 a year in addition, that he might be able to marry. This request was granted; but Miss Andrews perhaps did not give her consent, or Nelson thought that £230 would not support a wife in much luxury, for she afterwards married a clergyman by the name of Farrer, and later Colonel Warne. Nelson evidently admired her greatly; for he wrote to his brother William, "She has such accomplishments, that, had I a million of money, I am sure I should at this moment make her an offer of them."

In the spring of 1784 he was appointed to the Boreas, of twenty-eight guns, and sailed for the Leeward Islands, taking with him Lady Hughes and her family to her husband, Sir Richard, who was in command at that station.

There were about thirty midshipmen on board, and to all Nelson was extremely kind and sympathetic. When a boy was at first afraid to go up the masts, Nelson would say, "I am going a race to the masthead, and beg that I may meet you there." When they met at the top, Nelson would speak cheerfully and say, "How much any person was to be pitied who could fancy there was any danger, or even anything disagreeable, in the attempt."

He was always the first to arrive on deck with his quadrant at noon. When he made visits of ceremony he always took some of his lads with him. When he went to dine with the governor of Barbadoes, he said, "Your Excellency must excuse me for bringing one of my midshipmen. I make it a rule to introduce them to all the good company I can, as they have few to look up to besides myself during the time they are at sea."

Through life Nelson showed this same thoughtfulness and tenderness for his men. He never lost the sensitiveness of his childhood, which made him cry bitterly when he had hurt a pet lamb in a shoemaker's shop, by accidentally opening a door against it. He was always opposed to harsh discipline, and ruled by love rather than by fear. No wonder it was said of him, when other great men were mentioned, "Nelson was the man to love."

At the Island of Nevis, Nelson fell in love for the third time. The lady was Mrs. Fanny Nisbet, whose husband, a physician, had died insane, eighteen months after their marriage. Her uncle, Mr. Herbert, was the president of Nevis. She had a son Josiah, several years old, to whom Nelson became attached; and this, of course, helped to win the favor of the mother.

Three months before their marriage he writes to her from Antigua, where he has Prince William Henry with him: "What is it to attend on princes! let me attend on you and I am satisfied. Some are born for attendants on great men; I rather think that is not my particular province. His Royal Highness often tells me he believes I am married, for he never saw a lover so easy or say so little of the object he has a regard for. When I tell him I certainly am not, then he is sure I must have a great esteem for you, and that it is not what is vulgarly—I do not much like the use of that word—called love.

"He is right; my love is founded on esteem, the only foundation that can make the passion last. I need not tell you what you so well know, that I wish I had a fortune to settle on you; but I trust I have a good name, and that certain events will bring the other about; it is my misfortune, not my fault. You can marry me only from a sincere affection; therefore I ought to make you a good husband, and I hope it will turn out that I shall."

Again he writes, "I daily thank God, who ordained that I should be attached to you. He has, I firmly believe, intended it as a blessing to me, and I am well convinced you will not disappoint his beneficent intentions."

These are certainly very different letters from those which he wrote in after years to Lady Hamilton, whom he idolized. Undoubtedly Nelson mistook loneliness of heart for love; as he wrote to Lady Hamilton years after, "I never did love any one else.... I have been the world around, and in every corner of it, and never yet saw your equal, or even one who could be put in comparison with you." Nelson and Mrs. Nisbet were married March 12, 1787, Prince William giving away the bride. Many of his friends in the service regretted that he had married before his honors had been more fully won. "The Navy," said Captain Pringle, the day after the wedding, "yesterday lost one of its greatest ornaments by Nelson's marriage. It is a national loss that such an officer should marry; had it not been for that circumstance, I foresaw that Nelson would become the greatest man in the service."

Nelson took his wife to England, arriving at Spithead July 4, about four months after their marriage. He had applied for a ship-of-the-line, but no notice was taken of the request. He retired with his wife to the parsonage at Burnham Thorpe, and at the request of his aged father remained there. He was in very poor health and living on half-pay. "From the 30th of November, 1787, to the 30th of January, 1793," says W. Clark Russell, in his life of the hero, "Nelson, whose delicate form enclosed the genius of the greatest sea-captain the world has ever produced, was compelled by departmental neglect to lie by in an almost poverty-stricken retirement."

Again and again he asked for employment. The prince recommended him to Lord Chatham, but nothing was done. In December, 1792, Nelson wrote, "If your lordships should be pleased to appoint me to a cockle-boat I should be grateful." He would have left the service, if he had had means to live on shore. He was irritated beyond measure by this neglect, and perhaps Mrs. Nelson did not find the parsonage a perfect haven of rest and peace.

Finally Nelson concluded to take refuge in France. That country had become a republic Sept. 21, 1792. She soon found herself, on account of her democratic principles, engaged in war with various countries, Great Britain among them. Feb. 1, 1793, she declared war against England, Holland, and Spain. Sardinia was already at war with France. As soon as England was involved in war, Nelson was needed; and he was assigned to the Agamemnon, a fine ship of sixty-four guns, called by the seamen, "Old Eggs-and-Bacon." She sailed for Gibraltar June 27, 1793, with Lord Hood's fleet, nineteen sail-of-the-line, and a convoy of merchant-ships.

When Lord Hood arrived in the Mediterranean, he stationed his ships off Toulon, which soon surrendered to the British, without firing a shot. Nelson was at once ordered to Naples with despatches for Sir William Hamilton, the British minister, and to ask for ten thousand Italian troops, to help in the preservation of Toulon.

King Ferdinand and his queen, Maria Caroline, the daughter of Maria Theresa of Austria, gave Nelson most cordial welcome at Court, feeling that the English were "the saviours of Italy." Sir William Hamilton told his wife that he was going to introduce her to a little man, not handsome, "but an English naval officer, who will become the greatest man that England ever produced. I know it from the few words I have already exchanged with him. I pronounce that he will one day astonish the world.... Let him be put in the room prepared for Prince Augustus."

Lady Hamilton received Nelson with her accustomed grace and cordiality. He wrote his wife, "She is a young woman of amiable manners, and who does honor to the station in which she is raised.... She has been wonderfully kind and good to Josiah."

Nelson was at this time about thirty-five, and Lady Hamilton five years younger, of the same age as his wife. She was a woman of remarkable beauty and great sweetness of manner. Southey said, "She was a woman whose personal accomplishments have seldom been equalled, and whose powers of mind were not less fascinating than her person." Her history had been a strange one. Born in extreme poverty, and early left an orphan by the death of her father, she was for some years a nursery-maid and servant, then a model for Romney, the famous artist, who painted her twenty-three times, as Bacchante, Saint Cecilia, a Magdalen, a Wood Nymph, Joan of Arc, etc., and thought her the most beautiful human being he had ever looked upon.

At this time she supported herself by her needle. Her beauty attracted the attention of Mr. Charles Greville, second son of Francis, Earl of Warwick, and Elizabeth, daughter of Lord Archibald Hamilton. He educated her, and she became skilled in music and languages. She played finely on the harp. Her stage talents were so great that she was offered two thousand guineas to sing for the season at the Opera House in London. Greville sent her to Naples with his uncle, Sir William Hamilton, with the avowed object of perfecting her in music, but in reality to abandon her, as he had become somewhat straitened in circumstances.

She loved Greville, and was deeply wounded at his treatment. Sir William, a younger son of Lord Archibald Hamilton, was at that time sixty-one, and Emma Lyon twenty-eight. He had married for his first wife a Welsh heiress, who had died nine years previously: In 1791, Sept. 6, he married Emma, who thus became Lady Hamilton. He was a student of art, an author of several volumes, and for thirty-six years minister to Italy.

However blameworthy the previous life of Lady Hamilton, Sir William was devoted to her, and said at his death, twelve years later, "My incomparable Emma, you have never, in thought, word, or deed, offended me; and let me thank you, again and again, for your affectionate kindness to me all the time of our ten years' happy union."

On leaving Naples, Nelson was despatched to Corsica and Sardinia, to protect British trade and that of the Grand Duke of Tuscany. He wrote to his wife, "This island is to belong to England, to be governed by its own laws, as Ireland, and a viceroy placed here with free ports. Italy and Spain are jealous of our obtaining possession; it will command the Mediterranean."

The town of Bastia was taken by Nelson. "I am all astonishment," he said, "when I reflect on what we have achieved ... four thousand in all, laying down their arms to twelve hundred soldiers, marines, and seamen! I always was of opinion, have ever acted up to it, and never had any reason to repent it, that one Englishman was equal to three Frenchmen."

At the siege of Calvi, by the bursting of a shell in the ground, sand and small gravel destroyed the sight of Nelson's right eye. For two years Nelson was almost constantly active. He wrote his wife, Aug. 2, 1796, "Had all my actions been gazetted, not one fortnight would have passed during the whole war without a letter from me; one day or other I will have a long gazette to myself. I feel that such an opportunity will be given me. I cannot, if I am in the field of glory, be kept out of sight; wherever there is anything to be done, there Providence is sure to direct my steps."

He had been made colonel of marines, and then commodore. The Agamemnon had been sent to Leghorn to refit, so badly had she been damaged by shot.

Corsica was finally evacuated, and Nelson proceeded to Gibraltar. Spain and France had now become allies. Off Cape St. Vincent, on the coast of Portugal, a severe battle was fought, February 14, 1797, between the English and Spanish fleets. The former had fifteen ships-of-the-line, with four frigates, a sloop, and a cutter. The latter had twenty-seven ships-of-the-line, with ten frigates, and a brig. Nelson, in the Captain, was at one time engaged with no less than nine line-of-battle ships. He and his seamen sprang aboard the San Nicolas and the San Josef, he exclaiming, it is recorded, "Westminster Abbey or victory!" received the swords of some of the Spanish officers, and in the midst of falling spars and blinding smoke, showed themselves heroic.

For this successful battle Nelson received the Knighthood and Order of the Bath, and was made Rear-Admiral. The sword of the Spanish admiral given to Nelson on board the San Josef was presented to the mayor and corporation of Norwich, the capital of the county in which he was born. The freedom of the city was voted to him.

His aged father wrote him, "The name and serviceso of Nelson have sounded through this city of Bath—from the common ballad-singer to the public theatre."

His wife begged him "never to board again. Leave it for captains.... You have been most wonderfully protected; you have done desperate actions enough."

On the night of July 3. 1797, Cadiz, off the coast of Spain, was bombarded. Nelson was in a most desperate action. In a barge with twelve men, he was attacked by a Spanish barge of twenty-six oars, with thirty in her crew. A hand-to-hand fight ensued. The Spanish commander and his launch were taken, and eighteen of his men were killed. The life of Nelson was saved by a trusted follower, John Sykes, who interposed his own head to receive the blow of a Spanish sabre. He recovered from his dangerous wound, "but did not live long enough," says Southey, "to profit by the gratitude and friendship of his commander."

On July 15 Nelson sailed in the ship Theseus for Teneriffe, off the coast of Africa. On the evening of July 24, he determined to attack the garrison of Santa Cruz. With the help of his step-son, Lieutenant Josiah Nisbet, he burned his wife's letters before starting to row ashore. Seeing that the young man was armed, he begged him to remain in the ship, saying, "Should we both fall, Josiah, what would become of your poor mother? The care of the Theseus falls to you; stay therefore, and take charge of her."

"The ship must take care of herself," said Nisbet; "I will go with you to-night if I never go again."

The expedition was a failure. Several of the boats missed the pier in the darkness, some were struck by shot and their men drowned—ninety-seven men went down in the fog—and Nelson was shot through the right elbow, as he was stepping out of his boat. As he fell young

Nisbet placed him in the bottom of the boat, and laid his hat over the arm, lest the sight of the blood should increase Nelson's faintness. Then taking a silk handkerchief from his own neck, he bound it above the elbow, thus saving the life of the admiral. One of the bargemen, Lovel, tore his shirt into shreds to make a bandage for the shattered arm.

When his boat reached the Theseus, Nelson declined to be helped on board, and twisted the rope thrown over the side of the ship round his left hand, saying, "Let me alone; I have yet my legs and one arm. Tell the surgeon to make haste and get his instruments. I know I must lose my right arm; so the sooner it is off, the better."

When asked by the surgeon if he wished the arm embalmed that he might send it to England for burial, he said, "Throw it into the hammock with the brave fellow that was killed beside me," whose body was about to be thrown overboard.

Nelson was greatly depressed after this failure, and said, "A left-handed admiral will never again be considered as useful; therefore the sooner I get to a very humble cottage the better, and make room for a sounder man to serve the state."

He returned to England in September, and went to Bath where his father and Lady Nelson were staying. She tenderly nursed her husband for three months, till his arm was healed. In December, 1797, at his request the following notice was read in St. George's Church, Hanover Square, London: "An officer desires to return thanks to Almighty God for his perfect recovery from a severe wound, and also for the many mercies bestowed on him."

This year, 1797, government settled a pension of a thousand pounds a year on Sir Horatio Nelson, and at St. James's Palace made him Knight Companion of the Bath. The freedom of the city of London was conferred upon him in December, and with it a gold box worth one hundred guineas.

April 1, 1798, he sailed in the Vanguard, of seventy-four guns, to join Lord St. Vincent and the fleet off Cadiz. It was known that Napoleon and the French fleet were preparing for an invasion of some country of the allied forces, either England, Spain, or Italy. Nelson's instructions were to "take, sink, burn, and destroy it." It is now known that Napoleon's expedition was against the East Indian Empire, to cripple England. The Mediterranean was searched for the French ships. Nelson wrote his wife: "I have not been able to find the French fleet.... I yet live in hopes of meeting these fellows; but it would have been my delight to have tried Bonaparte on a bowline, for he commands the fleet as well as the army. Glory is my object and that alone."

After some months of fruitless search, Nelson obtained a fresh supply of provisions in July at Syracuse. A treaty between Naples and France forbade more than two English ships to enter any Neapolitan or Sicilian port, and it is said that Lady Hamilton gained the needed concession from her friend, Queen Maria Caroline, without which

Nelson (in his Will, on the last day of his life) declared he could never have gone to Egypt and fought the glorious battle of the Nile.

On the morning of Aug. 1, 1798, Nelson was off the city of Alexandria in Egypt. His force amounted to thirteen seventy-four gun ships, one of fifty guns, and one brig, all carrying 8,068 men, with 1,012 guns. The French had also thirteen ships of the line, with eight frigates, brigs, and bomb vessels. They had 11,230 men, with 1,226 guns. The French had come to anchor in Aboukir Bay, at the mouth of the Nile.

The British were overjoyed at finding the French fleet. Nelson had scarcely eaten or slept for days; but, now that the enemy were in sight, he ordered dinner to be served on the Vanguard, and, on rising from the table, is said to have exclaimed to his officers, "Before this time to-morrow I shall have gained a peerage or Westminster Abbey."

After talking over the plan of battle with his officers, one of them said with enthusiasm, "If we succeed, what will the world say?"

"There is no if in the case," replied the admiral; "that we shall succeed is certain; who may live to tell the story is a very different question."

A little after six in the evening, Aug. 1, the fierce battle began. Nelson had six colors flying in different parts of his rigging, lest they should be shot away. The first two ships of the French line were dismasted in a quarter of an hour; the third, fourth, and fifth were taken at half-past eight.

Nelson received a severe wound in the head, which, though he supposed it would prove fatal, Southey says the admiral would not allow touched until the other wounded had been cared for. "I will take my turn with my brave fellows," he said.

About nine the L'Orient, the flagship of the French Admiral de Brueys, of one hundred and twenty guns, was seen to be on fire. Brueys was dead. He had received three wounds, but would not leave his post. A4 fourth cut him nearly in two. He requested to be left to die on the deck, and expired a quarter of an hour afterwards.

When Nelson saw the ship on fire, he gave orders that boats should be sent to the enemy. About seventy of her crew were saved by the English boats. So heroic were her men that they continued to fire from the upper decks after the lower were in flames. Between ten and eleven the huge ship exploded. Officers and men jumped overboard, and most were lost in that frightful commingling of fire and falling timbers which had been shot high into the air.

Both fleets seemed paralyzed, and for a quarter of an hour no gun was fired. All was darkness and silence save the groans of the dying, and the swell of the ingulfing sea. Among those who perished were Commodore Casabianca and his brave little son of ten or twelve, whom Mrs. Hemans has immortalized in her poem:—

"The boy stood on the burning deck
Whence all but he had fled;
The flame that lit the battle's wreck
Shone round him o'er the dead.

Yet beautiful and bright he stood,
As born to rule the storm;
A creature of heroic blood,
A proud, though child-like form."

The battle raged till three in the morning. The French were overwhelmingly defeated. "Victory is not a name strong enough for such a scene; it is a conquest," said Nelson.

Of thirteen French sail-of-the-line, nine were taken and two burned; of the four frigates, one was sunk and another was burned. Of the French, 5,221 were taken, drowned, burned, and missing. The English lost 218 killed and 677 wounded. Long after the battle a great number of bodies floated about the bay in spite of all efforts to sink them. Many were cast up on Nelson's Island, and the sailors raised mounds of sand over them. For four leagues the shore was covered with wrecks. The day after the battle, Aug. 2, at two o'clock, Nelson's ship gave public thanksgiving to God. Other ships were recommended to do the same as soon as convenient.

Part of L'Orient's mainmast was picked up by the English ship Swiftsure, Benjamin Hallowell, captain. A coffin was made from this and presented to Nelson with the note:—

"My lord, herewith I send you a coffin made of part of L'Orient's mainmast, that when you are tired of this life you may be buried in one of your own trophies; but may that period be far distant, is the sincere wish of your obedient and much obliged servant,

Ben Hallowell."

Nelson was greatly pleased with this gift, and ordered it placed upright in his cabin. Finally, at the request of his friends, it was carried below. He was eventually buried in it.

The joy at Napoleon's defeat was inexpressible. England made Nelson a baron, with a pension of £2,000 a year while he lived, to descend to his two male successors. The East India Company voted him £10,000, as they had thus been saved from French conquest. The Emperor Paul of Russia sent him his portrait set in diamonds, in a gold box. The Sultan of Turkey sent a pelisse of sable fur valued at five thousand dollars, and a diamond aigrette valued at eighteen thousand dollars, taken from the royal turbans. The Sultan's mother sent a box set in diamonds valued at five thousand dollars; the King of Sardinia a gold box set in diamonds; the King of the Two Sicilies a sword which once belonged to Charles III. of Spain. His friend Alexander Davison sent medals to the officers and men costing £2,000. These were all greatly prized by the men.

Italy was as rejoiced at the defeat of the French as was England. When the news reached Naples, both the queen and Lady Hamilton fainted. Lady Hamilton wrote to Nelson of the queen, "She cried, kissed her husband, her children, walked frantic about the room; cried, kissed and embraced every person near her, exclaiming, O brave Nelson! O God, bless and protect our brave deliverer! O Nelson, Nelson, what do we not owe you! O victor, saviour of Italy! Oh that my swollen heart could now tell him personally what we owe him!" She was the sister of Marie Antoinette, and, of course, felt no love for the people who had put her beautiful sister to death.

On Sept. 22 Nelson and his ships appeared off Naples. Hundreds of boats and barges went out to meet them with music and banners. He describes the scene in a letter to Lady Nelson, "I must endeavor to convey to you something of what passed; but if it were so affecting to those who were only united to me by bonds of friendship, what must it be to my dearest wife, my friend, my everything which is most dear to me in this world? Sir William Hamilton and his wife came out to sea, attended by numerous boats with emblems, etc. They, my most respectable friends, had nearly been laid up and seriously ill; first from anxiety, and then from joy....

"Alongside came my honored friends; the scene in the boat was terribly affecting; up flew her ladyship, and exclaiming, 'O God! is it possible?' she fell into my arms more dead than alive. Tears, however, soon set matters to rights; when alongside came the king. The scene was in its way as interesting; he took me by the hand, calling me his 'Deliverer and Preserver,' with every expression of kindness." ...

The poor of Italy were no less enthusiastic. They brought cages of birds, and opening them, allowed the little creatures to fly about the ship, and alight upon the admiral's shoulder.

Nelson had been very ill, and was taken to the house of Sir William Hamilton, where his wife nursed the admiral back to health. She arranged a celebration for him on his fortieth birthday, Sept. 29. Eighteen hundred people were entertained at a cost of two thousand ducats. "Every ribbon, every button, has Nelson," etc., writes the admiral. "The whole service is marked H. N., Glorious 1st of August!"

Encouraged by the victory of Nelson, a second coalition was now formed against Napoleon, composed of Russia, Austria, England, Portugal, Naples, and Turkey. Ferdinand of Naples engaged to raise eighty thousand soldiers for the common cause. A force of thirty-two thousand Italians were sent to Rome to drive out the French, but were defeated, and the French in turn entered Naples and compelled the royal family to fly for safety to Palermo.

Lady Hamilton, with great skill and courage, after having

explored a subterranean passage from the royal8 palace to the seaside, had two millions and a half of royal treasures, paintings and the like, removed to the English ships. She also assisted the king and his family secretly to reach Nelson's barges on the night of Dec. 21. They were carried to the Vanguard in a heavy sea.

On the night of Dec. 23 the fleet sailed. A dreadful storm arose; Nelson says, "the worst I ever experienced since I have been at sea." Almost all were ill, and Lady Hamilton, who was a good sailor, soothed and comforted them. Sir William sat with a pistol in his hand, prepared to shoot himself if the vessel sank. The little Prince Albert was taken ill on the morning of Dec. 25, and died at seven o'clock that evening in Lady Hamilton's arms.

Naples for a time was transformed by the French into the Parthenopæan Republic, which later was abolished, and the insurgents put to death by Ferdinand. Nelson has been censured, and justly, for the execution, on board one of his ships, the Foudroyant, of Francesco Caracciolo, who belonged to one of the noble families of Naples, and, with others, had been promised protection by a British officer. Caracciolo was tried and condemned as a rebel by officers of his own country, and Nelson decided not to interfere. The prisons of Naples were indeed slaughter pens; but wars are never humane, and struggles between despotism and liberty are rarely bloodless.

Ferdinand rewarded Nelson with the Sicilian dukedom of Brontë, with an estate worth about £3,000 per annum. Nelson at once gave from this estate an annuity of £500 for life to his father. He had already given out of the £10,000 voted him by the East India Company, fivehundred pounds each to his father, his brother-in-law, Mr. Bolton, his sister, Mrs. Matcham, and his brothers Maurice and William. When his brother Maurice died in April, 1801, Nelson gave his blind widow £100 a year while he lived, and Lady Hamilton cared for her after his death. He wrote to his wife, "If I were rich I would do more. To my father say everything which is kind. I love, honor, and respect him as a father and as a man, and as the very best man I ever saw. May God Almighty bless you, my dear father, and all my brothers and sisters, is the fervent prayer of your affectionate—Nelson."

The Queen of Naples gave Nelson the king's picture set in diamonds and emeralds. She gave Lady Emma Hamilton her portrait set with diamonds, with the words "Eterna Gratitudine" on the back, hanging it round her neck by a chain of gold; to Sir William a gold snuffbox, with a picture of the king and herself set in diamonds; the king sent Sir William and his wife each a picture of himself richly set in jewels, worth a thousand guineas. Lady Hamilton also received two coach-loads of costly dresses from Queen Caroline, and a superb diamond necklace, with the cipher of the names of all the royal children, ornamented by locks of their hair. Emperor Paul of Russia sent her the cross of the Order of Malta, the first Englishwoman upon whom the honor was ever bestowed.

The Island of Zante sent Nelson a golden-headed sword and a truncheon set round with diamonds, thanking him "for having by his victory preserved that part of Greece from the horrors of anarchy."

The French having been driven out of Italy, Nelson, in poor health, asked to return to England. Sir Williamo Hamilton had been superseded by Hon. Arthur Paget, so he and his wife decided to return at the same time. The queen and some of her children accompanied them to Vienna. Here Prince Esterhazy entertained the party in regal style for four days, a hundred grenadiers, six feet high, waiting at table. At Dresden the party remained eight days, when two vessels were fitted up for their conveyance down the Elbe to Hamburg. Everywhere great crowds gathered to see the hero of the Nile. At Hamburg he met a venerable clergyman who had travelled forty miles to ask the admiral to write in the parish Bible. Here Nelson called upon the poet Klopstock. He also bought some elegant lace trimming for a court dress for his wife.

On Oct. 31 they started for England on a mail packet, and reached Yarmouth Nov. 6, 1800, after an absence of two years and seven months. On landing in a harbor radiant with flags, his carriage was drawn by the eager multitude to the inn; the freedom of the town was given him; and then, with his officers and people of the town, he went to the church to return thanks for his safe return to his country. He reached London Sunday, Nov. 9, and went to Nerot's hotel, King Street, St. James's, where his father and Lady Nelson had come from Norfolk to meet him. On the following day the people took his horses from his carriage and drew him from Ludgate Hill to Guild Hall, where he received the thanks of the common council, and a golden-hilted sword studded with diamonds.

Rumors of Nelson's devotion to Lady Hamilton had already reached England and his wife. She received him coldly. Shortly after this, while Lord and Lady Nelson were with the Hamiltons at the theatre, Lady Nelson, unable to control her feelings, fainted in the box where they were sitting.

For two months Lord Nelson and his wife lived, as might be supposed, most unhappily, when he determined to leave her forever, settling upon her £1,600 per year. He wrote to his friend Davison, "Sooner than live the life I did when last I came to England, I would stay abroad forever." The last time he saw her, Jan. 13, 1801, before he left for the Baltic, he said at parting, "I call God to witness there is nothing in you or your conduct I wish otherwise."

In 1801 England found herself engaged in conflict with Denmark, which had become an ally of Russia, Prussia, and Sweden, in naval rights. On March 12, 1801, a fleet of fifty-two sail was sent into the Baltic from England, Nelson acting as second in command under Sir

Hyde Parker. On March 16 the ship Invincible, of seventy-four guns, struck on a sand-bank called Hammond's Knowl, and went down, taking four hundred persons with her.

The harbor of Copenhagen was most strongly fortified. The city was protected by defences which stretched a distance of about four miles. The Danes had removed all the buoys, so that Nelson was obliged to make soundings and replace them.

On the morning of April 1, the British fleet anchored within two leagues of Copenhagen. On April 2, at five minutes past ten in the forenoon, the battle began. Nelson's squadron being received with the fire of more than a thousand guns. As some of his ships had become disabled, Admiral Parker, at a distance, thinking that the fire was too hot for Nelson, threw out the signal to retreat, knowing that if Nelson could possibly continue the battle he would do so.

When told of the signal, Nelson put his glass to his blind eye, saying, "I really do not see the signal! Keep mine for closer battle flying! That's the way I answer such signals. Nail mine to the mast!"

The men fought heroically on both sides. The battle lasted for five hours, men fighting knee-deep among the dead on the decks. The Danes lost 1800 men, including prisoners, 6,000, and the English 253 killed and 688 wounded.

Nelson said, "I have been in one hundred and five engagements in the course of my life, but this has been the most terrible of all."

An armistice was effected, and the Crown Prince of Denmark gave a grand banquet to the Danish commissioners and English officers. At the banquet, Nelson praised the bravery of the Danes, and asked to be introduced to Lieutenant Villemoes, a youth of seventeen, who, on a floating battery or raft, with six small cannon and twenty-four men, came under the very stern of Nelson's ship, the Elephant, and attacked her. Twenty of his men were killed; but the boy-commander, standing up to his waist among his dead comrades, fought till the truce was proclaimed. Southey gives the number of guns as twenty-four, and the men one hundred and twenty.

When the lad was brought before Nelson, he embraced him, and told the prince that the youth deserved to be made an admiral. "If, my lord," was the answer, "I were to make all my brave officers admirals, I should have no captains or lieutenants in my service."

Nelson, brave to rashness himself, admired it in others. When, early in 1800, in the Mediterranean, Le Généreux, one of the ships that had escaped at the battle of the Nile, was captured, Nelson patted the head of a little midshipman, who was very pale, and asked him how he relished the music. He told the boy how Charles XII. ran away from the first shot he heard, but was afterwards called "the Great" for his bravery. "I therefore hope much from you in future," said the admiral.

Nelson was made a viscount for the battle of Copenhagen. His estates and titles were to go to his father, to his brother William, and

66

then to the male heirs of Nelson's sisters, Mrs. Bolton, and next Mrs. Matcham.

In very poor health he returned to England, and was welcomed to the home of Sir William Hamilton, at 23 Piccadilly.

By the wish of Nelson, Lady Hamilton purchased a country home for him, called Merton Place, in Surrey, eight miles from London. "It would make you laugh," wrote Sir William, "to see Emma and her mother fitting up pig-stys and hen-coops, and already the canal is enlivened with ducks, and the cock is strutting with his hens about the walks.... I have lived with our dear Emma several years. I know her merit, have a great opinion of the head and heart that God Almighty has been pleased to give her, but a seaman alone could have given a fine woman full power to choose and fit up a residence for him without seeing it himself."

On Oct. 29, 1821, Viscount Nelson took his seat in the House of Lords. The following year, in May, the Rev. Edmund Nelson, the father of the admiral, was coming to live with his son and the Hamiltons at Merton Place; but he died at Burnham Thorpe, April 26, at the age of seventy-nine.

During the summer of 1802, Nelson journeyed to Wales with the family of his brother, the Rev. William Nelson, and the Hamiltons, and everywhere received the homage of the people. Oxford gave him the freedom of the city in a gold box, and the degree of D.C.L. to him and to Sir William. He passed under triumphal arches, medals were struck in his honor, and crowds escorted him with lighted torches.

The next year, 1803, England and France, or, in reality, England and Napoleon, were again at war. Nelson wrote a characteristic note to the Premier:—

"House of Lords, 4 o'clock, March 9, 1803.

"Whenever it is necessary, I am your admiral.

Nelson and Brontë."

April 6, 1803, Sir William Hamilton died, holding his wife's and Nelson's hands, saying, "Protect my dear wife; and may God bless you, and give you victory and protect you in battle!" He bequeathed to Nelson a copy of a picture of his wife by Madame Le Brun in enamel. To her he gave a legacy of £800, and an annuity of £800 for life. Sir William's pension of £1,200 a year closed with his death, and, as the government did not continue it, in spite of Sir William's dying wishes, Nelson gave the amount to her, in monthly portions, while he lived.

A month after Sir William's death, Nelson was appointed to the command of the Mediterranean squadron, to take part in the war between England and France. He sailed from Spithead, May 20, in the Victory, and for two years, lacking ten days, did not step out of his ship. They were long, weary years of much illness and loneliness, but devotion to duty. He returned to Merton on the morning of Aug. 20, 1805.

A month later he was again called to serve his country. A third coalition had been formed by England, Russia, Austria, and Sweden against France. Spain had become the ally of the latter.

"I will do my best," he wrote to a friend, "and I hope God Almighty will go with me. I have much to lose, but little to gain; and I go because it is right, and I will serve the country faithfully."

He left Merton Friday night, Sept. 13, at half-past ten, taking a sad leave of his sisters and Lady Hamilton, and kneeling by the bedside of their little girl, Horatia, earnestly prayed that God would protect and bless her. This child was at that time about four and a half years old, having been born in January, 1801.

Nelson writes in his private diary that evening, "At half-past ten drove from dear, dear Merton, where I left all which I hold dear in this world, to go to serve my king and country.... If it is His good providence to cut short my days upon earth, I bow with the greatest submission, relying that He will protect those so dear to me that I may leave behind. His will be done. Amen! Amen! Amen!"

A great crowd gathered to see him embark. Many were in tears, and many knelt before him and blessed him as he passed. He remarked to his dear friend, Captain Hardy, "I had their huzzas before; I have their hearts now."

Sept. 28 the fleet anchored off Cadiz, on the coast of Spain. Nelson knew there must be a fearful battle, and seems to have expected to be killed in it. He took much exercise daily, generally walking the deck for six or seven hours. Such was the activity of his mind that he rarely slept more than two hours at a time. He never thought of himself. He exposed his body, frail as it was, in all kinds of weather, and would not change his clothing when wet through. He disliked to depend much on others, as he was obliged to do, from having but one arm and one eye.

He was very prompt, and made good use of time. He once said to General Twiss, "Time, Twiss, time is everything. Five minutes makes the difference between a victory and a defeat."

He was extremely generous. When one of his men, Captain Parker, died, he paid his debts and funeral expenses, about £200. He spent very little for himself, and much for others.

It was thought that there would be a battle on Saturday, Oct. 19; and Nelson wrote two letters, one to "my dearest angel," little Horatia, and the other to Lady Hamilton, whom he would have married, had the divorce laws of England permitted. To her he writes, "May the God of battles crown my endeavors with success; at all events, I will take care that my name shall ever be most dear to you and Horatia, both of whom I love as much as my own life."

On Monday, Oct. 21, the fleets, now off Cape Trafalgar, below

Cadiz, were ready for action. The English had twenty-seven sail-of-the-line and four frigates; the French and Spanish thirty-three sail-of-the-line and seven frigates. The English had 2,542 guns; the French and Spanish, 3,042 guns.

Nelson told the men who removed the picture of Lady Hamilton, which always hung in his cabin in the Victory, to "take care of his guardian angel." He wore a miniature of her next his heart. Then he wrote an earnest prayer, and a codicil to his will, in which he asked his country to reward Lady Hamilton for her services, leaving her and his child, Horatia, "a legacy to my king and country, that they will give her Lady Hamilton an ample provision to maintain her rank in life. These are the only favors I ask of my king and country, at this moment when I am going to fight their battle."

He wore his admiral's coat, which bore on the left breast his decorations. When fears were expressed that these would make him a mark for the enemy, he said, "In honor I gained them, and in honor I will die with them."

He gave orders for that well-known signal, "England expects that every man will do his duty," which was received with tremendous cheering. "You must be quick," he said to Lieutenant Pasco, "for I have one more to make, which is for close action."

"Now," said Nelson, "I can do no more. We must trust to the great Disposer of all events, and the justice of our cause. I thank God for this great opportunity of doing my duty."

The Royal Sovereign, one hundred guns, under Vice-Admiral Collingwood, was the first to get into action, a little past noon. The men were ordered to lie down upon the decks as she swept into the foe. She gave the great Spanish ship, Santa Ana, a broadside with double-shotted guns, killing and wounding four hundred men. Nelson shouted, "Bravo! What a glorious salute the Royal Sovereign is in!"

Seven or eight ships soon opened on the Victory. As Nelson and Captain Hardy walked the deck a splinter struck the foot of the latter, tearing the buckle from his shoe. "This is too warm work, Hardy, to last long," said Nelson with a smile.

About half-past one, as they were walking, Nelson was shot by Sergeant Robert Guillemard of the French ship Redoubtable, who was stationed in the rigging of his ship, singling out officers for his aim.

Nelson fell on his face, in the blood where his secretary, Scott, had been killed. "They have done for me at last, Hardy," he said; "my backbone is shot through."

He was lifted and carried below, among the dead and dying. On the way thither, using one hand, he covered his face and his decorations with his handkerchief, that his men might not see who had fallen.

He was laid on a midshipman's bed, and covered with a sheet. As often as a ship surrendered, the men of the Victory cheered, and

Nelson's dying face would light up with joy. Nothing could be done for the hero, but to fan him with paper and give him lemonade to quench his thirst. His thoughtfulness of others was strong even in his dying hour. A poor fellow near him was jarred or hurt by another in passing, and Nelson reproved the man for his carelessness.

He frequently asked for Captain Hardy, whom he loved; but Hardy was not able to leave his post till an hour and ten minutes after Nelson was wounded.

When he came, they shook hands in silence, and Hardy turned away to conceal his grief. "Well, Hardy, how goes the battle?"—"Very well, my lord. We have got twelve or fourteen of the enemy's ships in our possession."

"I hope," said Nelson, "that none of our ships have struck?"

"No, my lord, there is no fear of that."

"I am a dead man, Hardy. I am going fast—it will be all over with me soon. Come nearer to me. Let my dear Lady Hamilton have my hair, and all other things belonging to me."

Hardy hastened to the deck and returned in about fifty minutes. Nelson exclaimed, "Anchor, Hardy, anchor! Don't throw me overboard, Hardy."

"Oh, no, certainly not," said Hardy.

"Then you know what to do. Take care of my dear Lady Hamilton, Hardy! take care of poor Lady Hamilton. Kiss me, Hardy."

The captain knelt and pressed his lips to his cheek. "Now I am satisfied," he said. "Thank God, I have done my duty." Hardy knelt again and kissed his forehead. "Who is that?" he said faintly. "It is Hardy." "God bless you, Hardy," said Nelson, and Hardy went again on deck.

To his chaplain, Dr. Scott, Nelson said, "Doctor, I have not been a great sinner," and after a short pause, "Remember that I leave Lady Hamilton and my daughter Horatia as a legacy to my country." His speaking now became difficult. "Thank God, I have done my duty," were his last words. At half-past four he passed away peacefully. He lived long enough to know that a great victory had been won.

Of the thirty-three ships in the French and Spanish fleets, nineteen were taken and destroyed by the English. Most of the rest became prizes, but were wrecked in a gale. The English lost in killed and wounded about three thousand; the French and Spanish about five thousand. "The greatest sea victory that the world had ever known was won," says W. Clark Russell, "but at such a cost, that there was no man throughout the British fleet—there was no man indeed in all England—but would have welcomed defeat sooner than have paid the price of this wonderful conquest."

The body of Nelson was carried in a cask of brandyo in the Victory till she reached Spithead, Dec. 12, five weeks after the battle. It was afterwards placed in the coffin made from the mast of L'Orient, enclosed in a leaden coffin, with a handsome wooden coffin outside of these.

All England was bowed with grief at the death of Nelson. He was the idol of the nation, despite his unhappy marriage and his unlawful love for the devoted Lady Hamilton. The king was unable to speak for a long time after he heard the news, and the queen wept aloud. In Naples, writes Coleridge, "Numbers stopped and shook hands with me because they had seen the tears on my cheek and conjectured that I was an Englishman; and several, as they held my hand, themselves burst into tears."

Nelson was buried Jan. 9, 1806, in St. Paul's Cathedral, London, at a public expense of £14,000. Ten thousand troops preceded the body of the hero to the tomb. The streets were lined with thousands of troops and hundreds of thousands of weeping spectators. The coffin was drawn uncovered, under a canopy, upon a car, having at its front and back a carved representation of the head and stern of the Victory.

At the burial, by a sudden impulse, the sailors who lowered the coffin seized the flag which covered it and tore it in shreds, to keep as mementoes of their great leader.

No such funeral had been seen in England. It was felt that the battle of Trafalgar had saved the nation from an invasion by Bonaparte, and therefore no honor was too great for her deliverer.

"The battle of Trafalgar," says Bourrienne, in his Memoirs of Napoleon, "paralyzed our naval force, and banished all hope of any attempt against England."

England raised monuments in many of her large cities to her heroic dead. In Trafalgar Square, London, stands the Nelson column, fluted, surmounted by his statue, while on the sides are representations of his four great battles, St. Vincent, the Nile, Copenhagen, and Trafalgar, cast in gun-metal taken from the enemy in these engagements. The four lions by Landseer are at the base.

The government awarded various honors to Nelson's family. An earldom was conferred on Nelson's brother, the Reverend William, with a pension of £5,000 a year, with £120,000 that he might purchase an estate; £20,000 of this gift were to be divided between Nelson's sisters, Mrs. Bolton and Mrs. Matcham. Lady Nelson received £2,000 per annum till her death, May 4, 1831, twenty-five years after the death of Lord Nelson.

Nelson's dying request for Lady Hamilton and their child, Horatia, was disregarded by the government. Nelson left her by will £2,000, an annuity for life of £500 charged on the Bronte estate, Merton Place, and the yearly interest on £4,000 settled on Horatia till she became eighteen.

Lady Hamilton survived Nelson nine years, dying Jan. 16, 1815, in apartments in the Rue Française at Calais, at the age of fifty-one. She lost Merton Place, in Surrey, through debts. She was imprisoned for debt at the King's Bench, 12 Temple Place, in 1813, and was discharged after some months, by a city alderman, J. J. Smith, who felt that she had been cruelly treated. Fearing re-arrest, she went to Calais in 1814, with Horatia, and died in less than a year. Her daughter, who was devoted to her, wrote, years later, "Although often certainly under very distressing circumstances, she never experienced actual want."

Lady Hamilton was buried in a cemetery just outside the city limits, which was soon after used as a timber-yard, and all traces of the graves disappeared. In accordance with her mother's last wishes, Horatia was taken to the home of Mrs. Matcham, Lord Nelson's sister, where she remained two years, and then resided with Mr. Bolton, Lord Nelson's brother-in-law, till her marriage, in February, 1822, to the Rev. Philip Ward, Vicar of Tenterden in Kent. She became the mother of a large family, and died March 6, 1881, in the eighty-first year of her age.

The Rev. William Nelson, made an earl by the successes of his brother, was succeeded in 1835 by his nephew, Thomas Bolton, as second earl, who took the name Nelson. Thomas was succeeded the same year by his son Horatio, the third earl. Lord Nelson is a graduate of Cambridge, where he took the degree of M.A. in 1844. He married a daughter of the second earl of Normanton in 1845.

JOHN BUNYAN

The first book which Benjamin Franklin owned was "Pilgrim's Progress." This he read over and over.

Sir Humphry Davy, the great scientist, could repeat a large part of "Pilgrim's Progress" before he could read it. Nathaniel Hawthorne read and loved it when he was six years old.

Rufus Choate, the great orator, says E. P. Whipple, "read 'Pilgrim's Progress' when he was six years old; and he not only got it by heart, but eloquently expounded it to his companions, dramatically reproducing the scenes, incidents, and characters of that wonderful allegory, so that the little people he addressed were made to see in it what he saw."

Dr. Thomas Arnold said, "I cannot trust myself to read the account of Christian going up to the celestial gate, after his passage through the river of death.... I hold John Bunyan," he said, "to have been a man of incomparably greater genius than any of them our old divines, and to have given a far truer and more edifying picture of Christianity."

"'Pilgrim's Progress' has been translated into more languages," says Canon Edmund Venables, in his life of John Bunyan, "than any other book in the English tongue;" and Southey thinks, "there is no European language into which it has not been translated."

Who wrote it? A travelling tinker, in prison; "A man," says James Anthony Froude, "whose writings have for two centuries affected the spiritual opinions of the English race in every part of the world more powerfully than any book or books except the Bible."

John Bunyan was born at Elstow, a little village about a mile from Bedford, England, in 1628. "Few villages," says Canon Venables, "are so little modernized as Elstow. The old, half-timbered cottages with overhanging stories, peaked dormers, and gabled porches, tapestried with roses and honeysuckles, must be much what they were in Bunyan's days."

The parish church is a part of the old Benedictine nunnery, founded here in 1078 by Judith, niece of William the Conqueror, in honor of the mother of the Emperor Constantine.

Thomas Bunyan, the father of the renowned author and preacher, was a tinker, "a mender of pots and kettles." He was married to his first wife, Anne Pinney, before he was twenty years of age. She died four years later, apparently without children; and Thomas was soon married again to Margaret Bentley, who became the mother of John Bunyan.

Poor as the parents were, "of that rank," says Bunyan, "that is meanest and most despised of all the families in the land ... it pleased

God to put it into their hearts to put me to school, to learn both to read and write."

There was a school at Bedford at this time, founded in Queen Mary's reign by the Lord Mayor of London, Sir William Harpur. Thither probably the lad walked day after day, but he seems to have learned little, and that little he soon forgot.

At an early age he was obliged to help his father at the forge, where, he says, he was "brought up in a very mean condition among a company of poor countrymen."

He soon learned bad habits from the men or boys around him. "From a child," he says, "I had but few equals (considering my years, which were then but tender and few) for cursing, swearing, lying, and blaspheming the holy name of God. Yea, so settled and rooted was I in these things, that they became as a second nature to me."

In the plain home he must have been taught some religious truths by his parents, for at ten years of age he was greatly disturbed on account of his sins. These "did so offend the Lord that even in my childhood he did scare and affright me with fearful dreams, and did terrify me with dreadful visions.... These things did so distress my soul, that then in the midst of my many sports and childish vanities, amidst my vain companions, I was often cast down and afflicted in my mind therewith; yet could I not let go my sins."

Books the lad did not read, except the not very edifying life of Sir Bevis of Southampton, because the poor tinker's home afforded none.

In the midst of his reckless living—he himself protests that he was never immoral—several remarkable preservations from death had a strong influence on his mind. Twice he narrowly escaped drowning, once in the river Ouse at Bedford, and again in "a creek of the sea." At another time, he says, "Being in the fields with one of my companions, it chanced that an adder passed over the highway; so I, having a stick in my hand, struck her over the back, and having stunned her, I forced open her mouth with my stick, and plucked her sting out with my fingers; by which act, had not God been merciful to me, I might, by my desperateness, have brought myself to my end."

When John Bunyan was about seventeen, he was for a time engaged in the civil wars of the reign of Charles I. Whether he fought for the king or with the Parliamentary forces will never be known. Dr. John Brown, minister at Bedford, thinks he was drafted to fight against the Royalist party.

Here again he was marvellously preserved. "When I was a soldier, I, with others, was drawn out to go to such a place to besiege it; but when I was just ready to go, one of the company desired to go in my room; to which, when I had consented, he took my place; and coming to the siege, as he stood sentinel, he was shot in the head and died. Here were judgment and mercy; but neither of them did awaken my soul to righteousness."

74

Before Bunyan was twenty, a most important matter came into his life. He met a poor girl, an orphan, whose name even is not known, and married her. "I lighted on a wife," he says, "whose father was counted godly. She also would be often telling me what a godly man her father was, and how he would reprove and correct vice, both in his house and amongst his neighbors; what a strict and holy life he lived in his day, both in word and deed...."

"This woman and I came together as poor as poor might be, not having so much household stuff as a dish or spoon betwixt us both. But she had for her portion two books, 'The Plain Man's Pathway to Heaven,' and 'The Practice of Piety,' which her father had left her when he died. In these two books I sometimes read with her. I found some things pleasing to me, but all this while I met with no conviction." However, they created in him "some desire to religion."

"The Practice of Piety," by Dr. Lewis Bayley, Bishop of Bangor in King James's time, was translated into several languages, and passed through more than fifty editions during a century. The other book was written by the Rev. Arthur Dent, the Puritan pastor of Shoebury in Essex.

Young Bunyan changed his outward life after his marriage. He says, "I fell in with the religion of the times, to go to church twice a day, very devoutly to say and sing as the others did, yet retaining my wicked life."

Exceedingly fond of athletic sports, it was the fashion of the day to enjoy them on Sunday after the sermon. Sometimes the people danced on the village green, or rang the bells for hours, or played tip-cat or other sports.

James I. had issued a proclamation that "his good people should not be disturbed, letted, or discouraged, after the end of the divine service from any lawful recreations, such as dancing, either of men or women; archery for men; leaping, vaulting, or any such harmless recreations."

Bunyan's minister, Vicar Hall, was opposed to these forms of Sabbath breaking, and denounced them from the pulpit in words which the young married man thought were especially aimed at him. He went home "with a great burden upon his spirit," but after dinner, "shook the sermon out of his mind," and went out to play tip-cat on the green.

As Bunyan was in the midst of the game, "having struck the cat one blow from the hole," he says, "just as I was about to strike it a second time, a voice did suddenly dart from heaven into my soul, which said, 'Wilt thou leave thy sins and go to heaven, or have thy sins and go to hell?' At this I was put into an exceeding maze. Wherefore, leaving my cat on the ground, I looked up to heaven, and was as if I had, with the eyes of my understanding, seen the Lord Jesus looking down upon me, as being very hotly displeased with me."

The impression soon wore away, and Bunyan became as reckless as ever. A month went by, and "one day," he says, "as I was standing at a neighbor's shop-window, cursing and swearing, and playing the madman, after my wonted manner, there sat within the woman of the house, and heard me; who, though she was a very loose, ungodly wretch, yet protested that I swore and cursed at that most fearful rate, that she was made to tremble to hear me; and told me further, that I was the ungodliest fellow for swearing that she ever heard in all her life; and that I, by thus doing, was enough to spoil all the youth in the whole town, if they came but in my company."

Bunyan was ashamed and hung his head. "While I stood there," he says, "I wished with all my heart that I might be a little child again, that my father might teach me to speak without this wicked way of swearing; for, thought I, I am so much accustomed to it, that it is in vain for me to think of reformation; for, I thought, that could never be.... How it came to pass I know not; but I did from this time forward so leave off my swearing, that it was a great wonder to myself to observe it. And whereas, before, I knew not how to speak unless I put an oath before and another behind, to make the words have authority; now I could speak better without it, and with more pleasantness than ever I could before."

He began to read the Bible at the suggestion of a friend, and attempted to keep the commandments. He had a hard struggle in giving up his amusements. While sure that bell-ringing was a foolish use of time, he "hankered after it still," and would for some time go and see his old companions ring. He could not bring himself to give up dancing for a full year.

His neighbors began to think him very pious, and he was "proud of his godliness.... I thought," he says, "I pleased God as well as any man in England."

His self-satisfaction was soon spoiled. "Upon a day," he says, "the good providence of God called me to Bedford, to work at my calling; and in one of the streets of that town I came where there were three or four women sitting at a door in the sun, talking about the things of God. And being now willing to hear what they said, I drew near, to hear their discourse—for I was now a brisk talker of myself in the matters of religion—but I may say, I heard, but understood not; for they were far above, out of my reach.

"Their talk was about a new birth—the work of God in their hearts; as also, how they were convinced of their miserable state by nature. They talked how God had visited their souls with his love in the Lord Jesus.... Methought, they spoke as if joy did make them speak. They spoke with such pleasantness of Scripture language, and with such appearance of grace in all they said, that they were to me, as if I had found a new world; as if they were people thato dwelt alone, and were not to be reckoned among their neighbors....

"I left, but their talk and discourse went with me; also my heart would tarry with them, for I was greatly affected by their words.... Therefore, I would often make it my business to be going again and again into the company of these poor people; for I could not stay away."

The result was "a very great softness and tenderness of heart, and a desire to meditate on good things."

These poor women could not have realized the wonderful work they were doing in reforming the life of this travelling vender of pots and kettles. They were simply using every opportunity for good which came in their way, and the seed was now destined to bring forth an hundred-fold.

They followed up the interest already awakened in Bunyan's heart. They were in earnest to serve their Lord. They introduced Bunyan to their minister, the Rev. John Gifford.

This Free Church was founded in Bedford in 1650, with twelve members. "Now the principle upon which they thus entered into fellowship one with another, and upon which they did afterwards receive those that were added to their body and fellowship, was faith in Christ and holiness in life, without respect to this or that circumstance or opinion in outward and circumstantial things." The Rev. John Gifford is usually spoken of as a Baptist, though Dr. Brown finds no proof for or against. In Gifford's last letter to his church, written just before his death, he appeals to them not to divide the church on such matters as "baptism, laying on of hands, anointing with oil, psalms, or any externals."

Bunyan himself, in a work written in 1673, "Differences in Judgment about Water Baptism no Bar to Communion," implies that he believes in immersion, but his children were baptized in their infancy.

Mr. Gifford had been a young major in the king's army, was defeated, and with eleven others condemned to the gallows. On the night before he was to be executed, his sister visited him in prison. The guards were asleep, and his fellow-prisoners were drunk. She urged him to escape to the fields. He did so, and for three days hid himself in a ditch, and lived on water. Coming to Bedford, he practised as a physician, but continued his bad habits, drinking and losing heavily through gambling.

In the midst of such a course of life he happened one day to take up a book written by an eminent scholar and Puritan preacher, the Rev. Robert Bolton, born at Blackburn, Lancashire, 1572. It was probably the volume entitled, "The Four Last Things, and Directions for Walking with God," published in 1626. Mr. Bolton died in 1631, with these words upon his lips: "By the wonderful mercies of God, I am as full of comfort as my heart can hold, and feel nothing in my soul but Christ, with whom I heartily desire to be."

Mr. Bolton's book was the means of the conversion of Gifford, who, in turn, led Bunyan into the light, and, consequently, to the writing of that wonderful book, "The Pilgrim's Progress," in which Gifford is supposed to be the Evangelist, who points out to Pilgrim the wicket gate. Who shall measure the power of a good book!

For months, even years, Bunyan passed through the struggles which Pilgrim found in his difficult journey.2 He has glowingly depicted these in his "Grace Abounding to the Chief of Sinners."

Sometimes he was in the depths of despair, because he felt that his sins had been too great to be forgiven. Then he feared that he was not one of the elect, or that he had committed the unpardonable sin against the Holy Ghost. Then doubts about the Bible and God took possession of him, till, under the mental strain, his health became affected, and consumption seemed imminent.

Sometimes a promise from the Bible would bring him the greatest joy. "I was now so taken with the love and mercy of God," he writes, "that I thought I could have spoken of it even to the very crows that sat upon the ploughed lands before me, had they been capable to have understood me."

In these days of alternate grief and joy, Bunyan came upon an old copy of Luther's "Commentary on the Galatians;" "so old, that it was ready to fall piece from piece if I did but turn it over.... I found my conditions as largely and profoundly handled, in his experience, as if his book had been written out of my heart. I do prefer this book of Martin Luther (excepting the Bible) before all the books that ever I have seen, as most fit for a wounded conscience."

This book was also most effective in the experience of John Wesley. "I went," Wesley wrote, "very unwillingly, to a society in Aldersgate Street, where one was reading Luther's Preface to the Epistle to the Galatians. About a quarter before nine, while he was describing the change which God works in the heart through faith in Christ, I felt my heart strangely warmed. I felt I did trust in Christ, Christ alone, for salvation, and an assurance was given me that he had taken away my sins."

Finally, "the peace of God which passeth understanding" came into Bunyan's heart. As he was walking in the field, he seemed to hear the sentence, "Thy righteousness is in heaven;" "and methought I saw," he says, "with the eyes of my soul, Jesus Christ at God's right hand, there I say, as my righteousness, so that wherever I was, or whatever I was doing, God could not say of me, he wants my righteousness, for that was just before him. Now did my chains fall off my legs indeed. Now went I home rejoicing for the grace and love of God."

During these years of anxiety, Bunyan worked hard with his hands, feeling, as did his honest father, that it was one of the first of duties to be "very careful to maintain his family." He had been moderately successful at his trade, as a contemporary biographer writes, that "God had increased his stores so that he lived in great credit among his neighbors."

In the year 1653, when he was twenty-five,—the year in which Oliver Cromwell was made Lord Protector of England,—he became a member of Mr. Gifford's church. He probably removed to Bedford from Elstow, two years later, and was made a deacon in the church.

About this time his lovely wife, to whom he owed so much, died, leaving four children, one of them, his idolized blind daughter, Mary, born in 1650. His beloved friend and pastor, Mr. Gifford, died in September of the same year as his wife.

The members of the church, realizing that the uneducated tinker was gifted in speech, and believing in his earnestness, asked him "to speak a word of exhortation unto them."

At first, modest and shrinking as he was, "it did much4 dash and abash his spirit," but being entreated, he spoke twice, "but with much weakness and infirmity."

After this he was asked to go with others and hold meetings in the country roundabout; and finally, "after solemn prayer, with fasting, he was set apart to the more ordinary and public preaching of the Word."

"My great desire," he says, "in my fulfilling my ministry, was to get into the darkest places of the country, even amongst those people that were furtherest off of profession.... I preached what I felt, what I smartingly did feel.... Indeed, I have been as one sent to them from the dead. I went myself in chains, to preach to them in chains; and carried that fire in my conscience, that I persuaded them to be aware of."

Later, he says, after two years "crying out against men's sins," he changed his manner of preaching; "I did labor much to hold forth Jesus Christ in all his offices, relations, and benefits unto the world."

On one occasion, having preached with much feeling, one of his friends took him by the hand, and spoke of the sweet sermon he had delivered. "Ay," said the self-searching preacher, "you need not remind me of that, for the devil told me of it before I was out of the pulpit."

Bunyan preached wherever there was an open door,—in a barn, a church, or on the village green. Crowds came to listen,—some from curiosity,—and great numbers were converted.

"No such preacher," says Froude, "to the uneducated English masses was to be found within the four seas."

Among the crowd gathered in a churchyard in Cambridgeshire on a week-day, was a Cambridge scholar, "none of the soberest," who had come to hear "the tinker prate," and gave a boy twopence to hold his horse while he listened. "But God met him there by his ministry, so that he came out much changed; and would by his good will hear none but the tinker for a long time after, he himself becoming a very eminent preacher in that country afterwards."

Another Cambridge University man asked Bunyan, "How dare you preach, seeing you have not the original, being not a scholar?"

"Have you the original?" asked Bunyan.

"Yes," said the scholar.

"Nay, but have you the very self-same original copies that were written by the penmen of the Scriptures, prophets and apostles?"

"No," was the reply, "but we have the true copies of these originals."

"How do you know that?" said Bunyan.

"How?" said the scholar, "why, we believe what we have is a true copy of the original."

"Then," said Bunyan, "so do I believe our English Bible is a true copy of the original." Then away rode the scholar.

Bunyan met with many obstacles in his preaching. When Dr. William Dell, the Puritan master of Caius College, Cambridge, asked him to preach in the parish church on Christmas, the orthodox parishioners were indignant. Some of the university professors were "angry with the tinker because he strove to mend souls as well as kettles and pans." Others declared him a witch, a highwayman, and accused him of nearly every vice. All these things deeply wounded the earnest man, but he kept steadily at work.

His first book, about two hundred pages, "SomeGospel Truths Opened according to the Scriptures," was published in London, in 1656, when Bunyan was twenty-eight years old. The Rev. John Burton, the pastor who succeeded Mr. Gifford, wrote the introduction, and commended the young author as one who had "neither the greatness nor the wisdom of the world to commend him ... not being chosen out of an earthly but out of a heavenly university,—the Church of Christ."

This book being replied to by Edward Burrough, a Quaker, defending his sect, Bunyan wrote a second book, "A Vindication of Gospel Truths Opened." His third book, published in 1658, a few days before Oliver Cromwell's death, was an exposition of the parable of the rich man and Lazarus. The volume went through nine editions in the author's lifetime. His fourth book, published in 1659, was entitled "The Doctrine of Law and Grace Unfolded."

All were written in simple language, with the earnestness of one, who, as he said, grieved more over the backsliding of one of his converts "than if one of my own children were going to the grave."

With the restoration of Charles II. the rule of Puritanism was over. Dissenters' chapels were shut up. The worshippers were commanded to attend the Established Church. Bunyan had preached for five years; and he could not give up his work, even now that his pulpit was closed by law. He continued to preach in barns and private houses.

On Nov. 12, 1600, he went to the little hamlet of Lower Samsell, near Harlington, to preach. Some one communicated this fact to a magistrate, and a warrant was issued for his arrest. This was told him, and he had time to escape; but he said if he were to flee, "the weak and newly converted brethren would be afraid to stand." He would never play the coward.

He opened the meeting with prayer, and began to speak from the words, "Dost thou believe on the Son of God?"

When the officers arrived, he was ordered to cease speaking. He replied "that he was about his Master's business, and must rather obey his Lord's voice than that of man." However, knowing that resistance was useless, as he was arrested in the king's name, he was led away to prison "with God's comfort," he says, "in my poor soul." He would not promise to discontinue preaching, saying rather, "If I were out of prison to-day, I would preach the gospel again to-morrow." He was sentenced to remain in prison for three months; if at the end of that time he refused to give up preaching, he would be sent away from his country, and if he came back without license, he would be hanged. Those were times of dreadful intolerance, and yet in this age we have not ceased to be intolerant of those whose beliefs are not like our own!

Bunyan had recently married a second time, and his wife was dangerously ill. He was a man of deep affections and loved his home. He said, "What a man is at home, that he is indeed. My house and my closet show most what I am, to my family and to the angels, though not to the world."

He wrote in prison, "The parting with my wife and poor children hath often been to me in this place as the pulling of my flesh from my bones; and that not only because I am too, too fond of those great mercies, but also because I should have often brought to my mind the hardships, miseries, and wants my poor family was like to meet with should I be taken from them, especially my poor blind child, who lay nearer my heart than all I had beside. Poor child, thought I, what sorrow art thou like to have for thy portion in this world! Thou must be beaten, suffer hunger, cold, nakedness, and a thousand calamities, though I cannot now endure the wind should blow on thee.

"But yet, thought I, I must venture all with God, though it goeth to the quick to leave you. I was as a man who was pulling down his house upon the head of his wife and children."

As the coronation of Charles II. took place in the spring of 1661, and it was customary to pardon prisoners under sentence for any offence short of felony, it was hoped by the followers of Bunyan that he would be released. As the local authorities did not put his name on the list of those who might properly be pardoned, his young wife, Elizabeth, scarcely recovered from her illness, travelled to London, and with great courage made her way to the House of Lords, and presented her petition to one of the peers. He received her kindly, but told her that her husband's case must be left with the judges at the next assizes.

Three times Elizabeth Bunyan, "with abashed face and trembling heart," stood before the judges, pleading for her husband. One of the judges, Sir Matthew Hale, was very kind to her, though he feared he

81

could not help her, as the law was against her husband. The other judge, Twisden, was brutal in his manner, so that she feared he would strike her.

Unsuccessful, the poor woman went back to her home, and John Bunyan remained for twelve long years in prison.

For the first six months Bunyan was allowed considerable liberty by his sympathetic jailer. He went to some of the meetings of the Baptists, and to his home. Some of the bishops heard of it, and sent a messenger from London to ascertain if this were really so. The officer was told to call at night at the prison. It happened that Bunyan had been allowed to remain at his home that night, but he became so uneasy that he told his wife he must go back to prison. It was so late when he returned that the jailer chided him for coming at all.

Soon afterward the messenger arrived. "Are the prisoners all safe?" he asked.

"Yes," was the reply.

"Is John Bunyan safe?"

"Yes."

"Let me see him."

Bunyan was called, and fortunately was able to appear. When the messenger was gone, the jailer said, "Well, you may go out again just when you think proper, for you know when to return better than I can tell you." Soon, however, the jailer was censured, and came near losing his position, while Bunyan himself was not permitted "to look out at the door." His name does not appear again at a church meeting for seven years.

Bunyan's prison life was a very busy one. He did not, says his friend and biographer, the Rev. Charles Doe, "spend his time in a supine and careless manner, or eat the bread of idleness. For there I have been witness, that his own hands have ministered to his and to his family's necessities, by making many hundred gross of long, tagged, thread laces, to fill up the vacancies of his time, which he had learned for that purpose since he had been in prison. There also I surveyed his library,o the least and yet the best that ever I saw, consisting only of two books, a Bible and the 'Book of Martyrs.'"

Bunyan's Bible and his Foxe's "Book of Martyrs" came into the possession of Mr. Bohn, the London publisher, and were purchased from him for the Bedford library, where they have been seen by thousands of visitors.

"With those two books," says Froude, "Bunyan had no cause to complain of intellectual destitution. Foxe's Martyrs, if he had a complete edition of it, would have given him a very adequate knowledge of history.... The Bible, thoroughly known, is a literature of itself—the rarest and richest in all departments of thought or imagination which exists."

Besides these books, he seems to have had a rosebush, about which he wrote a poem:—

> "This homely Bush doth to mine eyes expose,
> A very fair, yea, comely, ruddy rose.
> This rose doth always bow its head to me,
> Saying, 'Come pluck me; I thy rose will be.'"

He also wrote verses about a spider whose habits he closely watched.

Bunyan's prison, if it had much of discomfort, gave him leisure to read and write—the one thing for which most persons of brain are struggling. "Prisons in those days," says Canon Venables, "and indeed long afterwards, were, at their best, foul, dark, miserable places. A century later John Howard found Bedford jail, though better than some, in what would now be justly deemed a disgraceful condition. One who visited Bunyan during his confinement speaks of it 'as an uncomfortable and close prison.'"

Once or twice his friends tried to regain his liberty for him, but he always left the matter with his Lord. When they failed to obtain his freedom, he said, "Verily, I did meet my God sweetly again, comforting of me and satisfying of me, that it was his will and mind that I should be there."

In prison Bunyan's pen was a source of great joy to himself, and a blessing to all the world. His earliest prison work was "Profitable Meditations" in verse. He put portions of the Old and New Testament into poetry. Froude calls the "Book of Ruth" and the "History of Joseph" "beautiful idylls."

He wrote in prose a treatise on prayer, entitled, "Praying in the Spirit;" a book on "Christian Behavior;" the "Holy City," an exposition of the closing chapters of Revelation; a work on the "Resurrection of the Dead and Eternal Judgment;" and "Grace Abounding," the story of his own conversion. The latter book, "if he had written no other," says Canon Venables, "would stamp Bunyan as one of the greatest masters of the English language of his own or any other age."

This book was published by George Larkin, in London, in 1666, in the sixth year of Bunyan's imprisonment.

Besides these, he wrote his "Confession of Faith," and his "Defence of the Doctrine of Justification by Faith."

Bunyan's imprisonment came to an end May 8, 1672. Through the Declaration of Indulgence, granted by Charles II., Nonconformists were once more allowed to worship God as they chose.

It seems probable, from Bunyan's later biographers, that "Pilgrim's Progress" was written during a subsequent imprisonment of six months in 1675, when the Nonconformists were again suffering the rigors of law.

The first edition appeared in 1678, when Bunyan was fifty years old. A second edition was issued the same year, and a third, with additions, the year following, 1679.

After it was written in prison, Bunyan, always distrusting his own abilities, consulted with his friends about the wisdom of publishing it, as will be seen from the metrical preface:—

"When at first I took my pen in hand,
Thus for to write, I did not understand
That I at all should make a little book
In such a mode; nay, I had undertook
To make another; which, when almost done,
Before I was aware I this begun.

* * * * * *

Well, when I had thus put my ends together,
I showed them others, that I might see whether
They would condemn them, or them justify:
And some said, 'Let them live;' some, 'Let them die.'
Some said, 'John, print it;' others said, 'Not so;'
Some said, 'It might do good;' others said, 'No.'
Now was I in a strait, and did not see
Which was the best thing to be done of me;
At last I thought, since you are thus divided,
I print it will, and so the case decided."

Bunyan was already famous. The day after he was released from prison, he began to preach in a barn standing in an orchard in Bedford, which one of the congregation, Josias Ruffhead, acting for the members of the church, had purchased, "to be a place for the use of such as doe not conforme to the Church of England, who are of the Persuasion commonly called Congregationall." The barn was so thronged that many were obliged to stay outside. Here he preached till his death, sixteen years afterward.

He had a general oversight of the churches far and near, and was often called Bishop Bunyan.

He was urged to reside in London, but he would not leave Bedford. Here he lived in a cottage which had three small rooms on the ground floor—such a house as laborers now use. Behind the cottage stood a small building which served as his workshop. A person visiting him found in his "study" the Bible, "Pilgrim's Progress," and a few other books, chiefly his own productions, "all lying on a shelf or shelves."

His beloved blind daughter, Mary, had died while he was in prison. The other children, Thomas, John, Joseph, Sarah, and

Elizabeth, four by the first mother, and two by the second, brightened the plain Bedford cottage. His son Thomas became a minister in 1673, the year after his father regained his liberty.

Whenever Bunyan went to London to preach, says Charles Doe, "if there were but one day's notice given, there would be more people come together than the meeting-house could hold. I have seen, by my computation, about twelve hundred at a morning lecture, by seven o'clock, on a working day, in the dark winter time. I also computed about three thousand that came to hear him one Lord's Day in London, at a town's-end meeting-house, so that half were fain to go back again for want of room, and then himself was fain at a back door to be pulled almost over people to get up-stairs to his pulpit." To what honor had the poor tinker already come!

It is said that Charles II. expressed his surprise to Dr. Owen that "a learned man, such as he, could sit and listen to an illiterate tinker."

"May it please your majesty," was the reply, "I would gladly give up all my learning if I could preach like that tinker."

The wonderful success attending the "Pilgrim's Progress" must have been a surprise to modest John Bunyan. Macaulay says, "He had no suspicion that he was producing a masterpiece." It spread his fame over Europe and the American settlements. It was translated into many foreign languages during his life.

Dr. Brown says: "It is found in Northern Europe—in Danish, Icelandic, Norwegian, Lithuanian, Finnish, Lettish, Esthonian, and Russ; in Eastern Europe—in Servian, Bulgarian, Bohemian, Hungarian, and Polish; and in Southern Europe—in French, Italian, Spanish, Portuguese, and Romaic, or modern Greek. In Asia, it may be met with in Hebrew, Arabic, Modern Syriac, Armeno-Turkish, Græco-Turkish, and Armenian. Farther to the south, also, it is seen in Pashtu, or Afghani, and in the great Empire of India it is found in various forms.

"It has been translated into Hindustani or Urdu, Bengali, Uriya or Orissa, Hindi, Sindhi, Panjabi or Sikh, Telugu, Canarese, Tamil, Malayaline, Marathi-Balbodh, Gujarati, and Singhalese.

"In Indo-Chinese countries there are versions of it in Assamese, Khasi, Burmese, and Sgau-Karen. It has been given to the Dyaks of Borneo, to the Malays, to the Malagasy, to the Japanese, and to the many-millioned people of China, in various dialects, both classical and colloquial."

It has also been translated into the languages of Western Africa, the Pacific Islands, the Mexicans, and various tribes of Indians.

The greatest minds of the world have been unanimous in its praise. Everybody agrees with Toplady, who wrote "Rock of Ages," that "it is the finest allegorical work extant."

Macaulay said, "Bunyan is the first of allegorists, as Shakespeare is the first of dramatists," and recommended the study of his simple style to any who wished to gain command over his mother tongue.

Coleridge said, "I know of no book, the Bible excepted as above all comparison, which I, according to my judgment and experience, could so safely recommend, as teaching and enforcing the whole saving truth, according to the mind that was in Christ Jesus, as 'The Pilgrim's Progress.'"

Fronde well says it has made Bunyan's "name a household word in every English-speaking family on the globe." Hallam calls his style "powerful and picturesque from concise simplicity." Green, the historian, thinks "Bunyan's English the simplest and homeliest English that has ever been used by any great English writer.... It is the English of the Bible."

The second part of "Pilgrim's Progress" was published seven years after the first, in 1685. In 1680 appeared the "Life and Death of Mr. Badman," a contrast to the good Pilgrim; in 1681, "Come and Welcome to Jesus Christ," which went through several editions; and in 1682, the "Holy War," which, Macaulay says, would have been our greatest allegory if "Pilgrim's Progress" had never been written. It represents the fall and recovery of man.

Several small books from Bunyan's pen appeared from year to year. In 1688, the year of his death, five of his works were published, "Jerusalem Sinner Saved, or a Help to Despairing Souls;" "The Work of Jesus Christ as an Advocate;" a poetical composition entitled, "The Building, Nature, and Excellency of the House of God;" the "Water of Life;" and "Solomon's Temple Spiritualized." "The Acceptable Sacrifice" was going through the press at the time of his death.

Besides these, Bunyan had prepared the manuscript of fourteen or more works. Ten were published soon after his death, by his devoted friend, Charles Doe, who said he thought the best work he could do for God was to get Bunyan's books printed and sold.

In the summer of 1688, a young man, in whom Bunyan was deeply interested, told him that his father was about to disinherit him, and begged the preacher to see him. Though scarcely recovered from an illness, he at once rode on horseback to Reading, met the father, obtained a promise of forgiveness, and returned homeward through London, where he was to preach near Whitechapel.

His forty miles to London were made through a pouring rain. Drenched and weary, he reached the home of his friend, Deacon John Strudwick, Holborn Bridge, Snow Hill. With his usual determination to do what he thought to be his duty, he preached Sunday, Aug. 19, 1688. Twelve days later, Aug. 31, he was dead. In two months he would have been sixty years old. He was buried in Mr. Strudwick's vault, in the Dissenters' burying-ground at Bunhill Field. The mother of John Wesley sleeps close by. This place was called Bunhill or Bonehill, from a vast quantity of human remains removed to it from the charnel house of St. Paul's Cathedral in 1549.

Bunyan died as he had lived, in complete trust and faith. He asked those who stood around his bedside to pray, and he joined fervently with them. "Weep not for me," he said, "but for yourselves. I go to the Father of our Lord Jesus Christ, who will, no doubt, through the mediation of his blessed Son, receive me, though a sinner, where I hope we ere long shall meet to sing the new song, and remain everlastingly happy, world without end, Amen."

His blind Mary had gone before him; and Elizabeth, his noble wife, died four years after him, in 1692.

Bunyan's preaching was natural, simple, and earnest, with now and then an appropriate comparison and anecdote. He said, "I have observed that a word cast in by-the-by hath done more execution in a sermon than all that was spoken besides. Sometimes, also, when I have thought I did no good, then I did the most of all; and at other times, when I thought I should catch them, I have fished for nothing."

The Rev. Charles Doe describes Bunyan "as tall of stature, strong-boned, though not corpulent; somewhat of a ruddy face, with sparkling eyes, ... hair reddish, but in his later days time had sprinkled it with gray, ... forehead something high, and his habit always plain and modest.... In his conversation he was mild and affable, not given to loquacity or much discourse in company.... He had a sharp, quick eye, with an excellent discerning of persons, being of good judgment and quick wit."

He was careful in preparing his sermons, usually committing them to writing after he had preached them. In composing his books his habit was, "first with doing, and then with undoing, and after that with doing again."

Froude says if Bunyan's "importance may be measured by the influence which he has exerted over succeeding generations, he must be counted among the most extraordinary persons whom England has produced.... To understand, and to make others understand, what Christ had done, and what Christ required men to do, was the occupation of his whole mind, and no object ever held his attention except in connection with it." Is it any wonder that the ministry of the poor, uneducated tinker was a marvellous success?

Visitors from all parts of the world go to Bedford yearly to look upon the scenes associated with Bunyan's life. In the Manor are seen his will, his cabinet, the Church Book, and various editions and foreign versions of the "Pilgrim's Progress."

Bunyan's chair is also shown, and the oak door with iron crossbars, once a part of Bedford jail, the home of the great preacher for twelve long years.

THOMAS ARNOLD

Dr. Thomas Arnold of Rugby, "England's greatest schoolmaster," was born at West Cowes, Isle of Wight, June 13, 1795. He was the youngest son and seventh child of William and Martha Arnold. His father died before he was six years old. His early education was intrusted to his mother's sister, Mrs. Delafield; and later, at the age of twelve, he was sent to Winchester.

This aunt he never forgot. When she was seventy-seven he wrote to her, "This is your birthday, on which I have thought of you, and loved you, for as many years past as I can remember. No tenth of September will ever pass without my thinking of you and loving you."

The shy, retiring boy was early fond of books. When he was three, he received a present from his father of Smollett's "History of England," "as a reward," says Dean Stanley, in his life of Arnold, "for the accuracy with which he had gone through the stories connected with the portraits and pictures of the successive reigns; and at the same age he used to sit at his aunt's table arranging his geographical cards, and recognizing by their shape at a glance the different counties of the dissected map of England."

His first childish literary work was at the age of seven,—a play, on "Piercy, Earl of Northumberland."o Between eight and twelve, when at school at Warminster, he rejoiced in Homer. A schoolmate writes: "Arnold's delight was in preparing for some part of the Siege of Troy; with a stick in his right hand, and the cover of a tin box, or any flat piece of wood, tied upon his left arm, he would come forth to the battle, and from Pope's Homer would pour forth fluently the challenge or the reproach.... Every book he had was easily recognized as his property by helmet and shields, and Hectors and Achilleses, on all the blank leaves; many of mine had some token of his graphic love of those heroes."

The home life seems to have been full of affection. Rose E. Selfe, in the World's Worker series, gives these letters. His brother Matthew writes him from school, in 1800, before he is five years old, asking him for a letter, "with all the news you can think of. What new books you have, whether you like the great Bible as well as you did, how your garden and the flowers come on."

"My darling little Tom...." his sister Susannah writes, "I shall expect to find you very much improved, particularly in your reading. As you know you are fond of kissing, give our DEAREST, DEAREST, DEAREST Mamma and Aunt ten each from Fan and myself. Oh, how I wish I could see and kiss them myself, and you, too, my sweet dear Tom! I should like to know very much if you are as fond of geography as you were last Christmas; tell me when you honour us with a letter. Adieu now, my lovely Boy. With sincerely wishing you health and happiness,

I remain, your truly affectionate and loving sister,

Sue Arnold."

This sister, an invalid for twenty years, was most unselfish and lovable in character. She died at Laleham in 1832.

At the Winchester school he was called the poet Arnold to distinguish him from another boy of the same name. He used to recite ballad poetry for the pleasure of his schoolmates, and wrote a long poem, "Simon de Montfort," in imitation of Scott's "Marmion."

He had read Gibbon and Mitford through twice before he left Winchester, at sixteen. At fourteen he enjoyed "the modest, unaffected, and impartial narratives of Herodotus, Thucydides, and Xenophon," and did not like "the numerous boasts which are everywhere to be met with in the Latin writers." He thought Roman history "scandalously exaggerated," and had no idea that he was thereafter, in his manhood, to write a fair and delightful Roman history himself.

In 1811 he was elected a scholar at Corpus Christi College, Oxford, and four years later became a Fellow at Oriel College. He gained in 1815 and in 1817 the Chancellor's prize for the two University essays, Latin and English. In college he had a passion for Aristotle and Thucydides. Next to these he loved Herodotus. Though delicate in appearance, he took long walks, in which he studied nature, being a lover of flowers, birds, and clouds.

His friendships were warm and lasting. John Keble, author of "The Christian Year," Whately, later Archbishop of Dublin, and Coleridge, afterwards chief-justice, were his especial friends.

During his four years as a Fellow in Oriel College, he took private pupils, and read in the Oxford libraries. His plan was to make himself master of some one period, like the fifteenth century, and write full notes upon it.

Oxford was always very dear to Arnold. He wrote years later, "If I live till I am eighty, and were to enjoy all the happiness that the warmest wish could desire, I should never forget or cease to look back with something of a painful feeling on the years we were together there, and on all the delights that we have lost."

During these college years he was often restless and weary of duty, inclined to indolence, and an early riser with the greatest difficulty. These things he overcame in later life. He had some religious doubts, which completely vanished as he studied and thought more deeply.

In 1819 Arnold removed to Laleham, with his mother, sister, and aunt, and remained here for the next nine years, preparing private pupils for the universities.

A year after coming to Laleham, he married, when he was twenty-five, Mary, youngest daughter of the Rev. John Penrose, in Nottinghamshire, and sister of one of his best college friends, Trevenen Penrose. She was a worthy helper through all the laborious years which followed.

Although Arnold had fitted himself for the Church, he loved the work of teaching. He wrote to a friend about to engage in a similar occupation. "I know it has a bad name, but my wife and I always happened to be fond of it.... I enjoyed and do enjoy the society of youths of seventeen or eighteen; for they are all alive in limbs and spirits at least, if not in mind, while in older persons the body and spirits oftener become lazy and languid without the mind gaining any vigor to compensate for it....

"The misery of private tuition seems to me to consist in this, that men enter upon it as a means to some further end; are always impatient for the time when they may lay it aside; whereas, if you enter upon it heartily as your life's business, as a man enters upon any other profession, you are not then in danger of grudging every hour you give to it....

"I should say, have your pupils a good deal with you, and be as familiar with them as you possibly can. I did this continually more and more before I left Laleham, going to bathe with them, leaping, and all other gymnastic exercises within my capacity, and sometimes sailing or rowing with them. They, I believe, always liked it, and I enjoyed it myself like a boy, and found myself constantly the better for it."

"Large private schools," he thought, "the worst possible system; the choice lies between public schools, and an education whose character may be strictly private and domestic."

The home at Laleham was very dear to him. Here six of his children were born. He loved the quiet walks along the banks of the Thames, his garden back of his house, where, he said, "there is always something to interest me even in the very sight of the weeds and litter, for then I think how much improved the place will be when they are removed," and the churchyard, where in after years his mother, his infant child, and now his distinguished son Matthew are resting.

One of his pupils at Laleham thus writes of Arnold: "His great power as a private tutor resided in this, that he gave such an intense earnestness to life. Every pupil was made to feel that there was a work for him to do,—that his happiness as well as his duty lay in doing that work well.... His hold over all his pupils perfectly astonished me. It was not so much an enthusiastic admiration for his genius or learning or eloquence which stirred within them; it was a sympathetic thrill caught from a spirit that was earnestly at work in the world....

"In all this there was no excitement, no predilection for one class of work above another ... but an humble, profound, and most religious consciousness that work is the appointed calling of man on earth, the

90

end for which his various faculties were given, the element in which his nature is ordained to develop itself."

Arnold used to say, "one must always expect to succeed, but never think he had succeeded."

Besides teaching, Arnold devoted his spare time to philology and history, preparing a Lexicon of Thucydides and articles on Roman History. He learned the German language that he might read Niebuhr's "History of Rome," and thereafter became deeply interested in German literature.

He wrote a friend concerning his little study "where I have a sofa full of books, as of old, and the two verse books lying about on it, and a volume of Herodotus; and where I sit up and read or write till twelve or one o'clock." Plato's "Phædo" was a great favorite. He thought it "nearly the perfection of human language."

To another he wrote, "One of my most useful books is dear old Tottle's (Aristotle's) 'Politics,' which give one so full a notion of the state of society and opinions in old times, that by their aid one can pick out the wheat from the chaff in Livy with great success."

Arnold was always a learner. He studied Hebrew when he was forty-three and Sanscrit when he wasforty-five. He urged ministers not to study works on "Divinity" only. "A man requires," he said "first, the general cultivation of his mind, by constantly reading the works of the very greatest writers, philosophers, orators, and poets, and next, an understanding of the actual state of society, ... and of political economy as teaching him how to deal with the poor.... Further, I should advise a constant use of the biography of good men."

Arnold's friends were urging him to a wider sphere of influence. Laleham had become too expensive for his means, and he had determined to move elsewhere. Just at this time the head-mastership of Rugby became vacant. There were about thirty applicants, and his testimonials were sent in late. His college friend, Dr. Hawkins, afterwards Provost of Oriel, wrote the twelve trustees a letter about Arnold, predicting that if he were elected, "he would change the face of education all through the public schools of England." He was elected in December, 1827, and the words of Dr. Hawkins were fully verified.

In 1828 he received the degree of D.D., and entered upon his new duties.

It cost the Arnold family many a struggle to leave Laleham. "I cannot tell you," Dr. Arnold writes J. T. Coleridge, "how we both love it, and its perfect peace seems at times an appalling contrast to the publicity of Rugby. I am sure that nothing could stifle this regret, were it not for my full consciousness that I have nothing to do with rest here, but with labor."

To another friend he writes, "On Tuesday, if God will, we shall leave this dear place, this nine years' home of such exceeding happiness. But it boots not to look backwards. Forwards, forwards, forwards,—should be one's motto."

For fourteen years Arnold lived at Rugby and did his great work, which has made his name known and honored among all educated nations. "What a pity," said some persons, "that a man fit to be a statesman should be employed in teaching school-boys."

But Arnold knew the greatness of his chosen work. "It is a most touching thing to me," he said, "to receive a new fellow from his father, when I think what an influence there is in this place for evil as well as for good. I do not know anything which affects me more. If ever I could receive a new boy from his father without emotion, I should think it was high time to be off."

With much firmness he united great tenderness. "Lenity is seldom to be repented of," he wrote a friend who had asked his advice in dealing with a difficult pupil. "In cases," says Dean Stanley, "when it might have been thought that tenderness would have been extinguished by indignation, he was sometimes so deeply affected in pronouncing sentence of punishment on offenders as to be hardly able to speak."

Once, when he heard of some great fault in one of his pupils, "I felt," he said—and his eyes filled with tears as he spoke, "as if it had been one of my own children, and, till I had ascertained that it was really true, I mentioned it to no one, not even to any of the masters."

At another time he said to one of the masters, speaking of a promising lad, "If he should turn out ill, I think it would break my heart."

He wrote a friend, "I believe that boys may be governed a great deal by gentle methods and kindness, and appealing to their better feelings, if you show that you are not afraid of them; I have seen great boys, six feet high, shed tears when I have sent for them up to my room and spoken to them quietly, in private, for not knowing their lesson, and I have found that this treatment produced its effect afterwards in making them do better. But of course deeds must second words when needful, or words will soon be laughed at."

When occasion demanded, Arnold could be very firm. If a boy were habitually idle, or doing harm in the school, he was expelled, for a time or permanently. "Often it would be wholly unknown who were thus dismissed or why," says Dean Stanley; "latterly, Arnold generally allowed such cases to remain till the end of the half-year, that their removal might pass altogether unnoticed."

Many parents were displeased, but Arnold never hesitated for a moment in what he believed to be his duty. The result was that the tone of the school became so elevated that more wished to come than could be accommodated.

He always appealed to the honor of the pupils. Once he said, with great spirit, in an address in which he had spoken of bad feeling amongst the boys, "Is this a Christian school? I cannot remain here if all is to be carried on by constraint and force; if I am to be here as a jailer, I will resign my office at once."

He said, "My great desire is to teach my boys to govern themselves—a much better thing than to govern them well myself."

At another time, when several boys had been sent away, and there was much discontent in consequence, he said, "It is not necessary that this should be a school of three hundred, or one hundred, or of fifty boys; but it is necessary that it should be a school of Christian gentlemen."

He trusted the boys, and never seemed to watch them. Their word was not doubted. "If you say so, that is quite enough; of course I believe your word," was his frequent statement.

"There grew up in consequence," says Stanley, "a general feeling that it was a shame to tell Arnold a lie—he always believes one." If falsehood was discovered, the punishment was severe.

He usually had great patience. When living at Laleham he once spoke sharply to a dull pupil. "Why do you speak angrily, sir?" said the youth, looking up in his face; "indeed, I am doing the best that I can."

Years afterward Arnold used to say to his children, "I never felt so much ashamed in my life—that look and that speech I have never forgotten."

For mere "intellectual acuteness" he had no admiration, unless united with goodness. "If there be one thing on earth which is truly admirable," he said, "it is to see God's wisdom blessing an inferiority of natural powers, where they have been honestly, truly, and zealously cultivated.... I would stand to that man hat in hand."

Arnold's consistent and noble life won the undying regard of his pupils. One pupil writes: "I am sure that I do not exaggerate my feelings when I say that I felt a love and reverence for him as one of quite awful greatness and goodness, for whom, I well remember, that I used to think I would gladly lay down my life.... I used to believe that I, too, had a work to do for him in the school, and did, for his sake, labor to raise the tone of the set I lived in."

Who can ever forget the description of Arnold in that natural and fascinating book, "Tom Brown's School Days"?

"And then came that great event in his, as in every Rugby boy's life of that day—the first sermon from the Doctor.... The tall, gallant form, the kindling eye, the voice, now soft as the low notes of a flute, now clear and stirring as the call of the light infantry bugle, of him who stood there Sunday after Sunday, witnessing and pleading for his Lord, the King of righteousness, and love, and glory, with whose spirit he was filled, and in whose power he spoke....

"But what was it, after all, which seized and held these three hundred boys, dragging them out of themselves, willingly or unwillingly, for twenty minutes on Sunday afternoon? True, there

93

always were boys scattered up and down the school, who in heart and head were worthy to hear and able to carry away the deepest and wisest words there spoken. But those were a minority always, generally a very small one....

"What was it that moved and held us, the rest of the three hundred scholars, childish boys, who feared the Doctor with all our hearts, and very little besides in heaven or earth; who thought more of our sets in the school than of the Church of Christ, and put the traditions of Rugby and the public opinion of boys in our daily life above the laws of God?

"We couldn't enter into half that we heard: we hadn't the knowledge of our own hearts or the knowledge of one another, and little enough of the faith, hope, and love needed to that end. But we listened, as all boys in their better moods will listen (ay, and men, too, for the matter of that), to a man whom we felt to be, with all his heart, and soul, and strength, striving against whatever was mean and unmanly and unrighteous in our little world."

Another pupil writes of these sermons: "I used to listen to them from first to last with a kind of awe, and over and over again could not join my friends at the chapel door, but would walk home to be alone; and I remember the same effects being produced by them, more or less, on others, whom I should think Arnold looked on as some of the worst boys in the school."

The influence at Rugby under Arnold was thoroughly Christian, though never sectarian. Harry East, the friend of Tom Brown (Thomas Hughes) went to Arnold to talk with him about being confirmed. "When I stuck," says East, "he lifted me, just as if I had been a little child; and he seemed to know all I'd felt, and to have gone through it all. And I burst out crying—more than I've done this five years; and he sat down by me and stroked my head; and I went blundering on.... And he wasn't shocked a bit, and didn't snub me, or tell me I was a fool ... and he didn't give me any cut-and-dried explanation. But when I'd done, he just talked a bit—I can hardly remember what he said yet; but it seemed to spread round me like healing, and strength, and light; and to bear me up and plant me on a rock, where I could hold my footing and fight for myself. I don't know what to do, I feel so happy."

While Arnold loved his boys, and felt the keenest interest in them, he did not forget his own mental requirements. "He is the best teacher of others," he said, "who is best taught himself; that which we know and love we cannot but communicate.... I hold that a man is only fit to teach so long as he is himself learning daily. If the mind once becomes stagnant, it can give no fresh draught to another mind; it is drinking out of a pond instead of from a spring.... I think it essential that I should not give up my own reading, as I always find any addition of knowledge to turn to account for the school in some way or other."

While his great desire for his boys was "moral thoughtfulness:

the inquiring love of truth going along with the devoted love of goodness," he insisted on liveliness in his teachers: "It is a great matter to make these boys understand that liveliness is not folly and thoughtlessness. A schoolmaster's intercourse is with the young, the strong, and the happy; and he cannot get on with them unless in animal spirits he can sympathize with them, and show them that his thoughtfulness is not connected with selfishness or weakness.... He who likes boys has probably a daily sympathy with them."

One great secret of Arnold's success was that he loved his work. Not that he had not strong ambitions like other men. He said, "I believe that, naturally, I am one of the most ambitious men alive," and thought that "the three great objects of human ambition" which would attract him, were "to be the prime minister of a great kingdom, the governor of a great empire, or the writer of works which should live in every age and in every country." But he felt that God had opened a great school to him, and that his path of duty was clearly marked out.

He grew tired, as do others, with what he felt to be very hard work, as all know who have tried teaching, and almost yearly took a journey on the Continent for rest and change.

"I hunger sometimes," he said, "for more time for writing; but I do not indulge the feeling, and on the other hand, I think my love of tuition rather grows upon me.... The work here is more and more engrossing continually, but I like it better and better; it has all the interest of a great game of chess, with living creatures for pawns and pieces." No one ever studied the game more intently.

"Do you see those two boys walking together?" he said to an assistant master. "I never saw them together before; you should make an especial point of observing the company they keep; nothing so tells the changes in a boy's character."

He deprecated such long terms for boys or masters as twenty-one weeks, and wished for more "co-operation in our system of public education, including both the great schools and the universities."

Besides his teaching, Arnold did much writing of pamphlets and books. "I must write or die," was an expression which he often used. His pamphlet on "The Christian Duty of Conceding the Roman Catholic Claims," in 1828, whereby many of their civil and political disabilities were to be removed, created great bitterness of feeling against him. Sir Robert Peel, the leader of the House of Commons, was also fighting the battles for the Roman Catholics of Ireland, and probably saved England from a civil war by his advocacy. But toleration was as rare nearly a century ago as it is to-day, and Arnold soon received abuse from pulpit and pew.

He was the devoted friend of the poor and the laborers. In 1831 Arnold started the Englishmen's Register, a weekly newspaper, with the hope of telling the people "the evils that exist, and lead them, if I can, to their causes and their remedies."

"If the clergy would come forward," he writes to his beloved sister Susannah, "as one man, from Cumberland to Cornwall, exhorting peaceableness on the one side and justice on the other, denouncing the high rents and the game laws, and the carelessness which keeps the poor ignorant, and then wonders that they are brutal, I verily believe they might yet save themselves and the State." ...

To the Rev. Augustus Hare, he writes; "Unquestionably our aristocratic manners and habits have made us and the poor two distinct and unsympathizing bodies; and from want of sympathy I fear the transition to enmity is but too easy when distress embitters the feelings, and the sight of others in luxury makes that distress still more intolerable. This is the plague-spot, to my mind, in our whole state of society, which must be removed, or the whole must perish."

He rejoiced that some of the leading manufacturers "are considering that their workmen have something else besides hands belonging to them, and are beginning to attend to the welfare of that something."

The Register soon died, because Arnold could not give all the time needed to conduct it, or the large amount of money necessary to start and carry on a weekly paper. His articles, however, about laborers were copied into the Sheffield Courant, and he was asked to continue his writings for its columns.

He was always a noble friend to the poor. At Laleham and Rugby he gave lectures in their interest, and was often seen in their homes. "I never knew such an humble man as the doctor," said the parish clerk at Laleham; "he comes and shakes us by the hand as if he was one of us." At his later home in Westmoreland a poor woman said, "He used to come into my house and talk to me as if I was a lady."

"Prayer and kindly intercourse with the poor," said Arnold, "are the two great safeguards of spiritual life; its more than food and raiment."

Dr. Arnold held that there "are but two things of vital importance," which Algernon Sidney calls Religion and Politics, "but which I would rather call our duties and affections toward God, and our duties and feelings toward men; science and literature are but a poor make-up for the want of these."

At one time Arnold was very anxious to start a journal, a portion of which should be devoted regularly to such subjects as history, statistics of different countries, and the like. "All instruction must be systematic," he said, "and it is this which the people want."

Without doubt Arnold was right. He could not then foresee how the newspapers of to-day, with their syndicate novels, travels, and biography, were to take the place of books in very many families. The life and times of Lincoln in the Century Magazine was a great step in the right direction. Sometime, it is to be hoped, our newspapers, instead of containing so much that is neither helpful nor lasting, will be the schools of the people, teaching history, political economy, and helpful biography.

While Arnold was, above all things, devoted to one central idea, "One name there is, and one alone—Jesus Christ, both God and man," yet he said, "I never wanted articles on religious subjects half so much as articles on common subjects written with a decidedly Christian tone. History and biography are far better vehicles of good, I think, than any direct comments on Scripture, or essays on evidences."

Arnold used to say, "Above all, be afraid of teaching nothing; it is vain now to say that questions of religion and politics are above the understanding of the poorer classes—so they may be, but they are not above their misunderstanding, and they will think and talk about them, so that they had best be taught to think and talk rightly."

In 1833 Arnold published a pamphlet on Church Reform. He believed in a union of Church and State, but wished to bring Dissenters within the pale of the Established Church. He would give them the use of the churches for worship, with different hours for their services. He did not believe in the Apostolical succession, and deprecated all divisions among Christians. He longed to see all united on one foundation stone, the Saviour of men.

The Church Reform pamphlet went rapidly through four editions, and aroused a perfect whirlwind of invective. Arnold was denounced by the Established Church because too liberal; by Dissenters as not liberal enough; by Conservatives in politics as one revolutionary in doctrine and too thoroughly a friend of the people; by other educators as the unwise head of a new system which bade fair to destroy the old. The sale of his sermons—he had published two or three volumes—was stopped. Some of his friends even dropped their intercourse with him.

"The strong, great man was startled," says Dean Stanley, "but not moved by this continued outcry."

He resolved not to answer anybody through the newspapers. "All that is wanted," he said, "is to inspire firmness into the minds of those engaged in the conduct of the school, lest their own confidence should beimpaired by a succession of attacks, which I suppose is unparalleled in the experience of schools."

When the controversy was at its height, he voted for the Liberal candidate, "foreseeing," as Stanley says, "as he must have done, the burst of indignation which followed."

"I should like," he said, "to write a book on 'The Theory of Tides,' the flood and ebb of parties. The English nation are like a man in a lethargy; they are never roused from their conservatism till mustard poultices are put to their feet."

He wrote in 1833, "May God grant to my sons, if they live to manhood, an unshaken love of truth and a firm resolution to follow it for themselves, with an intense abhorrence of all party ties, save that one tie which binds them to the party of Christ against wickedness."

Two years later he wrote, "The only hope is with the young, if by any means they can be led to think for themselves without following a party, and to love what is good and true, let them find it where they will."

Arnold went steadily forward with his scholarly work, bringing out in 1835 the last volume of his edition of Thucydides, and resumed his labor on his "Roman History." He thought "brevity and simplicity" two of the greatest merits which style can have, and applied these rules to his own accurate and thorough workmanship.

His eyes were often turned towards America, which he foresaw would solve many of the old world problems. To Jacob Abbott he wrote concerning "The Young Christian," "The publication of a work like yours in America was far more delightful to me than its publication in England could have been. Nothing can be more important to the future welfare of mankind, than that God's people, serving Him in power and in love, and in a sound mind, should deeply influence the national character of the United States."

Later he writes to his friend Chevalier Bunsen, "so beautifully good, so wise, and so noble-minded!" "I hear, both from India and the Mediterranean, the most delightful account of the zeal and resources of the American missionaries, that none are doing so much in the cause of Christ as they are. They will take our place in the world, I think not unworthily, though with far less advantages, in many respects, than those which we have so fatally wasted."

While the storm raged around him, he enjoyed great peace and comfort in his home life. He romped with his children, gathered flowers with them, and climbed mountains like a boy. "I do not wonder," he said, "that it was thought a great misfortune to die childless in old times, when they had not fuller light—it seems so completely wiping a man out of existence." He wrote Coleridge, "What men do in middle life without a wife and children to turn to, I cannot imagine; for I think the affections must be sadly checked and chilled, even in the best men, by their intercourse with people, such as one usually finds them in the world.... But with a home filled with those whom we entirely love and sympathize with, and with some old friends, to whom one can open one's heart fully from time to time, the world's society has rather a bracing influence to make one shake off mere dreams of delight."

Archbishop Whately said of Arnold, "He was attached to his family as if he had no friends; to his friends as if he had no family; and to his country as if he had no friends or relations."

Dr. Arnold's married life was very happy. He wrote his "Dearest Mary" on their wedding-day; "How much of happiness and of cause for the deepest thankfulness is contained in the recollections of this day;

for in the ten years that have elapsed since our marriage, there has been condensed, I suppose, as great a portion of happiness, with as little alloy, as ever marked any ten years of human existence."

To his servants he was extremely kind and considerate, as are all true gentlemen and well-bred women. "He was in the habit," says Stanley, "whether in travelling or in his own house, of consulting their accommodation and speaking to them familiarly as to so many members of the domestic circle."

In 1832 Arnold had purchased a small estate, Fox How, between Rydal and Ambleside, among the English lakes. "It is," he said, "with a mixed feeling of solemnity and tenderness that I regard our mountain nest, whose surpassing sweetness, I think I may safely say, adds a positive happiness to every one of my waking hours passed in it." He loved every tree, every rock, every flower, "as a child loves them." The three roads he often used to walk upon with his children he called "Old Corruption," an irregular, grassy path; "Bit-by-Bit Reform;" and "Radical Reform," a straight, good road.

The mountains were an especial delight. The impression they gave him, he said, "was never one of bleakness or wildness, but of a sort of paternal shelter and protection to the valley."

Here the work went on as elsewhere. "All the morning, till one o'clock," he wrote, "I used to sit in one corner of the drawing-room, not looking towards Fairfield lest I should be constantly tempted from my work,9 and there I worked on at the 'Roman History' and the 'Tudor Tables,' and Appius Claudius and Cincinnatus, and all the rest of them."

The "Roman History" was never finished. The third volume, published after his death, Archdeacon Hare thinks the first history which "has given anything like an adequate representation of the wonderful genius and noble character of Hannibal."

Dr. Arnold took an active part in the opposition to "The Tracts for the Times," when John Henry Newman went from the High Church Party of Oxford to the Roman Catholic Church, and became a cardinal. "I groan," he said, "over the divisions of the church, of all our evils I think the greatest ... that men should call themselves Roman Catholics, Church of England men, Baptists, Quakers, all sorts of appellations, forgetting that only glorious name of Christian, which is common to all, and a true bond of union."

In 1835 Arnold accepted a fellowship in the Senate of the new London University, with the hope that he could make it as he said, "Christian, yet not sectarian." He wished an examination in the Scriptures to be a part of the University work, but as the University from its charter was intended for all denominations, without regard to belief, he was overruled, and resigned his position. While he thanked Parliament "for having done away with distinctions between Christian and Christian"—Dissenters had been excluded heretofore from degrees at the universities because not belonging to the Established Church—"I would pray," he said, "that distinctions be kept up between Christians and non-Christians."

It is surprising to read that a man so broad and greato as Dr. Arnold thought the Jews, because unbelievers, "have no claim whatever of political right,"—"no claim to become citizens, but by conforming to our moral law, which is the Gospel,"—and petitioned against the removal of their civil disabilities. Mr. Gladstone was also against the removal, but happily changed his opinions, and spoke in behalf of the Jews in 1847.

When the Chartists were demanding a people's charter with universal suffrage for men, and other reforms, Arnold was greatly moved. He began a correspondence with Carlyle, urging that a society be formed "for drawing public attention to the state of the laboring classes throughout the kingdom." He believed that the "upper classes would make sacrifices," if the real condition of the poor and the workers could be brought to their knowledge. "Men do not think of the fearful state in which we are living," he said; and he did not despair of a remedy, "even though it is the solution of the most difficult problem ever yet proposed to man's wisdom, and the greatest triumph over selfishness ever yet required of his virtue."

We in America are facing the same problems; and there was never more need for the "upper classes to make sacrifices," and live unselfish lives for the good of their country, than now. We need to keep ever before us the Bible message, "For none of us liveth to himself."

Arnold believed rightly in each one doing his share of the world's work and duties. "There is no earthly thing," he said, "more mean and despicable in my mind than an English gentleman destitute of all sense of his responsibilities and opportunities, and only revelling in the luxuries of our high civilization, and thinking himself a great person."

He wrote to a pupil who had become a physician, "It is a real pleasure to me to find that you are taking steadily to a profession, without which I scarcely see how a man can live honestly. I use the term 'profession' in rather a large sense ... a definite field of duty, which the nobleman has as much as the tailor, but which he has not, who, having an income large enough to keep him from starving, hangs about upon life, merely following his own caprices and fancies."

Again he writes to a friend, "I would far rather send a boy to Van Diemen's Land, where he must work for his bread, than send him to Oxford to live in luxury, without any desire in his mind to avail himself of his advantages." As the years went by, the spirit of opposition against Arnold seemed to die out, and the school at Rugby gained continually in numbers and influence. He was presented to the Queen; he went up to Oxford to see degrees conferred upon Wordsworth and Bunsen; he published more volumes of sermons—six in all—and two volumes of his admirable "Roman History."

100

In 1841 he was appointed by Lord Melbourne, Regius Professor of Modern History at Oxford, the chair being made vacant by the death of Dr. Nares. This gave him great pleasure, and with enthusiasm he began to prepare his lectures.

He gave his first lecture Dec. 2, 1841, in the "theatre," the usual lecture-rooms in the Clarendon Buildings being too small for the hundreds who crowded to hear him. "It was an audience," says Dean Stanley, "unprecedented in the range of academical memory."

He designed to give a yearly course of eight lectures, beginning with the fourteenth century. Some of his lectures were to be biographical: "The life and times of Pope Gregory, or the Great," Charlemagne, Alfred, Dante, and "the noblest and holiest of monarchs, Louis IX."

He wrote Coleridge before going to Oxford, "If I do go up, many things, I can assure you, have been in my thoughts, which I wished gradually to call men's attention to; one in particular, which seems to me a great scandal—the debts contracted by the young men, and their backwardness in paying them. I think that no part of this evil is to be ascribed to the tradesmen, because so completely are the tradesmen at the mercy of the undergraduates, that no man dares refuse to give credit; if he did, his shop would be abandoned."

Arnold still continued his work at Rugby, remaining in part because two of his sons were being educated there. He was also making final arrangements for an edition of St. Paul's Epistles.

The last lecture of his first year at Oxford, June 2, 1842, was abandoned for the time, on account of a brief, but sudden illness. June 5 he preached his farewell sermon to the Rugby boys, before the vacation; and Friday, June 10, was the public-day for school speeches.

Saturday he was in high spirits, taking his usual walk and bath, and conversing with his guests on social and historical topics. In the evening he gave a supper to some of the higher classes of the school.

He wrote in his diary that evening, June 11, 1842: "The day after to-morrow is my birthday, if I am permitted to live to see it—my forty-seventh birthday since my birth. How large a portion of my life on earth is already passed.... But above all, let me mind my own personal work—to keep myself pure and zealous and believing—laboring to do God's will, yet not anxious that it should be done by me rather than by others, if God disapproves of my doing it."

Between five and six o'clock on Sunday morning he awoke with a sharp pain across his chest. He lay with his hands clasped and his eyes raised upwards, while he repeated, "And Jesus said unto him, Thomas, because thou hast seen me, thou hast believed: blessed are they that have not seen, and yet have believed."

Against Arnold's wish, his wife sent for a physician. Meantime she read to him in the Prayer Book, the fifty-first psalm. The twelfth

101

verse, "O give me the comfort of thy help again, and establish me with thy free spirit," he repeated after her very earnestly.

The physician soon came, and Arnold, asking the cause of the pain, was told that it was spasm of the heart.

"Is it generally fatal?" asked Arnold. "Yes, I am afraid it is," was the reply.

Soon after the doctor left the house for medicine, and the son Thomas entered the room. "Thank God, Tom," said Arnold, "for giving me this pain; I have suffered so little pain in my life, that I feel it is very good for me; now God has given it to me, and I do so thank Him for it."

His son said, "I wish, dear papa, we had you at Fox How." He made no reply, but smiled tenderly upon the boy and his mother.

The doctor soon came; and as he was dropping the laudanum into a glass, Arnold asked what medicine it was. On being told, he replied, "Ah, very well."

In a moment there was a convulsive struggle, then a few deep gasps, and the work of the great teacher was over.

Five of their nine children were waiting for their father at Fox How, to celebrate his forty-seventh birthday, and returned to Rugby for the burial. The news brought bewilderment and deep sorrow to Rugby, to Oxford, to London, and indeed to the whole of England.

On the following Friday he was buried in the chancel, immediately under the communion-table. How many of us Americans have stood by that sacred spot, and remembered how one good man can bring honor to his work and nation!

Out of gratitude for his services in the cause of education, a public subscription was at once started. The money subscribed was used to erect his monument in Rugby Chapel, Chevalier Bunsen writing an epitaph for it in imitation of those on the tombs of the Scipios, and of the early Christian inscriptions; and for scholarships, first to be used by his sons, and afterwards for the promotion of general study at Rugby, and history at Oxford.

WENDELL PHILLIPS

The great orator, thinker, and leader was of the best blood of New England. Educated, brilliant, aristocratic, he gave his life to the lowly. No such self-sacrifice can ever be forgotten. His name will live as long as American history is read.

Wendell Phillips was born in a stately mansion on Beacon Street, Boston, Nov. 29, 1811, the eighth in a family of nine children. The father was the Hon. John Phillips, a rich merchant, a judge of the Court of Common Pleas, a member of the corporation of Harvard College, and of the convention which revised the Constitution of the State; elected to the House of Representatives, and later to the Senate till his death; the first mayor of Boston; honored for a noble heart as well as for gifts of speech, and worthy to be the parent of such a son as Wendell.

Sally Walley, the mother, the daughter of a wealthy merchant, well-educated and of strong nature, soon perceived the unusual talents of her son. Her earliest gift to him was a Bible, which was one of his most prized treasures for seventy years.

Affectionate and domestic by nature, "Wendell's love for his mother was a passion," says the Rev. Carlos Martyn, in his life of Phillips. Her advice to him always was, "Be good and do good; this is my whole desire for you." From her he learned his Bible and the catechism; and years after, when he stood like a great oak in the forest, beat upon by wind and storm, he never forgot to keep his trust where his mother first taught him to place it.

From her knowledge and common sense in political and mercantile affairs, he judged that other women must be able to take part in the world's work, and therefore through life he asked for them an equal place in home and state.

When a child he enjoyed tools, and would have made a good carpenter or engineer. As his ancestors were mostly preachers—he was descended from the Rev. George Phillips, who came from Great Britain in 1630, and was settled at Watertown, Mass., for fourteen years, till his death—Wendell seemed inclined to follow in their footsteps; for when he was four or five years old, he would put a Bible in the chair before him, and arranging other chairs in a circle, would address them by the hour.

"Wendell," said his father, "don't you get tired of this?"

"No," said the boy, "I don't get tired, but it's rather hard on the chairs!"

His most intimate playmate was J. Lothrop Motley, afterward the celebrated historian. Often, in the Motley garret, they dressed themselves in fancy costume, and declaimed poetry and dialogue; a good preparation for the after years.

At eleven years of age Wendell was sent to the Boston Latin School, then on School Street, where the Parker House now stands. Here he met and became the warm friend of the studious Charles Sumner.

While noted for his love of books and power in declamation, he was also fond of sports,—boating, horseback-riding, and all gymnastic exercises. He was tall, graceful, and handsome.

In 1827, when he was sixteen, he entered Harvard College, whose buildings, noble trees, and shaded walks have become dear to thousands, and will be through all time. The widowed mother—John Phillips had been dead four years—gave her promising boy her blessing, and sent him out into the world to make a man of himself by virtuous and noble living, or to spoil himself by yielding to temptation, as he should elect. He chose the former course.

He became the intimate friend of Edmund Quincy, the son of the president of the college, Josiah Quincy. He stood high in his classes, besides reading extensively in general history and mechanics. He was also greatly interested in genealogy.

Sir Walter Raleigh, Sir Harry Vane, Oliver Cromwell, Lady Mary Wortley Montague, and James Watt were among his English heroes, and Benjamin Franklin, Samuel Adams, and Eli Whitney among his American. Scott and Victor Hugo were great favorites. Elizabeth Barrett Browning he regarded as the first of modern poets. Through life he was an omniverous reader of newspapers.

He was versed in several languages,—German, Italian, and Spanish, but French was his favorite among the modern tongues. He was always skilled in Latin.

Already his life had become more serious through the preaching of Dr. Lyman Beecher. The Rev. Dr. O. P. Gifford relates that Phillips once told a friend that he asked God "that whenever a thing be wrong it may have no power of temptation over me; whenever a thing be right, it may take no courage to do it. From that day to this it has been so. Whenever I have known a thing to be wrong, it has held no temptation. Whenever I have known a thing to be right, it has taken no courage to do it."

The Rev. Dr. Edgar Buckingham, secretary of the class of 1831, says: "I remember well his appearance of devoutness during morning and evening prayers in the chapel, which many attended only to save their credit with the authorities. Doddridge's 'Expositor' Wendell bore to college in his Freshman year (a present, I think, from his mother, a new volume), to be his help in daily thought and prayer."

Another of his classmates says: "Before entering college he had been the subject of religious revival. Previous to that he used to give way to violent outbursts of temper, and his schoolmates would sometimes amuse themselves by deliberately working him into a passion. But after his conversion they could never succeed in getting him out of temper."

"He had a deep love for all that was true and honorable," said his room-mate, the Rev. John Tappan Pierce of Illinois, "always detested a mean action. His Bible was always open on the centre-table. His character was perfectly transparent; there were no subterfuges, no pretences about him. He was known by all to be just what he seemed.... As an orator, Phillips took the highest stand of any graduate of our day. I never knew him to fail in anything or hesitate in a recitation."

Dr. Buckingham speaks of his "kindly, generous manner, his brightness of mind, his perfect purity and whiteness of soul; ... with a most attractive face, 'a smile that was a benediction,' with manners of superior elegance, with conversation filled with the charms of literature, with biography and history, full of refined pleasantry, ... it was no wonder that his society was courted and respected by those who had wealth at their command, and still more by those young men who came from the South."

He was a member of the "Phi Beta Kappa," on account of his scholarship, and president of the exclusive "Porcellian" and "Hasty-Pudding Club."

After graduation Phillips entered the Harvard Law School, under the brilliant Judge Story, and was admitted to the bar when he was twenty-three.

His first honor, after leaving the law school, was the invitation to deliver a Fourth of July address at New Bedford.

Charles T. Congdon, the well-known journalist, says: "When Phillips stood up in the pulpit, I thought him the handsomest man I had ever seen. When he began to speak, his elocution seemed the most perfect to which I had ever listened.... He was speaking of the political history of the State, and of its frequent isolation in politics, and electrified us all by exclaiming, 'The star of Massachusetts has shone the brighter for shining alone!'" How little he foreknew his own isolation and the brightness of the star which shone almost alone for so many years!

He opened an office on Court Street, Boston, and began regular work, knowing that idleness brings no fame. He drew up legal papers, wills, etc., and, as he told a friend, during "those two opening years I paid all my expenses, and few do it now."

On the afternoon of Oct. 21, 1835, sitting beside ano open window on Court Street, he saw a noisy crowd on Washington Street; and curiosity prompted him to put on his hat, and learn the reason of the commotion. He found a mob of four or five thousand men trying to force their way into the office of the Anti-Slavery Society, No. 46 Washington Street, where the Boston Female Anti-Slavery Society was holding its meeting. Warning handbills had been circulated about the city, and threats had been heard concerning the women if they attempted to assemble; yet nobody really believed that, in a rich and cultivated city, a company of thirty women would be mobbed on account of free speech. It had not then become apparent that the North was bound hand and foot by the slave-power.

While the women prayed, the "broadcloth" mob, of well-dressed men, in large part "gentlemen of property and standing," were yelling and cursing outside. Mayor Lyman appeared on the scene, and commanded the women to disperse, as he was powerless to protect them from bloodshed. He besought the mob to lay down their arms; but they pushed their way into the hall, appropriated the Testaments and Prayer-books, and then began to search for William Lloyd Garrison, who was in an adjoining room. He escaped across a roof, by the advice of the Mayor, but was caught by the mob, who coiled a rope around his body, and dragged him, bare-headed, and with torn garments, into State Street, toward the City Hall, shouting, "Kill him!" "Hang the Abolitionist!"

He was taken to the Mayor's room, provided with needful clothing, thrust into a closed carriage, and driven rapidly to jail, "as a disturber of the peace," but in reality to save his life. The mob clung to the wheels, dashed open the doors, seized the horses, and tried to upset the carriage; but the driver laid his whip on horses and heads of rioters alike, and Garrison was finally safely locked in a cell.

Wendell Phillips looked on bewildered, and seeing, near by, the colonel of his own Suffolk regiment, in which he also was an officer, said, "Why does not the Mayor call out the regiment? We would cheerfully take arms in such a case as this."

The reply was, "Don't you see that the regiment is in the mob?"

The young lawyer went back to his office sadly and thoughtfully.

He said, twenty years later, before the anti-slavery meeting on the anniversary of this mob: "Let me thank the women who came here twenty years ago, some of whom are met here to-day, for the good they have done me. I thank them for all they have taught me. I had read Greek and Roman and English history; I had by heart the classic eulogies of brave old men and martyrs; I dreamed, in my folly, that I heard the same tone in my youth from the cuckoo lips of Edward Everett;—these women taught me my mistake. They taught me that down in those hearts, which loved a principle for itself, asked no man's leave to think or speak, true to their convictions, no matter at what hazard, flowed the real blood of '76, of 1640, of the hemlock-drinker of Athens, and of the martyr-saints of Jerusalem. I thank them for it!"

The year after the Garrison mobbing scene, Phillips began to take part in the lyceum lectures, which at that time were popular, as the University Extension lectures are now. He spoke usually upon some topic in natural science, being more fond of this evidently than of the law.

The colored people were refused admittance to lectures; and this fact so incensed Emerson, Sumner, George William Curtis, and Phillips, that they refused to speak where the negroes were not admitted. This refusal soon broke the exclusive and unnatural custom.

In this year, 1836, Phillips met a young lady two years younger than himself, Ann Terry Greene, the daughter of a wealthy Boston merchant. Her cousin, Miss Grew, was to go by stage-coach with her intended husband to Greenfield, Mass., and Miss Greene was to accompany them. Phillips was asked to join the party. The brilliant young woman, as she herself said, "talked abolition to him all the way up." Mr. Phillips was never a great talker, but a good listener. He said, "I learn something from every one."

Both parents were dead; and she had been received as a daughter into the home of her uncle and aunt, Mr. and Mrs. Henry G. Chapman, who lived in Chauncy Place, near Summer Street. Both were warm friends of Garrison, and deeply interested in the anti-slavery movement. The young girl, with all the enthusiasm of youth, and the impulse of a strong and noble nature, espoused the cause of the slave, and was not afraid to stand for the right in a choice so unpopular among the rich and aristocratic.

The acquaintance begun on the stage-coach resulted in an engagement the same year; and the following year, Oct. 12, 1837, they were married. Like Mrs. Browning, Miss Greene was an invalid at the time of her marriage, and remained thus all her life.

"Of Mr. Phillips's unbounded admiration and love for his wife," writes Francis Jackson Garrison in his memorial sketch of "Ann Phillips," "of his chivalrousdevotion to her, and absolute self-abnegation through the more than forty-six years of their married life, and of his oft-confessed indebtedness to her for her wise counsel and inspiration, matchless courage, and unswerving constancy, the world knows in a general way; but only those who have been intimately acquainted with them both can fully realize and appreciate it all. They also know how ardent was her affection for him, and how great her pride in his labors and achievements."

When his speeches were first published in book form, in 1863, he wrote on the title-page of one volume, and gave it to his wife, "Speeches and Lectures. By Ann Phillips." Thus thoroughly did he appreciate her helpfulness.

Mrs. Phillips wrote to a friend regarding her husband, whom she called her "better three-quarters," "When I first met Wendell, I used to think, 'It can never come to pass; such a being as he is could never think of me.' I looked upon it as something as strange as a fairy-tale."

A month after her marriage, she wrote a friend, Nov. 19, 1837: "Only last year, on my sick-bed, I thought I should never see another birthday, and I must go and leave him in the infancy of our love, in the dawn of my new life; and how does to-day find me? the blessed and happy wife of one I thought I should never perhaps live to see. Thanks be to God for all his goodness to us, and may he make me more worthy of my Wendell! I cannot help thinking how little I have acquired, and Wendell, only two years older, seems to know a world more."

And yet, with all this depreciation of self, she had such a fine mind and sound judgment that Phillips deferred to her constantly, talked over with her the arguments of his speeches, and valued her approval more than that of all the world beside. As in the case of John Stuart Mill and his wife, intellectual companionship seemed the basis of their extremely happy married life.

Four years later they moved into a modest brick house, 26 Essex Street, given to Mrs. Phillips by her father, where they lived for forty years. From here Mrs. Phillips writes to a friend concerning herself: "Now what do you think her life is? Why, she strolls out a few steps occasionally, calling it a walk; the rest of the time from bed to sofa, from sofa to rocking-chair; reads generally the Standard and Liberator, and that is pretty much all the literature her aching head will allow her to peruse; rarely writes a letter, sees no company, makes no calls, looks forward to spring and birds, when she will be a little freer.... I am not well enough even to have friends to tea, so that all I strive to do is to keep the house neat and keep myself about. I have attended no meetings since I helped fill 'the negro pew.' What anti-slavery news I get, I get second-hand. I should not get along at all, so great is my darkness, were it not for Wendell to tell me that the world is still going.... We are very happy, and only have to regret my health being so poor, and our own sinfulness. Dear Wendell speaks whenever he can leave me, and for his sake I sometimes wish I were myself again; but I dare say it is all right as it is."

In 1846 Mrs. Phillips writes: "Dear Wendell has met with a sad affliction this fall in the death of his mother.... She was everything to him—indeed, to all her children; a devoted mother and uncommon woman.... So poor unworthy I am more of a treasure to Wendell than ever, and a pretty frail one. For his sake I should love to live; for my own part I am tired, not of life, but of a sick one. I meet with but little sympathy; for these long cases are looked upon as half, if not wholly, make-believes,—as if playing well would not be far better than playing sick."

On the same sheet of paper Mr. Phillips writes: "Dear Ann has spoken of my dear mother's death. My good, noble, dear mother! We differed utterly on the matter of slavery, and she grieved a good deal over what she thought a waste of my time, and a sad disappointment to her; but still I am always best satisfied with myself when I fancy I can see anything in me which reminds me of my mother. She lived in her children, and they almost lived in her, and the world is a different one, now she is gone!"

Nearly a dozen years later Mr. Phillips writes to a friend: "We are

108

this summer at Milton, one of the most delightful of our country towns, about ten miles from Boston. Ann's brother has a place here, and we are with him. She is as usual—little sleep, very weak, never goes downstairs, in most excellent and cheerful spirits, interested keenly in all good things, and, I sometimes tell her, so much my motive and prompter to every good thing, that I fear, should I lose her, there'd be nothing of me left worth your loving."

After they had been married thirteen years, having no children of their own, Mr. and Mrs. Phillips took into their home, as a daughter, Phœbe Garnaut, twelve years old, the daughter of the lovely Eliza Garnaut, who had died of cholera the year before, through her unselfish devotion to others. This child remained to brighten the Phillips' home for ten years, when she married Mr. George Washburn Smalley, the London correspondent of the New York Tribune, and made her home abroad.

Dr. Buckingham says truly that Wendell Phillips "was a lover all his life,—not with the instinctive love of youth alone, but with the secured attachment, the quiet confidence of the heart, the beautiful affectionateness, which, in the later years of the pure and good, is a far superior development of character, and a far richer enjoyment, than the effervescence of youthful days. She was, as he wrote me once, his counsel, his guide, his inspiration."

As long as Mr. Phillips lived, whenever he was at home, he visited the markets daily, searching for things which should tempt the appetite of "Ann." Lovely flowers were in her windows from one year's end to the other, placed there by his thoughtfulness or that of other dear friends. Fond of music, he daily left her money for the hand-organs played beneath her window. Her love, her cheer, her enthusiastic devotion to the great causes which he pleaded with inimitable grace and power, more than paid him for all his care and self-sacrifice.

Two months after their marriage came the event which made him, like Byron, "awake to find himself famous."

On Nov. 7, 1837, the Rev. Elijah P. Lovejoy was murdered by a pro-slavery mob in Alton, Ill. He was a Presbyterian clergyman from Maine, a graduate of Waterville College. Going West, he became the editor of the St. Louis Observer, a weekly religious paper of his own denomination.

A negro having been chained to a tree and burned to death for killing an officer who attempted to arrest him, the judge decided in favor of the mob. Rev. Mr. Lovejoy protested against such barbarity, and hisprinting-office was at once destroyed by the lawless. He moved his paper to Alton, Ill., but the slavery sympathizers destroyed his press. Some citizens reimbursed him for the loss. Another press was purchased and destroyed, and then another. The fourth press, the mayor and law-abiding citizens determined should be defended.

In the evening a mob gathered from the saloons,—their usual place of starting,—and threatened to burn the building where it was stored. The officials seemed powerless, the building was fired, and the Rev. Mr. Lovejoy received three balls in his breast.

The death of this young minister in a free State sent a thrill of indignation throughout the North. Dr. William Ellery Channing and one hundred others called a meeting at Faneuil Hall, Boston, for the morning of Dec. 8.

The Hon. Jonathan Phillips, a relative of Wendell Phillips, presided over the crowded assemblage. Dr. Channing spoke eloquently. Soon in the gallery, James T. Austin, the Attorney-General of Massachusetts, a prominent lawyer, and member of Dr. Channing's congregation, arose and declared that Lovejoy "died as the fool dieth," and compared his murderers to the men who destroyed the tea in Boston harbor. The audience was intensely excited.

Young Phillips, twenty-six years old and comparatively unknown, standing among the people,—there are no seats in the hall,—said to his neighbor, "Such a speech in Faneuil Hall must be answered in Faneuil Hall."

"Why not answer it yourself?" whispered the man.

"Help me to the platform and I will," was the reply; and pushing his way through the turbulent crowd he reached the rostrum.

He began with all the grace and self-control which characterized him in after years. There were mingled cries of, "Question," "Hear him," "Go on," "No gagging," and the like.

"Riding the whirlwind undismayed," says George William Curtis, in his eulogy, "he stood upon the platform in all the beauty and grace of imperial youth—the Greeks would have said a god descended—and in words that touched the mind and heart and conscience of that vast multitude, as with fire from heaven, recalling Boston to herself, he saved his native city and her cradle of liberty from the damning disgrace of stoning the first martyr in the great struggle for personal freedom."

"Mr. Chairman," he said, "when I heard the gentleman lay down principles which place the murderers of Alton side by side with Otis and Hancock, with Quincy and Adams, I thought those pictured lips (pointing to the portraits on the wall) would have broken into voice to rebuke the recreant American—the slanderer of the dead.... Sir, for the sentiments he has uttered, on soil consecrated by the prayers of Puritans and the blood of patriots, the earth should have yawned and swallowed him up."

This was received with applause and hisses, with cries of, "Make him take back 'recreant.' He sha'n't go on till he takes it back."

As soon as he could proceed he said, "Fellow-citizens, I cannot take back my words. Surely the Attorney-General, so long and well-

110

known here, needs not the aid of your hisses against one so young as I am,—my voice never before heard within these walls!"

"In the annals of American speech," says Curtis, "there had been no such scene since Patrick Henry's electrical warning to George the Third.... Three such scenes are illustrious in our history. That of the speech of Patrick Henry at Williamsburg, of Wendell Phillips in Faneuil Hall, and of Abraham Lincoln in Gettysburg—three, and there is no fourth."

From this time Wendell Phillips was famous; but, save for the approbation of his young wife, he stood nearly alone. He had already spoken once before an Anti-Slavery Convention at Lynn, Mass. He was now a despised abolitionist. His family were disappointed, his college was surprised, his law constituency well-nigh disappeared. He was socially ostracized.

James Russell Lowell, who also knew what it cost to be on the unpopular side, spoke thus nobly of Phillips:

> "He stood upon the world's broad threshold; wide
> The din of battle and of slaughter rose;
> He saw God stand upon the weaker side,
> That sank in seeming loss before its foes;
> Many there were, who made great haste and sold
> Unto the cunning enemy their swords;
> He scorned their gifts of fame and power and gold,
> And, underneath their soft and flowery words,
> Heard the cold serpent hiss; therefore he went
> And humbly joined him to the weaker part,
> Fanatic named, and fool, yet well content
> So he could be the nearer to God's heart,
> And feel its solemn pulses sending blood
> Through all the wide-spread veins of endless good."

Mr. Phillips turned his time and thought more than ever to the lecture platform, because in this way he could mould public opinion. He began to deliver "The Lost Arts," in 1838, which gives a glimpse of earlycivilization in glass-making, in gems, colors, metals, canals, etc., and gave it over two thousand times during the next forty-five years, receiving for it, Dr. Martyn says, which statement he heard from Phillips's own lips, a net result of $150,000.

When asked to lecture he would state his price if he were to speak on science or biography, of which he was especially fond, but would make no charges and pay his own expenses if he might speak on slavery or temperance. If he spoke once he was sure to be sought again, and sooner or later the people heard concerning the subjects to which he had dedicated his life.

Having been made the general agent of the Massachusetts Anti-

Slavery Society, Phillips organized a strong lecture force, and made every schoolhouse and church where he was allowed to enter the centre for discussions. Mrs. Phillips's health seeming to fail more and more, it was deemed wise to cross the ocean for her sake. They accordingly sailed from New York for London, June 6, 1839, arriving in July. They visited France, Italy, and Germany, and remained abroad two years, without, however, any improvement for the invalid wife.

On June 12, 1840, a World's Anti-Slavery Convention began its sessions in London. A call had been issued, addressed to the "Friends of the slave of every nation and of every clime." American societies sent delegates, Wendell Phillips and his wife, already abroad, Lucretia Mott, the distinguished Quaker, Garrison, and many others.

When they reached England, the women were refused as delegates. They asked Wendell Phillips to plead their cause. When he left the house in London to do so, his wife said to him, "Wendell, don't shilly-shally."

He spoke with his usual politeness and power: "It is the custom there America not to admit colored men into respectable society; and we have been told again and again that we are outraging the decencies of humanity when we permit colored men to sit by our side. When we have submitted to brickbats and the tar-tub and feathers in America, rather than yield to the custom prevalent there of not admitting colored brethren into our friendship, shall we yield to parallel custom or prejudice against women in Old England?

"We cannot yield this question if we would, for it is a matter of conscience, ... and British virtue ought not to ask us to yield."

The women were not admitted, however, and were obliged to sit in the gallery as spectators. None the less the women of both nations owe Phillips hearty thanks for his appreciation and his justice. Father Mathew, the great temperance leader of Ireland, deeply regretted the exclusion of the women delegates.

After the convention, Phillips and his wife went, by way of Belgium and the Rhine, to Kissingen, in Bavaria. He writes to a friend in England: "To Americans it was especially pleasant to see at Frankfort the oldest printed Bible in the world, and two pairs of Luther's shoes, which Ann would not quit sight of till I had mustered German enough to ask the man to let the 'little girl' feel of them."

Again he writes: "We started for Florence, by Bologna, that jewel of a city; ... for she admits women to be professors in her university, her gallery guards their paintings, her palaces boast their sculptures. I gloried in standing beside a woman-professor's monument, set up side by side with that of the illustrious Galvani."

To Garrison he writes from Naples, having then the same sympathy for the poor and the laborer which he showed through life: "When you meet in the same street a man encompassed with all the equipage of wealth, and the beggar, on whose brow disease and starvation have written his title to your pity, the question is, involuntarily, Is this a Christian city? To my mind the answer is, No....

"I hope the discussion of the question of property will not cease until the Church is convinced that, from Christian lips ownership means responsibility for the right use of what God has given; that the title of a needy brother is as sacred as the owner's own, and infringed upon, too, whenever that owner allows the siren voice of his own tastes to drown the cry of another's necessities.... None know what it is to live till they redeem life from monotony by sacrifice."

After the return of the Phillipses, the anti-slavery work was taken up more vigorously than ever. Colored children were not allowed to study in the schools with white in Boston. Phillips agitated till separate colored schools were abolished. He appealed to the Legislature of his native State to compel railroads, as common carriers, to admit the negro to the cars, and finally was successful.

He shared, like Henry Ward Beecher and Lucretia Mott, the discomforts of the colored man. Frederick Douglass said, in his oration on Phillips, given before his own race, in Washington, 1884: "On one occasion, after delivering a lecture to the New Bedford Lyceum, before a highly cultivated audience, when brought to the railroad station (as I was not allowed to travel in a first-class car, but was compelled to ride in a filthy box called the 'Jim Crow' car), he stepped to my side, in the presence of his aristocratic friends, and walked with me straight into this miserable dog-car, saying, 'Douglass, if you cannot ride with me, I can ride with you.'

"On the Sound, between New York and Newport, in those dark days, a colored passenger was not allowed abaft the wheels of the steamer, and had to spend the night on the forward deck, with horses, sheep, and swine. On such trips, when I was a passenger, Wendell Phillips preferred to walk the naked deck with me to taking a state-room. I could not persuade him to leave me to bear the burden of insult and outrage alone."

In 1850 the "irrepressible conflict" between freedom and slavery was reaching its climax. The Fugitive-Slave Law, fathered by Henry Clay, and, to the dismay of a large portion of the North, upheld by Daniel Webster in his 7th of March speech, had been signed by the President, Millard Fillmore, Sept. 18, 1850. This bill made slave-hunting and the return of slaves to their masters a duty.

A great company, presided over by Charles Francis Adams, and addressed by Phillips and others, in Faneuil Hall, protested; but the North was powerless or suppliant. Mobs broke up anti-slavery meetings in New York City. Colored men, on one pretext or another, were seized and carried back to slavery.

On April 3, 1851, Thomas Sims, a slave, was arrested in Boston, and, after a hurried examination before the United States Commissioner, was given up to his pursuers. The poor slave youth begged this favor: "Give me a knife," he said, "and when the commissioner declares me a slave, I will stab myself to the heart, and die before his eyes."

At midnight the Mayor of Boston, with two or three hundred policemen, heavily armed, placed Sims on board the ship Acorn, and sent him back into bondage.

Great meetings were held on Boston Common and in Tremont Temple to protest against this action, but they were of no avail. A year later, on the anniversary of the rendition of Sims, Phillips gave a thrilling address at the Melodeon. Looking towards the future, he said, "I know what civil war is.... And yet I do not know that, to an enlightened mind, a scene of civil war is any more sickening than the thought of a hundred and fifty years of slavery. Take the broken hearts, the bereaved mothers, the infant wrung from the hands of its parents, the husband and wife torn asunder, every right trodden under foot, the blighted hopes, the imbruted souls, the darkened and degraded millions, sunk below the level of intellectual life, melted in sensuality, herded with beasts, who have walked over the burning marl of Southern slavery to their graves, and where is the battle-field, however ghastly, that is not white—white as an angel's wing—compared with the blackness of that darkness which has brooded over the Carolinas for two hundred years?"

Meantime, what had become of Sims? On arriving at Savannah he was severely whipped, and confined in a cell for two months. He was then sent to a slave-market at Charleston, and thence to another market at New Orleans. Finally he was purchased by a brick-mason, taken to Vicksburg, and in 1863 he escaped to the besieging army of Grant, and was given transportation to the North.

Three years later, May 14, 1854, Anthony Burns, a slave, was arrested, and on June 2, marched through Court Street and State Street, over the ground where Crispus Attucks, a colored man, fell as the first victim in the Boston Massacre in the Revolution, to the wharf, in the centre of a concourse of people, guarded by companies of militia and protected by cannon. The streets were draped in black by the indignant citizens, and the bells tolled a dirge, as the bound slave was thrust into the hold of a vessel ready to start for Virginia. Burns was the last black man carried back to his masters from Massachusetts.

Meantime, Wendell Phillips had been fighting other battles. In October, 1850, the first National Woman Suffrage Convention was held at Worcester, Mass. Nine States responded. Phillips spoke earnestly, but no full report of his address or of others was taken.

The next year, 1851, at Worcester, he made a brilliant speech at the second National Woman Suffrage Convention. Of that speech, given in full in Mr. Phillips's "Speeches and Lectures" published in 1863, Mr. Curtis says, in his eulogy of Phillips: "In his general statement of principle nothing has been added to that discourse; in vivid and effective eloquence of advocacy it has never been surpassed."

"What we ask is simply this," said Phillips, "what all other classes have asked before: Leave it to woman to choose for herself her profession, her education, and her sphere. We deny to any portion of the species the right to prescribe to any other portion its sphere, its education, or its rights.... The sphere of each man, of each woman, of each individual, is that sphere which he can, with the highest exercise of his powers, perfectly fill. The highest act which the human being can do, that is the act which God designed him to do.... The tools, now, to him or her who can use them...."

"While woman is admitted to the gallows, the jail, and the tax-list, we have no right to debar her from the ballot-box."

He had no fears that woman's natural grace or tenderness would be marred by depositing her vote in the ballot-box. "Let education," he said, "form the rational and moral being, and nature will take care of the woman."

On another occasion Mr. Phillips gave this illustration: "Goethe said, that, 'if you plant an oak in a flower-pot, one of two things was sure to happen,—either the oak will be dwarfed, or the flower-pot will break.' So we have planted woman in a flower-pot, hemmed her in by restrictions; and, when we move to enlarge her sphere, society cries out, 'Oh, you'll break the flower-pot!' Well, I say, let it break. Man made it, and the sooner it goes to pieces the better. Let us see how broadly the branches will throw themselves, and how beautiful will be the shape, and how glorious against the moonlit sky or glowing sunset the foliage shall appear!"

He thought the idea that woman would have no time for political matters an absurdity, when the soldier, the busy manufacturer, the lawyer, the president of a college, and the artisan have time to vote.

"Responsibility," he said, "is one instrument—a great instrument—of education, both moral and intellectual. It sharpens the faculties. It unfolds the moral nature. It makes the careless prudent, and turns recklessness into sobriety.... Woman can never study those great questions that interest and stir most deeply the human mind, until she studies them under the mingled stimulus and check of this responsibility.... The great school of this people is the jury-box and theballot-box.... Great political questions stir the deepest nature of one-half the nation; but they pass far above and over the heads of the other half. Yet, meanwhile, theorists wonder that the first have their whole nature unfolded, and the others will persevere in being dwarfed."

In 1861, in Cooper Institute, New York, Mr. Phillips said: "Let public opinion only grant that, like their thousand brothers, those women may go out, and, wherever they find work to do, do it without a stigma being set upon them. Let the educated girl of twenty have the same liberty to use the pen, to practise law, to write books, to serve in a library, to tend in a gallery of art, to do anything that her brother can do." And he asked for woman equal wages with man for the same work.

The anti-slavery war was still waging. The Kansas and Nebraska Act, by which the people were left to fight out the battle of slavery or freedom on their own soil, resulted, as might have been expected, in bloodshed. Among those who went to Kansas, determined to help make it a free State, was John Brown, whose pathetic life has been written recently by that eminent anti-slavery worker and author, Frank B. Sanborn, Esq., of Concord, Mass.

During those dreadful years of civil war in Kansas, Brown and his family suffered all manner of hardships. Some of his sons were in prison, and some murdered. He had always wished to free the slaves, had helped many to escape, and in 1859 carried out a plan, long in his mind, to establish a station in Virginia, near enough to a free State, where fugitive slaves could defend themselves for a time, till they could be helped into Canada.

On Sunday evening, Oct. 16, 1859, Brown, with eighteen men, arrived at Harper's Ferry, broke down the armory-gate, and took possession of the village, without firing a gun. The citizens soon armed, several men were killed, and, before the next night, Brown and his company, now reduced to six, were barricaded in the engine-house. Colonel Robert E. Lee, afterwards the Confederate general, arrived with some United States marines from Washington, and Brown was ordered to surrender, which he refused to do. When he was finally captured, his two sons were dead, and he was thought to be dying from his wounds.

He met his death bravely on the scaffold at Charlestown, Va., Dec. 2. 1859.

He wrote a friend, a short time before his death, "I think I cannot better serve the cause I love so much than to die for it; and in my death I may do more than in my life."

The day he died, he wrote on a piece of paper and handed it to one of the guards, "I, John Brown, am now quite certain that the crimes of this guilty land will never be purged away but with blood. I had, as I now think vainly, flattered myself that without very much bloodshed it might be done."

As he rode on the wagon to the scaffold, at eleven o'clock, looking out over the two thousand Virginian soldiers, the distant hills, and the Blue Ridge Mountains, he said, "This is a beautiful country; I have not cast my eyes over it before—that is, in this direction." He thanked his jailer for his kindness, and said, "I am ready at any time—do not keep me waiting;" and died without a tremor.

Victor Hugo said, "His hangman is the whole American Republic.... What the South slew last December was not John Brown, but slavery."

Brown's body was delivered to his wife, and she bore it to New York. Wendell Phillips met the funeral company at that city, and they carried the body to North Elba, in the Adirondack Mountains. He was buried Dec. 8, 1859, Mr. Phillips speaking eloquently and touchingly at the grave. "He has abolished slavery in Virginia," said Phillips.... "History will date Virginia emancipation from Harper's Ferry. True, the slave is still there. So, when the tempest uproots a pine on yon hill, it looks green for months—a year or two. Still, it is timber, not a tree. John Brown has loosened the roots of the slave system; it only breathes,—it does not live,—hereafter."

How strange it was that only a few short months afterward thousands of Union soldiers were marching to battle, singing that inspiring strain,—

> "John Brown's body lies a-mouldering in the grave,
> And his soul is marching on!"

While Brown lay in prison at Charlestown, Va., a meeting was held in Tremont Temple, Boston, to raise money for his impoverished family. John A. Andrew, not then governor, presided. Emerson, Phillips, and the Rev. J. M. Manning, Congregationalist, of the "Old South" Church, made earnest addresses. The latter said, "I am here to represent the church of Sam Adams and Wendell Phillips; and I want all the world to know that I am not afraid to ride in the coach when Wendell Phillips sits on the box."

In New York a meeting for the same purpose was confronted by a fierce mob. On Staten Island, when Phillips attempted to lecture, George William Curtis presiding, a mob gathered on the road and sidewalk. Ao lady driving up, a man from West Brighton rushed to the carriage-door, followed by several rough men, and exclaimed, "I advise you, madam, not to go in; there is going to be trouble."

"What trouble, sir?" said she calmly.

"Two hundred of us," said the leader, "have sworn to tear this man from the desk and plant him in the Jersey marshes."

"I don't think that will be allowed, sir," she replied.

"Well, if you have force enough to prevent it, go ahead."

"I do not say any such thing," she answered; "but this is not a political meeting. I have come to hear a literary lecture, and I think there will be decent men enough here to check any disturbance."

The bravery of the woman seemed to abash the crowd. Though some climbed on ladders to the windows of the church and shouted, "Fetch him out!" they did not attempt to batter down the doors. They threw stones and cursed after the lecture was over, but Phillips was not harmed.

An attempt was made to mob him in Philadelphia. He wrote to his wife's cousin, Miss Grew, "I have become so notorious, that at Albany, Kingston, and Hartford the Lyceum could not obtain a church for me; and the papers riddled me with pellets for a week; but that saved advertising, and got me larger houses gratis. At Troy they even thought of imitating Staten Island, and getting up a homœopathic mob, but couldn't."

Phillips was becoming accustomed to mobs. He had, says Mr. Higginson, "a careless, buoyant, almost patrician air, as if nothing in the way of mob-violence were worth considering." Dec. 2, 1860, on the anniversary of John Brown's execution, being debarred from speaking in Tremont Temple, a crowded meeting was held in the Belknap-street colored church. The mob determined to get him into their hands, says Charles W. Slack, in George Lowell Austin's life of Phillips, and were only prevented "by a cordon of young men, about forty or more in number, who with locked arms and closely compacted bodies, had Phillips in the centre of their circle, and were safely bearing him home."

On Jan. 24, 1861, the annual meeting of the Massachusetts Anti-slavery Society was held in Tremont Temple. Mrs. Lydia Maria Child describes the scene: "Soon the mob began to yell from the galleries. They came tumbling in by hundreds.... Such yelling, screeching, and bellowing I never heard....

"Mr. Phillips stood on the front of the platform for a full hour, trying to be heard whenever the storm lulled a little. They cried, 'Throw him out! Throw a brickbat at him! Your house is afire; go put out your house!' Then they'd sing, with various bellowing and shrieking accompaniments, 'Tell John Andrew, tell John Andrew, John Brown's dead!' I should think there were four or five hundred of them. At one time they all rose up, many of them clattered down-stairs, and there was a surging forward toward the platform. My heart beat so fast I could hear it; for I did not then know how Mr. Phillips's armed friends were stationed at every door, and in the middle of the aisle. At last it was announced that the police were coming. Mr. Phillips tried to speak, but his voice was again drowned. Then ... he stepped forward and addressed his speech to the reporters stationed directly below him."

He said to the reporters—the noisy crowd shouted, "Speak louder! We want to hear what you're saying!"—"While I speak to these pencils, I speak to a million of men. What, then, are these boys? We have got the press of the country in our hands.... My voice is beaten by theirs, but they cannot beat types. All hail and glory to Faust, who invented printing, for he made mobs impossible." Nothing seemed to fire the great orator like opposition. He was the very soul of courage.

The Civil War had begun. Phillips, who had been in favor of disunion, because he and other anti-slavery men and women wished no union with slavery, now that the first shot had been fired on April 12, 1861, became a firm supporter of the Union.

He said in his lecture "Under the Flag," delivered in Music Hall, April 21, 1861, and contained in the first volume of his speeches: "The cannon shot against Fort Sumter has opened the only door out of this hour. There were but two. One was compromise; the other was battle....

118

The South opened this with cannon shot, and Lincoln shows himself at the door. The war, then, is not aggressive, but in self-defence, and Washington has become the Thermopylæ of liberty and justice. Rather than surrender that capital, cover every square foot of it with a living body; crowd it with a million of men, and empty every bank vault at the North to pay the cost. Teach the world once for all, that North America belongs to the Stars and Stripes, and under them no man shall wear a chain."

The speech was reported for the Boston Journal; but fearing that the war Democrats would not be pleased, it was suppressed. The friends of Phillips, learning of this, had it printed as an extra, and scattered one hundred thousand copies of it.

Through these early years of the war Phillips was urging the arming of the negroes; and when some white men doubted their courage, he lectured through the land upon Toussaint L'Ouverture, the great leader of Hayti, whom he thus pictures:—

"Of Toussaint, Hermona, the Spanish general, who knew him well, said, 'He was the purest soul God ever put into a body.' Of him history bears witness, 'He never broke his word.'"

When he was captured by the French and taken to France, "As the island faded from his sight, he turned to the captain and said, 'You think you have rooted up the tree of liberty, but I am only a branch; I have planted the tree so deep that all France can never root it up.'"

He was thrown into a stone dungeon, twelve feet by twenty. "This dungeon was a tomb. The story is told that, in Josephine's time, a young French marquis was placed there, and the girl to whom he was betrothed went to the Empress and prayed for his release. Said Josephine to her, 'Have a model of it made and bring it to me.' Josephine placed it near Napoleon. He said, 'Take it away, it is horrible!' She put it on his footstool, and he kicked it from him. She held it to him the third time, and said, 'Sire, in this horrible dungeon you have put a man to die.' 'Take him out,' said Napoleon, and the girl saved her lover.

"In this tomb Toussaint was buried, but he did not die fast enough. Finally the commandant was told to go into Switzerland, to carry the keys of the dungeon with him, and to stay four days; when he returned, Toussaint was found starved to death....

"'No RETALIATION,' was his great motto and the rule of his life; and the last words uttered to his son in France were these, 'My boy, you will one day go back to St. Domingo; forget that France murdered your father.'"

Early in 1863 Phillips saw colored troops, the Fifty-fourth and Fifty-fifth Regiments, march through the same street where Garrison had been mobbed and Anthony Burns carried back into slavery by United States troops, singing the John Brown song. Times were indeed changed since Phillips himself was mobbed for suggesting negro soldiers.

When the war was over, and Abraham Lincoln lay dead, Phillips spoke in Tremont Temple to a hushed and mourning company: "What the world would not look at, God has set to-day in a light so ghastly bright that it dazzles us blind. What we would not believe, God has written all over the face of the continent with the sword's point, in the blood of our best and most beloved. We believe the agony of the slave's hovel, the mother, and the husband, when it takes its seat at our own board....

"He was permitted himself to deal the last staggering blow which sent rebellion reeling to its grave; and then, holding his darling boy by the hand, to walk the streets of its surrendered capital, while his ears drank in praise and thanksgiving which bore his name to the throne of God in every form piety and gratitude could invent; and finally to seal the sure triumph of the cause he loved with his own blood. He caught the first notes of the coming jubilee, and heard his own name in every one. Who among living men may not envy him?"

In the great matters of reconstruction andconstitutional changes, Phillips took an ardent and helpful part. He criticised sharply, perhaps not always wisely, (for who can be infallible in judgment?) but he was always earnest and unselfish. When asked to let his name be used for Congress, he refused, preferring to hold no party allegiance where principle was at stake.

He constantly urged the ballot for the negro. "Reconstruct no State," he said, "without giving to every loyal man in it the ballot. I scout all limitations of knowledge, property, or race. Universal suffrage for me; that was the Revolutionary model. Every freeman voted, black or white, whether he could read or not. My rule is, any citizen liable to be hanged for crime is entitled to vote for rulers. The ballot insures the school."

When the slavery question was settled, Wendell Phillips could not stop working. He wrote to a meeting of his old abolition comrades, two months before his death, "Let it not be said that the old abolitionist stopped with the negro, and was never able to see that the same principles claimed his utmost effort to protect all labor, white and black, and to further the discussion of every claim of humanity."

He said to a friend, "Now that the field is won, do you sit by the camp-fire, but I will put out into the underbrush."

He had for years been a total abstainer, and now more than ever was an earnest advocate of prohibition. In Tremont Temple, Jan. 24, 1881, he reviewed Dr. Crosby's "Calm view of Temperance."

Phillips stood manfully for the temperance pledge. "We make a pledge by joining a church," he said. "The husband pledges himself to his wife, and she to him, for life. Is the marriage ceremony, then, a curse, a hindrance to virtue and progress?

120

"Society rests in all its transactions on the idea that a solemn promise, pledge, assertion, strengthens and assures the act.... The witness on the stand gives solemn promise to tell the truth; the officer about to assume place for one year, or ten, or for life, pledges his word and oath; the grantor in a deed binds himself for all time by record; churches, societies, universities, accept funds on pledge to appropriate them to certain purposes and no other.... No man ever denounced these pledges as unmanly.... The doctor's principle would unsettle society; and if one proposed to apply it to any cause but temperance, practical men would quietly put him aside as out of his head."

Phillips told this story concerning the pledge. A man about sixty came to sit beside him as he was travelling in a railway car. He had heard Phillips lecture on temperance the previous evening. "I am master of a ship," said he, "sailing out of New York, and have just returned from my fiftieth voyage across the Atlantic. About thirty years ago I was a sot, shipped, while dead drunk, as one of the crew, and was carried on board like a log. When I came to, the captain sent for me. He asked me, 'Do you remember your mother?' I told him she died before I could remember anything. 'Well,' said he, 'I am a Vermont man. When I was young I was crazy to go to sea. At last my mother consented I should seek my fortune in New York.'

"He told how she stood on one side the garden gate and he on the other, when, with his bundle on his arm, he was ready to walk to the next town. She said to him, 'My boy, I don't know anything about towns, and I never saw the sea; but they tell me those great towns are sinks of wickedness, and make thousands of drunkards. Now, promise me you'll never drink a drop of liquor.'

"He said, 'I laid my hand in hers and promised, as I looked into her eyes for the last time. She died soon after. I've been on every sea, and seen the worst kinds of life and men. They laughed at me as a milksop, and wanted to know if I was a coward; but when they offered me liquor, I saw my mother across the gate, and I never drank a drop. It has been my sheet-anchor. I owe all to that. Would you like to take that pledge?' said he."

He took it. "It has saved me," he said. "I have a fine ship, wife and children at home, and I have helped others."

Dr. Crosby favored license. Phillips said, "The statute books in forty States are filled with the abortions of thousands of license laws that were never executed, and most of them were never intended to be."

"No one supposes," said Phillips later, "that law can make men temperate.... But law can shut up those bars and dram-shops which facilitate and feed intemperance, which double our taxes, make our streets unsafe for men of feeble resolution, treble the peril to property and life, and make the masses tools in the hands of designing men to undermine and cripple law."

121

Phillips also worked untiringly for labor reform. He wrote to Mr. George J. Holyoake, in England, "There'll never be, I believe and trust, a class-party here, labor against capital, the lines are so indefinite, like dove's-neck colors. Three-fourths of our population are to some extent capitalists; and, again, all see that there is really, and ought always to be, alliance, not struggle, between them." Again he said, "Capital and labor are only the two arms of a pair of scissors,—useless when separate, and only safe when fastened together, cutting everything before them."

He urged fewer hours for labor, better wages, and united effort among workingmen. He said to them, "Why have you not carried your ends before? Because in ignorance and division you have let the other side have their own way. We are ruled by brains.... You want books and journals.... When men have wrongs to complain of they should go to the ballot-box and right them.... Men always lose half of what is gained by violence. What is gained by argument is gained forever."

In an address in 1872 he said to labor, "If you want power in this country, if you want to make yourselves felt, ... write on your banner, so that every political trimmer can read it, so that every politician, no matter how short-sighted he may be, can read it: 'We never forget! If you launch the arrow of sarcasm at labor, we never forget; if there is a division in Congress, and you throw your vote in the wrong scale, we never forget.'"

Mr. Phillips carried out his ideas of labor under his own roof. So kind and considerate was he to his servants, that his cook, who was his nurse in childhood, used to leave the door open into the kitchen, that she might hear him pass and repass. She said, "Bless him, there is more music in his footfall than in a cathedral organ!"

When she was too old for work, he placed her in a home of her own, and went to see her every Saturday, when possible, with many gifts for her comfort, till she died. He paid the best wages to servants of anybody in the neighborhood. "Good pay, good service," he used to say.

He was always generous. One day on the cars he met a woman thinly clad, a lecturer from the South, a niece of Jefferson Davis, as he afterwards learned. She had received five dollars for her work. Mr. Phillips said, "I don't want to give offence, but you know I preach that a woman is entitled to the same as a man if she does the same work. Now, my price is fifty or a hundred dollars; and, if you will let me divide it with you, I shall not have had any more than you, and the thing will be even."

The lady at first refused, but was persuaded to take it. When she reached home she found there were fifty dollars—all he had received for his lecture at Gloucester.

In 1870 Phillips accepted the nomination for the governorship of Massachusetts from the prohibition and the labor parties, though he said, and undoubtedly with truth, that he had no desire to be governor. He received over twenty thousand votes.

When blamed because he favored General Butler for governor, he replied that he did not know a man among all the candidates whom he would make a saint of. "The difficulty is," said he, with his natural love of humor, "saints do not come very often; and, when they do, it is the hardest thing in the world to get them into politics."

When Andrew Johnson was not impeached, as Phillips hoped he would be, he used to say, "Congress has deposed him without impeachment. 'Friend, I'll not shoot thee,' said the Quaker to the footpad, 'but I'll hold thy head in the water until thee drown thyself.' The Republican party has taken a leaf out of that scrupulous Christian's book."

Phillips was a Protectionist. In early life he was a0 free-trader, but changed his views. "Under free trade," he said, "our country would be wholly agricultural.... Should we lose our diversified occupations, we would suffer a great loss, though there might be a pecuniary gain.... If all the world were under one law, and every man raised to the level of the Sermon on the Mount, free trade would be so easy and charming! But while nations study only how to cripple their enemies,—that is, their neighbors,—and while each trader strives to cheat his customer, and strangle the firm on the other side of the street, we must not expect the millennium."

He smiled at the "shoals of college-boys, slenderly furnished with Greek and Latin, but steeped in marvellous and delightful ignorance of life and public affairs, filling the country with free-trade din."

Phillips pleaded the cause of the Irish in his wonderful lecture on Daniel O'Connell. He was also the friend and advocate of the Indian.

He opposed capital punishment, because he thought the old Testament law—about which scholars disagree—was no more binding upon us than scores of others given to the Jews about "abstaining from meats offered to idols, and from blood and from things strangled," etc. Once men were hanged in England for stealing a shilling. We are gradually learning that reform is what society needs—not revenge.

Mr. Phillips spoke on finance before the American Social Science Association. His plan was, says Austin: "Take from the national banks all right to issue bills; let the nation itself supply a currency ample for all public needs; reduce the rate of interest."

In the summer of 1880 Mr. Phillips and his wife spent some time at Princeton, Mass. He was then sixty-nine years old. He wrote a friend: "I laze and ride on horseback, exploring the drives.... The rest of the time I sleep. I weigh a hundred and seventy-five pounds, and don't feel as old as I am."

To another friend he wrote of the extreme stillness of the place: "A passer-by is an event. The only noise ever made is by the hens. The only thing that ever happens is when we miss the cat. But we always keep awake at the sunsets, they are splendid."

The next year, June 30, 1881, he was asked to give the address at Harvard College, on the Centennial Anniversary of the Phi Beta Kappa. His subject was "The Scholar in a Republic."

"It was," says Thomas Wentworth Higginson, "the tardy recognition of him by his own college and his own literary society, and proved to be, in some respects, the most remarkable effort of his life. He never seemed more at his ease, more colloquial and more extemporaneous; and he held an unwilling audience spellbound, while bating absolutely nothing of his radicalism."

He pleaded for the great reforms for which he had labored all his life. "The fathers," he said, "touched their highest level when, with stout-hearted and serene faith, they trusted God that it was safe to leave men with all the rights he gave them. Let us be worthy of their blood, and save this sheet-anchor of the race,—universal suffrage,— God's church, God's school, God's method of gently binding men into commonwealths in order that they may at last melt into brothers....

"These agitations are the opportunities and the means God offers us to refine the taste, mould the character, lift the purpose, and educate the moral sense of the masses, on whose intelligence and self-respect rests the State. God furnishes these texts. He gathers for us this audience, and only asks of our coward lips to preach the sermons....

"If in this critical battle for universal suffrage ... there be any weapon, which, once taken from the armory, will make victory certain, it will be, as it has been in art, literature, and society, summoning woman into the political arena.... The literary class, until half a dozen years, has taken note of this great uprising only to fling every obstacle in its way.

"The first glimpse we get of Saxon blood in history is that line of Tacitus in his 'Germany,' which reads, 'In all grave matters they consult their women.' Years hence, when robust Saxon sense has flung away Jewish superstition and Eastern prejudice, and put under its foot fastidious scholarship and squeamish fashion, some second Tacitus, from the Valley of the Mississippi, will answer to him of the Seven Hills, 'In all grave questions we consult our women.' ...

"To be as good as our fathers we must be better.... With serene faith they persevered. Let us rise to their level. Crush appetite and prohibit temptation if it rots great cities."

In the winter of 1882 he made his last lecture tour, when he was seventy-one. He had the same noble presence, the same exquisitely toned voice which began his speech as in ordinary conversation, the same calm self-poised manner, as in middle life. The eyes were blue and small, the smile sweet, the figure straight, the whole bearing one of perfect mastery of both self and audience. I have heard, "his attitude was a study for the sculptor—yet unconscious and natural," truly says

124

Mr. Martyn. "The weight of the body was usually supported upon the left foot, with the right slightly advanced at an easy angle—an attitude of combined firmness and repose."

His speeches were never written out. He disliked writing, and thought it "a mild form of slavery—a man chained to an ink-pot." He said, "The chief thing I aim at is to master my subject. Then I earnestly try to get the audience to think as I do."

He once wrote a young man, who had asked him about public speaking: "I think practice with all kinds of audiences the best of teachers. Think out your subject carefully. Read all you can relative to the themes you touch. Fill your mind; and then talk simply and naturally. Forget altogether that you are to make a speech or are making one.... Remember to talk up to an audience, not down to it. The commonest audience can relish the best thing you can say if you say it properly. Be simple, be earnest."

"He faced his audience," says Curtis, "with a tranquil mien, and a beaming aspect that was never dimmed. He spoke, and in the measured cadence of his quiet voice there was intense feeling, but no declamation, no passionate appeal, no superficial and feigned emotion. It was simply colloquy—a gentleman conversing. Unconsciously and surely the ear and heart were charmed.

"How was it done? Ah! how did Mozart do it, how Raphael? The secret of the rose's sweetness, of the bird's ecstasy, of the sunset's glory—that is the secret of genius and of eloquence."

Phillips's habit in travelling was to carry a large shawl, which he always spread between the sheets of his bed in the various hotels, to prevent a cold; an example to other speakers. His supper before an address was usually, it is said, three raw eggs and a cup of tea.

Mr. Phillips had already moved his home from 26 Essex Street, in the spring of 1881, to No. 37 Common Street, not far away, as his home had to be torn down for the widening of the street. It was a severe trial to both, but it did not remain their earthly home for long.

Mr. Phillips made his last public address at the unveiling of Anne Whitney's statue of Harriet Martineau at the "Old South" Church, Boston, Dec. 26, 1883.

His wife was seriously ill through January, and he watched most devotedly by her bedside. On the 26th of the month he was taken ill with angina pectoris. He felt that the end was near. He said, "I have no fear of death. I have long foreseen it. My only regret is for poor Ann. I had hoped to close her eyes before mine were shut." To a friend who spoke to him of his always expressed belief in the divinity of Christ, though many of his friends were Unitarian, he said, quoting the words of an eminent Semitic scholar: "I find the whole history of humanity before him and after him points to him, and finds in him its centre and its solution. His whole conduct, his deeds, his words, have a supernatural character, being altogether inexplicable from human

125

relations and human means. I feel that here there is something more than man."

"Then you have no doubt about a future life?" said the friend.

"I am as sure of it as I am that there will be a to-morrow," was the reply.

On Saturday evening, Feb. 2, 1884, at fifteen minutes past six, he closed his eyes calmly and quietly forever.

All Boston, all America, was moved at the death of the great leader—patrician born, yet the people's advocate. The funeral was held at eleven o'clock Wednesday, Feb. 6, at Hollis-street Church, and then the body was borne to Faneuil Hall, two colored companies forming a guard of honor.

There, where he had won his first fame in youth at the Lovejoy meeting, where he had stirred the whole land by his eloquence in the cause of the oppressed, it was fitting he should sleep at last.

The Irish National League of Boston sent a mound of flowers, three feet by four, with the word "Humanity" in the centre, in violets on a bed of carnations. The Irish-American Societies of Boston sent a harp four feet high of ivy leaves and japonicas, with the word "Ireland" in the centre. One of the harp strings was broken. Others sent a sheaf of ripened wheat, a crown of ivy and roses, and a wreath of laurel.

From one o'clock till four, thousands passed the form of their beloved dead; rich and poor, Irish and American, black and white, children and adults. One old colored woman, with tears flowing down her cheeks, said, "Our Wendell Philips has gone." Another said, "He was de bes' fren' we ever hed. We owes him a heap!"

Frederick Douglass looked on in sorrow. "I wanted to see this throng," he said, "and to see the hold that this man had upon the community. It is a wonderful tribute."

Thousands were unable to enter Faneuil Hall, and filled every available inch of space in the street, and windows and balconies of buildings. A vast crowd followed up State Street to Washington, up School to Tremont, to the old Granary burying-ground, where the body was laid in the family vault.

Mrs. Phillips died Saturday, April 24, 1886, two years after her husband. She had been closely confined to her home for the greater part of fifty years. "She lay as if asleep," says Francis J. Garrison, "with all the purity and guilelessness of her youthful face ripened into maturity. It seemed transfiguration."

The body of Wendell Phillips was carried with that of his wife to Milton, a beautiful suburb where they had often spent their summers; and both were buried in the same grave, side by side, in a lot which he had purchased a year or two before his death. A noble pine-tree stands near the spot. On a plain slab at the head of the grave are the words, "Ann and Wendell Phillips."

HENRY WARD BEECHER

"The most brilliant and fertile pulpit-genius of the nineteenth century, and the most widely influential American of his time," says John Henry Barrows in his masterly life of Henry Ward Beecher. "To the sensitive heart of a woman, he added a lion-like courage, and a Miltonic loftiness of spirit. To the more than royal imagination of Jeremy Taylor, he added a zeal as warm as Whitefield's. In him the wit of Sydney Smith was combined with the common-sense of John Bunyan.

"In the annals of oratory his place is near that of Demosthenes. Among reformers he need fear no comparison with Wendell Phillips, John Bright, Mazzini, or Charles Sumner. In moral genius for statesmanship he was the brother of Abraham Lincoln; and, in the annals of the pulpit, he can only be mentioned with the greatest names,—Chrysostom, Bernard, Luther, Wesley, Chalmers, Spurgeon."

Dr. Mark Hopkins, in Edward W. Bok's "Memorial Volume," said of Henry Ward Beecher's forty years in Plymouth pulpit, "No such instance of prolonged, steady power at one point, in connection with other labors so extended and diversified, and magnificent in their results, has ever been known."

Dr. Thomas Armitage of the Fifth-avenue Baptist Church, New York, his life-long friend, gave Beecher "the first place among the preachers of the world to-day." Dr. Robert Collyer said, "To my mind, he was the greatest preacher on this planet.... Men will be his debtors for ages to come."

June 24, 1891, the statue of this great American leader, by John Quincy Adams Ward, was unveiled in front of Brooklyn City Hall. Three hundred children from Plymouth Church Sunday-school sang his favorite hymn,—

"Love divine, all love excelling,"

accompanied by the band of the Thirteenth Regiment.

Henry Ward Beecher, the son of the Rev. Lyman Beecher and Roxana Foote, was born in Litchfield, Conn., June 24, 1813. The father was an eloquent, fearless, great-hearted man, the son and grandson of a sturdy blacksmith; the mother a refined, dignified, intellectual, beautiful, and superior woman. Her family connections were of the best in New England. Her ancestor, James Foote, an English officer, aided Charles II. of England to hide himself in the Royal Oak which grew in a field of clover, and for this was knighted; the family coat-of-arms bearing an oak for its crest with a clover-leaf in its quarterings.

Roxana, the granddaughter of General Ward of Revolutionary

fame, was remarkably well educated for the times. She was versed in literature and history, which she studied while she spun flax, tying her books to the distaff,—no wonder that her great son was an omniverous reader,—she wrote and spoke the French language fluently, drew with the pencil, and painted with the brush on ivory, sang and played on the guitar, and was an expert with her needle.

After her marriage with Mr. Beecher, she opened a school for girls in their parish at East Hampton, Long Island, to eke out a living on their four hundred dollars salary. From here they were called in 1810, eleven years after their marriage, to the hilly, lonely town of Litchfield, Conn., bringing their six little children with them.

Henry Ward was the ninth child, the eighth then living.

So many cares and privations broke down the beautiful mother, who died when Henry was three years old.

A friend of the family writes: "She told her husband that her views and anticipations of heaven had been so great that she could hardly sustain it, and if they had been increased she should have been overwhelmed, and that her Saviour had constantly blessed her; that she had peace without one cloud, and that she had never during her sickness prayed for life. She dedicated her sons to God for missionaries, and said that her greatest desire was that her children might be trained up for God....

"She attempted to speak to her children; but she was extremely exhausted, and their cries and sobs were such that she could say but little. She told them that God could do more for them than she had done or could do, and that they must trust him."

After Lyman Beecher had prayed, "she fell into a sweet sleep from which she awoke in heaven. It is a moving scene to see eight little children weeping around the bed of a dying mother."

"They told us," says Mrs. Harriet Beecher Stowe, "at one time that she had been laid in the ground, at anothero that she had gone to heaven. Whereupon Henry, putting the two things together, resolved to dig through the ground and go to find her; for being discovered under sister Catherine's window one morning digging with great zeal and earnestness, she called to him to know what he was doing, and, lifting his curly head, with great simplicity he answered, 'Why, I am going to heaven to find ma!'"

The benign influence of this lovely mother was never forgotten by Henry Ward Beecher. He said: "I have only such a remembrance of her as you have of the clouds of ten years ago, faint, evanescent, and yet, caught by imagination and fed by that which I have heard of her, and by what my father's thought and feeling of her were, it has come to be so much to me that no devout Catholic ever saw so much in the Virgin Mary as I have seen in my mother, who has been a presence to me ever since I can remember.... Do you know why so often I speak what must seem to some of you rhapsody of woman? It is because I had

128

a mother, and if I were to live a thousand years I could not express what seems to me to be the least that I owe to her....

"She has been part and parcel of my upper life—a star whose parallax I could not take, but nevertheless, shining from afar, she has been the light that lit me easier into the thought of the invisible and the presence of the Divine."

Again her distinguished son wrote: "There are few born into this world that are her equals. She was a woman of extraordinary graces and gifts; a woman not demonstrative, with a profound philosophical nature, of a wonderful depth of affection, and with a serenity that was simply charming. From her I received my love of the beautiful, my poetic temperament; from her also I received simplicity and childlike faith in God."

When Henry Ward was eighteen, he found some letters of his mother to his father. He wrote in his diary: "O my mother! I could not help kissing the letters. I looked at the paper and thought that her hand had rested upon it while writing it. The hand of my mother! She had formed every letter which I saw. She had looked upon that paper which I now looked upon. She had folded it. She had sent it."

The Rev. Lyman Beecher said of her, "I never heard a murmur, ... I never witnessed a movement of the least degree of selfishness; and if there ever was any such thing in the world as disinterestedness, she had it."

Henry Ward repeats this incident told him by his father: "One day, being much annoyed by some hogs that kept getting into his garden, he seized his gun and rushed to the door. My mother anxiously followed, and cried, 'O father, don't shoot the poor things!' He flashed back at her, 'Woman, go into the house!' and when he was telling me of it years afterwards he said: 'Without a word or look she turned, quietly, majestically, and went in—but she didn't get in before I did. I threw my arms around her in an agony of self-reproach, and cried "Forgive me, oh, forgive me!" She uttered no word, but she looked at me like a queen—and smiled—and kissed my face; my passion was gone, and my offence forgiven.' Up to the last of his life he never spoke of her but with intensest admiration and loving remembrance."

About a year after Roxana's death, Dr. Lyman Beecher found an estimable woman willing to be a mother to the eight motherless children, and to take summer boarders to help support the family, whose income was eight hundred dollars a year. She must have been a woman of great self-sacrifice.

Young Henry thought her saintly, but cold. "Although I was longing to love somebody," he writes, "she did not call forth my affection; and my father was too busy to be loved. Therefore I had to expend my love on Aunt Chandler, a kind soul that was connected with our family, and the black woman that cooked, who was very kind to me. My mother that brought me up I never thought of loving. I revered her, but I was not attracted to her.... I knew that about twilight she prayed; and I had a great shrinking from going past her door at the time. I had not the slightest doubt that she had set her affections on things above, and not on things beneath."

At four years of age Henry went to Ma'am Kilbourn's school, where he repeated his letters twice a day, and later to the district school, for which he had in those days no affection. "In winter," he says, "we were squeezed into the recess of the farthest corner, among little boys, who seemed to be sent to school to fill up the chinks between the bigger boys. We were read and spelt twice a day, unless something happened to prevent, which did happen about every other day. For the rest of the time we were busy in keeping still.

"And a time we always had of it. Our shoes always would be scraping on the floor or knocking the shins of urchins who were also being educated. All our little legs together (poor, tired, nervous, restless legs with nothing to do!) would fill up the corner with such a noise that, every ten or fifteen minutes, the master would bring down his two-foot hickory ferule on the desk with a clap that sent shivers through our breasts to think how that would have felt if it had fallen somewhere else; and then with a look that swept us all into utter extremity of stillness, he would cry, 'Silence in that corner!' ...

"Besides this our principal business was to shake and shiver at the beginning of the school for very cold; and to sweat and stew for the rest of the time before the fervid glances of a great iron box stove, red-hot." Those of us who have attended district schools in New England will recognize the truthfulness of the picture.

Henry longed for birds and flowers and books, as indeed he did all through college, and was ever a deeper student of nature than of books. And yet in after years he was glad for some of these school experiences. "I am thankful," he says, "that I learned to hem towels—as I did. I know how to knit suspenders and mittens. I know a good deal about working in wood-sawing, chopping, splitting, planing, and things of that sort. I was brought up to put my hand to anything; so that when I went West, and was travelling on the prairies and my horse lost a shoe, and I came to a cross-road where there was an abandoned blacksmith's shop, I could go in and start the fire, and fix the old shoe and put it on again. What man has done man can do; and it is a good thing to bring up boys so that they shall think they can do anything. I could do anything."

The lad was sensitive to praise or blame, and extremely diffident. "To walk into a room where 'company' was assembled, and to do it erect and naturally, was as impossible as it would have been to fly.... Our backbone grew soft, our knees lost their stiffness, the blood rushed to the head, and the sight almost left our eyes. We have known something of pain in after years, but few pangs have been more acute than some sufferings from bashfulness in our earlier years."

130

Mr. Beecher felt all through his life that he owed much to a colored man, Charles Smith, who worked on his father's farm when he was a boy. "He used to lie upon his humble bed," says Mr. Beecher, "(I slept in the same room with him) and read his Testament, unconscious, apparently, that I was in the room.... I never had heard the Bible really read before; but there, in my presence, he read it, and talked about it to himself and to God.... He talked to me about my soul more than any member of my father's family."

Henry was taken to Bethlehem, seven miles from Litchfield, to the school of the Rev. Mr. Langdon; but he seems here also to have loved the woods and flowers so much better than books, that he was finally sent to Hartford to the care of his sister Catherine, who taught a school for young ladies. Though a favorite on account of his sunny disposition, he proved a poor scholar, and was sent home at the end of six months. When the boy was thirteen, Dr. Lyman Beecher moved with his family to Boston, having been called to the pastorate of the Hanover-street Congregational Church at the North End.

Here he loved Christ Church chimes, listened to their music "with a pleasure and amazement," he says, "which I fear nothing will ever give me again till I hear the bells ring out wondrous things in the New Jerusalem," and studied ships as he strolled along the docks, or lingered in Charlestown Navy Yard.

At the latter place he stole a six-pound shot, and not knowing how to get it home unobserved, carried it rolled in a handkerchief on the top of his head under his hat. With the greatest difficulty he brought it home, and then did not know what to do with it, not daring to show it, nor tell where he got it.

"But after all," he says, "that six-pounder rolled a good deal of sense into my skull. I think it was the last thing I ever stole; and it gave me a notion of the folly of coveting more than you can enjoy, which has made my whole life happier."

The boy who had so loved the country among the hills of Connecticut, became gloomy and restless shut in by the treeless city. His father gave him the lives of Nelson and Captain Cook to read, and the lad resolved to go to sea. He could not bring himself to run away without telling his father, which he did. With rare tact Dr. Beecher replied that Henry would not wish to be an ordinary sailor.

"No," said the boy. "I want to be a midshipman, and after that a commodore."

"I see," said the father; "and in order for that you must begin a course of mathematics and study navigation.... I will send you up to Amherst next week, to Mount Pleasant, and there you'll begin your preparatory studies, and if you are well prepared I presume I can make interest to get you an appointment."

At fourteen the lad entered Mount Pleasant Institute, the father hoping and praying that his boy "would be in the ministry yet."

131

With Lord Nelson and other great commanders in mind, he determined to master his studies and be somebody. Hard mathematics became easier, and he liked the drill in elocution. He enjoyed sport among the boys, and the semi-military methods of the school, but best of all he liked spending his play-hours in caring for beds of pansies and asters.

During a revival at Mount Pleasant, Henry was much moved, and wrote to his father, who advised his coming home to join the church. He did so, though he felt afterwards that the change in his life was not as thorough as he could have wished. However, it obliterated the desire of being a sailor, and turned his thoughts toward the ministry.

When he was seventeen, in 1830, he entered Amherst College. The great beauty of the scenery always had for him an especial charm. "I used to look across the beautiful Connecticut River valley, and at the blue mountains that hedged it in, until my heart swelled and my eyes filled with tears."

In college he was fond of athletic sports, ready in wit, beginning to show his eloquence in debate, an ardent temperance advocate, a lover of rhetoric, botany, and geology, and a warm friend to his classmates. He cared little for the classics; but he read much, especially the old English authors, Spenser, Shakespeare, Milton, and others.

Dr. Roswell D. Hitchcock, who was at Amherst with young Beecher, says, "He was by all odds the best debater of his college generation. I should be glad to know how he acquired his mastery of the English language.... The four books which probably helped him most were the Bible, Shakespeare, Milton's 'Paradise Lost,' and Bunyan's 'Pilgrim's Progress.'"

"He was," said Dr. John Haven, a classmate, "a great reader, and probably had more general knowledge than any one of his classmates when he graduated."

He necessarily used the greatest economy in college, his board costing him but one dollar and fifty cents a week, a mile from college grounds; and when vacation came he walked more than a hundred miles to Boston, because he had no money to pay the stage-coach fare.

Charles Beecher, the youngest of Roxana's children, was in college with his brother Henry. Dr. Beecher became so straitened in money matters that it seemed probable that the sons must leave college. He and his wife talked the matter over till finally he said, "Well, the Lord always has taken care of me, and I am sure he always will." The mother lay awake after she had gone to bed, and cried over it; evidently she was not as cold at heart as the young Henry Ward thought.

The next morning was the Sabbath. The door-bell rang, and a one hundred dollar bill was handed in from Mr. Homes, as a thank-offering for the conversion of one of his children. The way was now opened for the boys to continue their college course.

After Henry had been at Amherst less than a year, in the spring vacation of 1831, he and another student walked fifty miles to the home of a classmate, and there fell in love with the sister of the latter, Eunice White Bullard, daughter of Dr. Artemas Bullard of West Sutton, Mass.

"After our outside work was done," writes Mrs. Beecher, years later, "mother and I took knitting and sewing and sat down with them. I was going to wind a skein of sewing-silk (that was before spools were common), and, as was my custom, put it over the back of a chair. More gallant and thoughtful, apparently, than his older companions, this young gentleman insisted upon holding it for me to wind. For some reason—perfectly unaccountable, if one judged only by his quiet, innocent face,without watching the eyes and mouth—that skein became as intricately tangled as if tied by Macbeth's witches.

"'A badly tangled skein is it not?' said he, when I had lost half my evening in getting it wound.

"'Rather more troublesome, I imagine, than if I had kept it on the chair,' I replied. 'It was a good trial of patience, anyhow,' was his response to the laugh that followed."

The students remained for several days, and had a merry time. One day, after some pies had been taken out of the old-fashioned brick oven, a few ashes falling upon one, the mother asked Eunice to get them off. Henry offered to help, and respectfully taking the pie from her hands carried it into the garden, where he and his two other college friends ate it up. "There, we have cleared the plate nicely," said Henry Ward, as he handed it back to the mother.

Dr. Bullard said of young Beecher, "He's smart. If he lives, he'll make his mark in the world."

The next winter, January, 1832, Henry Ward taught school near the town where Eunice was teaching. He asked, "If she would go to the West with him as a missionary?" and was referred to her parents. Mrs. Bullard was grieved; but Dr. Bullard was angry, and said, "Why, you are a couple of babies. You don't know your own minds yet, and won't for some years to come." Young Beecher was a little over eighteen, and Miss Bullard ten months older.

About this time Henry earned five dollars for giving a temperance lecture, using the money to buy for his future wife the unusual love-gift of Baxter's "Saints' Rest."

Soon after, he walked to Brattleborough, Vt., fifty miles each way, gave a lecture, for which he received ten dollars, and with a part of the money bought an engagement-ring for Miss Bullard, which was also her wedding-ring, and with the rest the works of Edmund Burke.

This money gave him great satisfaction. "Oh, that bill!" he says. "How it warmed me and invigorated me! I looked at it before going to sleep; I examined my pocket the next morning, to be sure that I had not dreamed it. How I pitied the poor students, who had not, I well knew, ten dollars in their pockets. Still, I tried to keep down pride in its offensive forms. I would not be lifted up."

After he had bought the books, he says, "I was a man that owned a library! I became conservative and frugal. Before, I had spent at least a dollar and a half a year for knickknacks; but, after I had founded a library, I reformed all such wastes, and every penny I could raise or save I compelled to transform itself into books!" When he graduated, he owned about fifty volumes.

Dr. Lyman Beecher having left Boston to become the President of Lane Theological Seminary at Cincinnati, Ohio, Henry and Charles went thither to study theology. The three years spent there were full of pathetic, and sometimes comic, incidents. In this, at that time far West, the fences were poor, and cattle were apt to stray at will over flower-beds and across the gardens. One day Henry found a strange cow lying down on the barn floor. He quickly drove her out, chased her down the street, and, hot and tired, came to the house and threw himself on the sofa.

"There, I guess I have taught one old cow to know where she belongs," he remarked to his father.

"What do you mean?" said the doctor, growingexcited. "Well, you have done it. I have just bought that cow, and had to wade the Ohio River twice to get her home; and, after I have got her safely into the barn, you have turned her out. You have done it, and no mistake." And the cow was vigorously hunted up.

During all these years affectionate letters were sent to Eunice Bullard. "What a noble creation E—— is," young Beecher writes in his journal. "I could have looked through ten thousand and never found one so every way suited to me. How dearly do I love her!"

Some of this time was darkened by doubt and disbelief; but, like John Bunyan, after about two years of unsettled condition of mind, peace was assured. "It came to me," he says, "like the bursting of spring. It was as if yesterday there was not a bird to be seen or heard, and as if to-day the woods were full of singing birds. There rose up before me a view of Jesus as the Saviour of sinners,—not of saints, but of sinners unconverted, before they were any better,—because they were so bad and needed so much; and that view has never gone from me.... Never for a single moment have I doubted the power of Christ's love to save me, any more than I have doubted the existence in the heaven of the sun by day and the moon by night."

The second Mrs. Beecher had died, triumphing in her faith. Dr. Beecher, tried for heresy, was fighting theological battles, which his son Henry learned to abhor.

"I see no benefit in a controversy," he wrote. "It will be a fierce technical dispute about propositions, at the expense in the churches of vital godliness.... Others may blow the bellows, and turn the doctrines in the fire, and lay them on the anvil of controversy, and beat them with all sorts of hammers into all sorts of shapes; but I shall busy myself with using the sword of the Lord, not in forging it."

Pro-slavery riots had begun, and the printing-press of James G. Birney was destroyed by a mob of Kentucky slaveholders. Young Beecher was sworn in as a special constable, and for several nights, well armed, patrolled the streets with others, to protect the colored people. He was learning bravery early, and he had need of it through life.

Mr. Beecher graduated in 1837 from Lane Seminary, and through the influence of a Yankee woman, Martha Sawyer, was asked to go to Lawrenceburg, Ind., to preach. "There was a church in that place," says Mr. Beecher, "composed of about twenty members, of which she was the factotum. She collected the money, she was the treasurer, she was the manager, she was the trustee, she was the everything of that church."

There were about fifteen hundred persons in the little town, situated at the junction of the Ohio and Miami Rivers. There were four big distilleries in the place, and a steamboat load of liquor was carried away from it every day.

"When I went there and entered upon my vocation of preaching," says Mr. Beecher, "I found a church, occupying a little brick building, with nineteen or twenty members. There was one man, and the rest were women. With the exception of two persons, there was not one of them who was not obliged to gain a livelihood by the labor of the hands. So you will understand how very poor they were....

"I was sexton in the church. There were no lamps there, so I went and bought some and filled them and lit them. I swept the church, and lighted my own fires. I did not ring the bell because there was none. I opened the church before every meeting, and shut and locked it after every meeting. I took care of everything in the church."

The salary was to be $300—it was raised from $250—of which the Home Missionary Society was to give $150.

His friends in Cincinnati opposed his going to so small a field; but he carried out the advice which he gave years afterward to theological students: "Don't hang round idle, waiting for a good offer. Enter the first field God opens for you. If he needs you in a larger one, he will open the gate for you to enter."

Young Beecher, having waited nearly seven years to claim his bride,—he was now but twenty-four,—wrote to Miss Bullard that he would be ready for the marriage Aug. 3. Arriving at her home on the evening of July 29, he picked over and stoned with her the raisins for the wedding-cake, beat the eggs, and in every way helped on the joyful event. At the hour chosen for the ceremony, a heavy thunder-storm came on. The bride determined to wait; and an hour after the appointed time, under a brilliant rainbow, they were married, and started for their missionary labors in the West.

They boarded for a short time, and then decided to go to

135

housekeeping. Mrs. Beecher, during the absence of her husband at a synodical meeting, found two rooms over a stable, at a rental of forty dollars per year. She went to Cincinnati by boat, to the home of the Beechers, and received, to help in furnishing these rooms, a bedstead, a stove, some sheets and pillow-cases, and a piece of carpet. Through the sale of her cloak for thirtydollars, she obtained a husk mattress, a table, wash-tubs, and groceries.

On Mr. Beecher's return he helped scrub the floors—the landlord objected to their being painted, as it would injure the wood!

Mrs. Beecher found in the back yard a broken table and shelves, which had been thrown away as useless; and covering the former with the skirts of Mr. Beecher's old coat, it became quite an elegant writing-table for the young minister. The flour-barrel and sugar-barrel—sent in by friends—were curtained from the rest of the room by a piece of four-cent calico.

Mrs. Beecher helped support the family by taking in sewing and keeping boarders. Mr. Beecher soon became the idol of his people. Mr. John R. Howard, in his life of Beecher, repeats these words of the famous preacher: "There lived over on the other side of the street in Lawrenceburg, a very profane man who was counted ugly. I understood that he had said some very bitter things of me. I went right over to his store, and sat down on the counter to talk with him. I happened in often—day in and day out. My errand was to make him like me. I did make him like me,—and all the children too; and when I left, two or three years later, it was his house that was opened to me and all my family for the week after I gave up my room. And to the day of his death, I do not believe the old man could mention my name without crying."

"Once," says a brother minister, "he called to a poor German emigrant woman that if she would bring him her clothes-line, he would show her how to get her winter's supply of fuel. She brought it, and he tied a stone to one end, and flinging it out from the shore over the logs, would draw them in. In a little while their combined efforts had brought in a dray-load."

Mr. Beecher began his work modestly: "I never expected that I could accomplish much," he said. "I merely went to work with the feeling: 'I will do as well as I can, and I will stick to it, if the Lord pleases, and fight his battle the best way I know how.' And I was thankful as I could be. Nobody ever sent me a spare-rib that I did not thank God for the kindness which was shown me. I recollect when Judge —— gave me his cast-off clothing, I felt that I was sumptuously clothed. I wore old coats and second-hand shirts for two or three years, and I was not above it, either, although sometimes, as I was physically a somewhat well-developed man, and the judge was thin and his legs were slim, they were rather a tight fit."

"At first," he says, "I preached some theology.... But my horizon grew larger and larger in that one idea of Christ.... After I had gone through two or three revivals of religion, when I looked around, he was all in all. And my whole ministry sprang out of that."

After two years at Lawrenceburg, Mr. Beecher was called to the Second Presbyterian Church of Indianapolis, then a place of four thousand inhabitants, with a salary of six hundred dollars. He declined the call twice, but finally, laying the matter before the Synod, was constrained to accept.

Here, as at Lawrenceburg, the church was filled to overflowing to hear the young, original, earnest preacher. During his ministry of eight years at Indianapolis, there were three seasons of revival. In the spring of 1842 about one hundred persons joined the church. One spring Mr. Beecher preached for seventy consecutive nights. He loved to recall those days. He said, "Talk of a young mother's feelings over her first babe—what is that compared with the solemnity, the enthusiasm, the impetuosity of gratitude, of humility, of singing gladness, with which a young pastor greets the incoming of his first revival? He stands upon the shore to see the tide come in! It is the movement of the infinite, ethereal tide! It is from the other world! There is no color like heart color. The homeliest things dipped in that forever after glow with celestial hues."

Other churches besides his own were blessed with his ministrations. He says, "For eight or ten years I labored for the poor and needy, in cabins, in camp-meetings, through woods, up and down, sometimes riding two days to meet my appointments. I had no books but my Bible; and I went from one to the other—from the Bible to men, and from men to the Bible."

Yet when he could be at home he was a diligent reader of other books,—the sermons of Jonathan Edwards, of Isaac Barrow, and of Robert South. He pored over Loudon's Encyclopædias of Horticulture, Agriculture, and Architecture. He became the editor of the Indiana Farmer and Gardener.

He loved to work among flowers and raise vegetables, which he often took to market before daylight. He believed in manual labor. He painted his own house, and did not hesitate to bring his groceries home in a wheelbarrow. He said: "It is my deliberate conviction that physical labor is indispensable to intellectual and moral health."

He was as fearless as he was industrious. One man had taken offence at Mr. Beecher's plain-speaking about some of his brutal acts. He stationed himself on the hotel steps, pistol in hand, to meet the pastor as he should return from the post-office.

"Did you say thus in your sermon yesterday?" asked the man.

"I did," was the reply.

"Did you intend those remarks for me, or were you meaning me?"

"I most certainly did."

"Then,"—with an oath, "take it back right here, or I'll shoot you on the spot."

"Shoot away," said Mr. Beecher, looking the man squarely in the face, and passed on. The man followed for a few steps, and then went down a side street.

Although one of Mr. Beecher's elders had said, "If an Abolitionist comes here, I will head a mob and put him down," the brave preacher sat on the platform at an Abolitionist meeting, and in his pulpit preached so earnestly against slavery that it was predicted that his influence for all time would be destroyed. He lectured as earnestly against intemperance and other sins; and these "Lectures to Young Men" became his first volume, dedicated to his father. The book had a wide reading, both in England and America.

While at Indianapolis his little son George died. Years later he said, "I remember, to-night, as well as I did at the time, the night that my eldest son died. That was my first great sorrow.... It was in March, and there had just come up a great storm, and all the ground was covered with snow.

"We went down to the graveyard with little Georgie, and waded through it in the snow. I got out of the carriage and took the little coffin in my arms, and walked knee-deep to the side of the grave, and looking in I saw the winter down at the very bottom of it.... If I should live a thousand years I could not help shivering every time I thought of it."

Mr. Beecher loved the West, and expected to remain permanently in it; but the East had learned of his earnestness and his eloquence, and called him to Brooklyn. For a long time he refused to consider it; but his wife having suffered much from chills and fever, he finally accepted the call to the newly organized Plymouth Church, with twenty-one members, in the fall of 1847, at a salary of fifteen hundred dollars. In two years the membership had grown to over four hundred, and a new church had been built—the other having been badly damaged by fire—at a cost of $36,000.

A month after Mr. Beecher's arrival in Brooklyn, his little girl, "Caty," died, and began, as he says, "her quiet march toward the once-opened gate, to rejoin the brother."

From this time onward till Mr. Beecher's death in 1887, for forty years, Plymouth Church became the centre of almost unparalleled influence. Dr. Barrows says with truth, "It is probable that, except Westminster Abbey, no other church of English-speaking nations has in this century been visited by so many men and women of renown."

The church, accommodating three thousand persons, was year by year crowded to repletion, often as many going away as could find standing-room within. Everybody wanted to hear the most eloquent pulpit orator in America.

When Mr. Beecher first came to Plymouth Church, some said he would not please the cultivated East, but his earnestness soon satisfied all cavillers. He had one message, as he said, "The love of Christ to men. This, to me, was a burning reality.... Consequently I went into this work with all my soul, preaching night and day."

The slavery question had now come to be the foremost question among the people. By the Missouri Compromise of 1821, slavery was not to extend north beyond latitude 36° 30´. When, in 1849, California asked admittance to the Union as a free State, the South, feeling that the balance of power would be on the side of freedom, bitterly opposed it. Henry Clay, the great compromiser, brought forward his "Omnibus Bill" in 1850, the principal features of which were that California should be a free State, and the Fugitive Slave Law should be more stringent, so that Southerners might reclaim slaves in the Northern States, and take them back to bondage, and it should be the duty of Northerners to help them. President Millard Fillmore signed these measures.

Mr. Beecher wrote for the New York Independent a three-column article, entitled, "Shall We Compromise?" The dying John C. Calhoun had it read twice to him. "The man who says that is right," he repeated. "There is no alternative. It is liberty or slavery."

When Daniel Webster, in his fatal speech of March 7, 1850, favored compromise, "Then it was that I flamed," said Mr. Beecher, and from that time till the Civil War was over he was at a white heat.

When Wendell Phillips was denied a place to speak because he was an Abolitionist, and no one dared to rent a hall for him through fear of a mob, Henry Ward Beecher opened Plymouth pulpit. He went to every trustee for his consent. It the man hesitated, Mr.9 Beecher said, "You and I will break if you don't give me this permission," and he signed.

A great audience assembled, and men were ready with revolvers to use them if the mob molested the speaker.

Mr. Beecher would not ride in omnibuses where colored persons were refused. He invited Frederick Douglass to sit beside him on the platform in Plymouth Church—he would not have a pulpit, which half hid the pastor from his people. Mr. Beecher's sister, Mrs. Stowe, had published "Uncle Tom's Cabin" as a serial in 1851, and in book form in 1852, which electrified the North and infuriated the South.

When Stephen A. Douglas proposed the repeal of the Missouri Compromise, which was carried in 1854, Kansas became a battleground between slaveholders and lovers of freedom. Houses were burned, men were murdered, and all the horrors of civil war continued for four years. Mr. Beecher's voice and pen were never silent: "Peace in Kansas," he said, "means peace everywhere; war there will be war all over the land.... What is done must be done quickly. Funds must be freely given, arms must be had, even if bought at the price mentioned by our Saviour: 'He that hath no sword, let him sell his garment and buy one.'"

He took up collections in Plymouth Church and elsewhere for Sharp's rifles, and for Bibles as well. Some of the rifles were sent, it is said, in boxes marked Bibles, though without his knowledge, and were therefore called "Beecher's Bibles."

When John C. Frémont was the first nominee of the Republicans in 1856, Mr. Beecher, with the hearty concurrence of his church, spoke for the party two or three times a week all through the State of New York. Ano amusing incident occurred at Rome, N.Y., which illustrated Beecher's graphic utterance.

He said: "My friends, in this great campaign there are but two sides, and we must range ourselves upon one side or the other; there is no middle ground for any of us. On the one side is Buchanan, with the black shield of slavery, and upon the other is Frémont, with the white banner of liberty, and with one or the other of these two you must take your stand; but who is this that I see crawling under the fence? Oh, that is Millard Fillmore." Immediately a little fellow in the front row jumped up, looked under the chairs, and shouted out, "Where is he?" The people laughed so heartily, that the lad got up and left the hall.

Mr. Beecher was always quick at repartee, either in conversation or address. Before an audience of ten thousand people in Chicago, he was lecturing on "Communism," and said, "The voice of the people is the voice of God." A man in the gallery shouted, "The voice of the people is the voice of a fool." Beecher replied simply, "I said the voice of the people, not the voice of one man."

In one of his anti-slavery speeches he said "that it was a penitentiary offence to teach a slave." A man in the corner of the gallery exclaimed, "It's a lie!"

"Well," said Beecher, "I shall not argue with the gentleman in the corner, as doubtless he has been there and ought to know."

Very stirring scenes were witnessed in these times. Two Edmonson sisters, of light complexion, whose mother was born a slave, but whose father was free, had been brought up in Washington. The former owner of the mother, finding that they were uncommonlyattractive, determined to send them to New Orleans to be sold in the slave market. The girls tried to escape, but could not.

Their heart-broken father went to New York to see if he could raise the two thousand dollars demanded for their purchase. He was advised to see Mr. Beecher. He reached his home in Brooklyn; but having met many rebuffs, he feared to ring the bell, and sat down on the steps, while tears coursed down his cheeks. Mr. Beecher finally heard his story and arranged for a meeting at the Broadway Tabernacle. He spoke with wonderful power, as did also the Rev. Dr. John Dowling, the father of the brilliant Rev. Dr. George Thomas Dowling. The sum of twenty-two hundred dollars was raised, and the girls were set free.

Mr. Beecher said, "I think that of all the meetings that I have attended in my life, for a panic of sympathy I never saw one that surpassed that. I have seen a great many in my day."

Mrs. Stowe became responsible for the education of the sisters, and later raised enough money to purchase the freedom of the mother and two other children.

Among several who were bought for liberty "on the auction-block of Plymouth pulpit," was "Pinky," a little colored girl. "She was bought and overbought," said Mr. Beecher. "The rain never fell faster than the tears fell from many that were here." Rose Terry Cooke threw her ring into the contribution box, and Mr. Beecher put it on the child's hand and told her "it was her freedom-ring." Her expression was such a happy one that Eastman Johnson, the artist, painted her on canvas, looking at her freedom-ring. Later she was sent for a year to Lincoln University at Washington, and went back to her own people to become a teacher and a missionary among them.

In these years of incessant toil, Mr. Beecher's home was gladdened by the birth of twin boys, Alfred and Arthur, in December, 1852. They both died on the fourth of July in the following year, and were buried in one grave. Mr. Beecher could not hear their names mentioned for years, so overwhelming was the loss to the man who idolized children.

In the autumn of 1854, by the aid of friends, he purchased a farm of nearly one hundred acres at Lenox, Berkshire County, Mass. He was a devoted lover of trees. Speaking of a large elm, he said, "It was with a feeling of awe that we looked up into its face; and when I whispered to myself, 'This is mine,' there was a shrinking, as if there were sacrilege in the very thought of property in such a creature of God as this cathedral-topped tree! Does a man bare his head in some old church? So did I, standing in the shadow of this regal tree, and looking up into that completed glory at which three hundred years have been at work with noiseless fingers!... Thou belongest to no man's hand, but to all men's eyes that do love beauty, and that have learned through beauty to behold God! Stand, then, in thine own beauty and grandeur! I shall be a lover and a protector, to keep drought from thy roots and the age from thy trunk."

Though he said, "The chief use of a farm is to lie down upon," knowing as all brain workers know, how restful it is to stretch one's self upon the ground, yet he always cultivated flowers and vegetables, and made the whole farm a thing of beauty.

He felt that he owed much to Ruskin's works. "The sky, the earth, and the waters are no longer what they were to us. We have learned a language and come to a sympathy in them more through the instrumentality of Ruskin's works than by all other instrumentalities on earth, excepting, always, the nature which my mother gave me—sainted be her name."

When the slavery struggles had culminated in war, and the South had fired the first gun at Fort Sumter, April 12, 1861, Beecher's heart was aflame. In his pulpit he said, "Give me war redder than blood and fiercer than fire, if this terrific infliction is necessary that I may maintain my faith in God, in human liberty, my faith of the fathers in the instruments of liberty, my faith in this land as the appointed abode and chosen refuge of liberty for all the earth!"

When his eldest son—he had already enlisted—said, "Father, may I enlist?" the instant reply was, "If you don't, I'll disown you."

After helping to fit out two regiments, Mr. Beecher took upon himself the entire equipping of a new one, called "The Long Island Volunteers," afterwards the Sixty-seventh New York.

Plymouth Church parlors became a workshop, where, under Mrs. Beecher's direction, women made articles for the soldiers at the front. By personal solicitation large sums were raised from families and merchants. Mr. Beecher told his wife to use all his salary except the smallest amount necessary for family expenses. He made patriotic addresses which were read and talked about the country over. "It is probable," said the well-known journalist, Frederick Hudson, "that there is not another man in the United States who is as much heard and read as Henry Ward Beecher, unless the other man is Wendell Phillips."

The first anniversary Sunday of the attack on Fort Sumter, Henry Ward Beecher said, "We will give every dollar that we are worth, every child that we have, and our own selves; we will bring all that we are and all that we have, and offer them up freely—but this country shall be one and undivided. We will have one Constitution and one liberty, and that universal. The Atlantic shall sound it, and the Pacific shall echo it back, deep answering to deep, and it shall reverberate from the Lakes on the North to the unfrozen Gulf on the South—'One nation, one constitution, one starry banner!' Hear it, England!—one country, and indivisible; one hope; one baptism; one constitution; one government; one nation; one country; one people—cost what it may, we will have it!"

He urged immediate and universal emancipation, with all the fire and eloquence of his nature. He became the warm friend of President Lincoln, with whom he had many confidential conferences. When the immortal Emancipation Proclamation was issued, declaring that after Jan. 1, 1863, the slaves "shall be thenceforward and forever free," Beecher said in his lecture-room talk, Dec. 31: "As for myself, let come what will come, I care not. God may peel me and bark me and strip me of my leaves, and do as he chooses with my earthly estate. I have lived long enough.... I have uttered some words that will not die, because they are incorporated into the lives of men that will not die."

In June, 1863, worn out with continuous speaking, Mr. Beecher went to Europe with Dr. John Raymond, then president of Vassar College. He had been over before, in 1850, thirteen years previously.

142

He travelled in Switzerland, Italy, and Germany, and at the request of the United States Minister, talked with King Leopold of Belgium, a wise and able man, about American affairs.

The king, asking Mr. Beecher what he thought of sending Maximilian to Mexico, he replied, "Your Majesty, any man that wants to sit upon a throne in Mexico, I would advise to try Vesuvius first; if he can sit there for a while, then he might go and try it in Mexico." His words proved true for the unfortunate Maximilian and Carlotta.

Henry Ward Beecher found in England much sympathy with the slave-holding South, and a disbelief in the ultimate success of the North, and continuance of the Union. Going to Europe for rest, he did not intend to speak, but was finally persuaded that it was his duty to win friends for the North, so that England should not declare for the Southern Confederacy.

The first meeting was held at Manchester, Oct. 9, 1863. The streets were placarded with huge posters in red ink, and threats were heard on every side that the speaker should never leave Free Trade Hall alive.

As soon as Beecher began to speak, there were hisses and yells by the mob, so that not a word could be heard. Standing erect before the howling crowd, he said, "My friends, we will have a whole night's session, but we will be heard." When not a word could reach the people, he leaned over to the reporters present, and said: "Gentlemen, be kind enough to take down what I say. It will be in sections, but I will have it connected by and by."

Finally by courage and wit and eloquence the crowd was subdued and won over to the speaker, who discussed the dire effects of slavery upon the manufacturing interests of the world, and stated the real condition of America in her struggle between slavery and liberty.

He said: "If the day shall come in one year, in two years, or in ten years hence, when the old stars and stripes shall float over every State of America; if the day shall come when that which was the accursed cause of this dire and atrocious war—slavery—shall be done away with; if the day shall come when through all the Gulf States there shall be liberty of speech, as there never has been; when there shall be liberty of the press, as there never has been; when men shall have common schools to send their children to, which they have never had in the South ... it will be worth all the dreadful blood and tears and woe."

Just as Beecher was closing, a telegram from London was read that "Her Majesty has to-night caused the 'broad arrow' to be placed on the rams in Mr. Laird's yard at Birkenhead." This meant the stoppage of the ships which were building for the South, to destroy our shipping as the Alabama had done. The whole audience rose and cheered, men waving their hats and women their handkerchiefs as they wept.

So moved were the people that a big fellow in the gallery, who could not shake hands with Mr. Beecher, cried out, "Shake my

143

umbrella," as he reached it down to the platform. Mr. Beecher did as requested. "By Jocks!" said the man, "nobody sha'n't touch that umbrella again."

On Oct. 13 Beecher spoke to an immense audience at Glasgow, telling them that in building ships to destroy free labor in America, "they were driving nails in their own coffins."

The interruptions, though great here, were not as bad as at Manchester. The next evening he spoke to a packed house at Edinburgh, being lifted over the people's heads to reach the platform. These speeches were reported verbatim all over England.

On Oct. 16 he spoke at the great Philharmonic Hall at Liverpool, at that time the headquarters of Southern sympathies. The meeting was a perfect bedlam. "Three cheers for Jeff Davis" were given every now and then, with cries of "Turn him out!" hisses and yells, till Beecher sat down on the edge of the platform and waited for a calm. For three hours, sentence by sentence, his voice was hurled against a threatening, hooting mob.

Four days later Henry Ward Beecher spoke to a dense crowd in Exeter Hall, London. With satire and pathos and burning eloquence, he spoke like one inspired. Dr. William M. Taylor, of the Broadway Tabernacle, New York, said, "I believe there has not been such eloquence in the world since Demosthenes."

Dr. Lyman Abbott and the Rev. S. B. Halliday, in their life of Mr. Beecher, say with truth, that "he changed the public sentiment, and so the political course of the nation, and secured and cemented an alliance between the mother country and our own land, which needs no treaties to give it expression, which has been gaining strength ever since, and which no demagogism on this side of the water, and no ignorance and prejudice on that, have been able to impair."

The physical strain while in England was great. "I thought at times," he says, "that I should certainly break a blood-vessel or have apoplexy. I did not care; I was willing to die as ever I was, when hungry and thirsty, to take refreshment, if I might die for my country."

Mr. Beecher on his return was welcomed with open arms and grateful hearts by the American people. Great receptions were given him at the Academy of Music, Brooklyn, and the Academy of Music, New York.

When the heart-breaking war was over, and General Lee had surrendered to General Grant under the apple-tree at Appomattox, April 9, 1865, and it was decided to raise over Fort Sumter, April 14, the flag that had been pulled down four years before, the great preacher and orator, who had helped to save the Union, was asked to deliver the address.

When Major-General Robert Anderson ran up the flag, it was saluted by a hundred guns from Fort Sumter and by a national salute from every fort that had fired upon Sumter at the beginning of the war.

Henry Ward Beecher's address was masterly; a review of the dreadful war, and our duties in the future.

That very night, April 14, 1865, President Lincoln was assassinated by the actor, J. Wilkes Booth. Mr. Beecher said in his sermon the following Sunday: "The blow brought not a sharp pang. It was so terrible that at first it stunned sensibility.... There was a piteous helplessness. Strong men bowed down and wept.... Men walked for days as if a corpse lay unburied in their dwellings. There was nothing else to think of. All business was laid aside. Pleasure forgot to smile.... Even avarice stood still, and greed was strongly moved to generous sympathy and universal sorrow. Rear to his name monuments, found charitable institutions, and write his name above their lintels; but no monument will ever equal the universal, spontaneous, and sublime sorrow that in a moment swept down lines and parties, and covered up animosities, and in an hour brought a divided people into unity of grief and indivisible fellowship of anguish."

Beecher took an active part in the reconstruction and readmission of the seceded States, urging that the greatest leniency be shown, now that they had surrendered; opposed the hanging of Jefferson Davis; urged the right of suffrage for the colored people:—"It is always inexpedient and foolish," he said, "to deny a man his natural rights." He did not believe that the freedmen should be cared for permanently by a military power at the South, placed there by the North. "We are to educate the negroes, and to Christianly educate them. We are to raise them in intelligence more and more, until they shall be able to prove themselves worthy of citizenship. For, I tell you, all the laws in the world cannot bolster a man up so as to place him any higher than his own moral worth and natural forces put him."

For a letter stating such views as these, written to the National Convention of Soldiers and Sailors held at Cleveland, O., in the autumn of 1866, Mr. Beecher was assailed all over the country. "The rage and abuse of excited men," he said, "I have too long been used to, now to be surprised or daunted.... I stood almost alone, my church, in my absence, full of excitement; all my ministerial brethren, with a few honorable exceptions, either aloof or in clamor against me; well-nigh the whole religious press denouncing me, and the political press furious."

He spoke boldly against the corrupt judges in New York City in the time of the Tweed dictatorship. Years later when Beecher voted and spoke for Grover Cleveland for the presidency, because he believed a change of parties wise for the country at the time, on account ofo "the corruption of too long held power," and did not trust James G. Blaine, the opposing candidate, the same denunciation and bitterness were shown; all of which proves that toleration for opinions differing from our own requires a very high type of character.

Beecher's liberal views in theology were likewise bitterly antagonized. The truth was that he cared little for creeds, believing that to preach Christ as the Saviour of the world was the paramount and vital need of men. He believed the theology of the future "would be far more powerful than the old—a theology of hope, and of love, which shall cast out fear." He felt with Whittier in the "Eternal Goodness,"—

"Yet, in the maddening maze of things,
And tossed by storm and flood,
To one fixed trust my spirit clings,—
I know that God is good!

And so beside the Silent Sea
I wait the muffled oar:
No harm from Him can come to me
On ocean or on shore.

I know not where His islands lift
There fronded palms in air;
I only know I cannot drift
Beyond His love and care."

His sermons were translated into German, French, Spanish, and Italian, and were read the world over; and men and women grew more gentle and lovable from the reading.

After the war the busy life went on as busy as ever. One volume of the "Life of Christ," rich in his wonderful imagination and beauty of language, was written. He did not live to complete the second volume. His one novel, "Norwood," a story of New England, was published as a serial in the New York Ledger in 1867, Mr. Bonner giving him $25,000 for it.

In 1870, having resigned the editorship of the Independent, Beecher became the editor of the Christian Union. In 1872 he gave a course of twelve lectures on "Preaching" to the Divinity School of Yale College, Mr. Henry W. Sage of Plymouth Church having founded at New Haven the Lyman Beecher Lectureship of Preaching.

When asked by Mr. John R. Howard if he knew what he should say at these lectures, he replied, "Yes; in a way. I know what I am going to aim at, but of course I don't get down to anything specific. I brood it, and ponder it, and dream over it, and pick up information about one point and another; but if ever I think I see the plan opening up to me, I don't dare to look at it or put it down on paper. If I once write a thing out, it is almost impossible for me to kindle up to it again. I never dare nowadays to write out a sermon during the week; that is sure to kill it. I have to think around and about it, get it generally ready, and then fuse it when the time comes."

Beecher was a great student of the Bible, reading it on the cars as he travelled to his lecture appointments, and, like Emerson, jotting down in little note-books thoughts and suggestions.

He prepared his Sunday morning sermon in an hour and a half, between breakfast and the time of service. Locked into his room, he wrote with his goose-quill pen the headings and a few illustrations. Then in the pulpit the eloquent words came pouring from his lips, born of the time and place. His evening sermon he prepared after tea. When asked how he was able to do so much work, he said it was partly owing to a good constitution; "much, also, to an early acquired knowledge of how to take care of myself, to secure invariably a full measure of sleep, to regard food as an engineer does fuel (to be employed economically, and entirely with reference to the work to be done by the machine); much to the habit of economizing social forces, and not wasting in needless conversation and pleasurable hilarities the spirit that would carry me through many days of necessary work; but, above all, to the possession of a hopeful disposition and natural courage, to sympathy with men, and to an unfailing trust in God; so that I have always worked for the love of working."

He never used stimulants except as a medicine. He wrote to a friend, "I am a total abstainer, both in belief and practice.... I hold that no man in health needs or is the better for alcoholic stimulants; that great good will follow to the whole community from the total disuse of them as articles of diet or luxury; and that so soon as the moral sense of society will sustain such laws, it will be wise and right to enact prohibitory liquor laws.... I should as soon think of offering a well man a dose of rhubarb as a dose of brandy."

Mr. Beecher was an earnest advocate of woman suffrage as well as temperance. He believed in equality of privilege in the pulpit, in medicine, everywhere, though he said, "People may talk about equality of the sexes!... The silent smile of a sensible, loving woman will vanquish ten men." Of woman, he said, "She is the right hand of the charities of the church.... She is not only permitted in the great orthodox churches of New England to speak in meeting, but when they send her abroad, ordained to preach the gospel to the heathen, there she is permitted to preach; and when they come home, women may still teach in a hall, but not in a church, and dear old men there are yet so conservative that they are reading through golden spectacles their Bibles, and saying: 'I suffer not a woman to preach.'"

Mr. Beecher found his recreation from hard work in his love of country life. His farm at Lenox, Mass., proving too far from Brooklyn, he bought, in 1859, thirty-six acres at Peekskill-on-the-Hudson, and named it Boscobel. The old farmhouse was said to have been the headquarters of General Israel Putnam of Revolutionary fame.

He watched like a child for the first note of the bluebird and robin, for the first arbutus, anemone, and violet of early spring. He

147

loved roses as fondly as Professor Child of Harvard College. He raised hollyhocks, dahlias, geraniums, pansies, lilies, and chrysanthemums. He said, "The wonder is, that every other man is not an enthusiast, and in the month of June a gentle fanatic. Floral insanity is one of the most charming inflictions to which man is heir."

He bought trees of almost every variety, chickens of various kinds, Jersey cows and honey-bees, and a large family of dogs,—a St. Bernard, a mastiff, an Eskimo, a terrier, and others.

He once said, "If the dog isn't good for anything else, it is good for you to love, and that is a good deal." Speaking of those at Peekskill, he said, "They are practically good for nothing, but I sometimes think they are worth more to me than the whole place."

He used to say that he felt really sorry that his dog Tommy could not talk. "If ever there was a dog that was distressed to think that he could not talk, that dog is. I sit by him on the bank, of a summer evening, and I say, 'Tommy, I am sorry for you;' and he whines, as much as to say, 'So am I.' I say, 'Tommy, I should like to tell you a great many things that you are worthy of knowing;' and I do not know which is the most puzzled, he or I—I to get any idea into his head, or he to get any out of mine."

Mr. Beecher finally built a beautiful house of granite and brick, natural woods throughout the interior: first story cherry; second, ash; and third, pine, where he gathered his valuable library. "Where is human nature so weak as in a book-store?" he said; and in books and flowers and works of art he found that money melted away, so that, say his sons, William C. Beecher and the Rev. Samuel Scoville, in the life of their father, "it was in part to meet this heavy outlay that he projected and carried out the series of lecture-tours that ran through the last ten years of his life."

He had learned what many another learns, that "the most profitable kind of land-owning" is to "enjoy all that there is of beauty and peacefulness in my neighbor's lands as much as they, without the responsibility or the taxes." And yet people have to build once, to learn not to build again.

In 1872, Mr. Beecher having preached for twenty-five years in Plymouth Church, a "Silver Wedding" was celebrated by his people. Monday, Oct. 7, was the first day of the jubilee. In the sunny afternoon the three thousand children in the three Sunday-schools connected with the church marched past Mr. Beecher's house, as he stood upon his doorstep, and each child laid a flower at his feet, until he stood "literally embanked in flowers." Each day through the week had its appropriate exercises. On Thursday, the historical day, the brilliant and learned Dr. Richard S. Storrs of Brooklyn gave an eloquent address. "May your soul," said the speaker, "as the years go on, be whitened more and more in the radiance of God's light, and in the sunshine of His love!"

That soul was soon to be tested and whitened in a furnace heated almost beyond endurance. Theodore Tilton, a member of Mr. Beecher's church, had, through the influence of the latter, become the editor of the Independent. Having lost his position, apparently by his own misdeeds, and made his family unhappy, Mr. and Mrs. Beecher advised his wife to separate from him. Tilton determined to drive Beecher from his pulpit, and forced his wife to criminate the latter in character, which statements she afterwards declared again and again were untrue in every particular. Plymouth Church dropped its obnoxious member. He took the case into the courts, asking one hundred thousand dollars damages. For six months the details were read all over the world. Mr. Beecher was acquitted by his church, by the jury, and by a National Advisory Council of one hundred and seventy-two churches. Mr. William A. Beach, the leading counsel for Tilton, said later, "I had not been four days on the trial before I was confident that he was innocent.... I felt and feel now that we were a pack of hounds trying in vain to drag down a noble man." Judge Neilson, who had not known Mr. Beecher previously, became his warm friend.

Most persons who will take the trouble to go over the testimony now, after twenty years have cooled thepassions of the hour, will agree with Mr. Beach. Dr. Barrows says truly, "That any man should have endured the fires which surrounded Mr. Beecher, and have come forth so radiant, so pure, so self-respecting, and so widely trusted and beloved, is a moral miracle, the parallel of which it would be difficult to find."

The expenses of the trial year were $118,000; and though Plymouth Church raised Mr. Beecher's salary for that year to $100,000, he found himself deeply in debt. To pay this indebtedness he gave a series of lectures during the next two or three years. "The Reign of the Common People," "The Burdens of Society," "Conscience," "The Uses of Wealth," "The Ministry of the Beautiful," "Evolution and Religion," were among his most popular lectures. Upon the last, though a deep subject, I have seen five thousand persons strangely moved by his eloquence.

Although in some places he was jeered at by the rabble, yet year by year he found great strength and comfort in the love of the people. He wrote home that preaching Sunday evening in Boston, "Ten thousand people couldn't get in. Shook hands with whole audiences. Papers next morning with kind notices. Went to Congregational ministers' meeting on Monday morning. Cheered and clapped when I entered. After prayer for day was finished it was moved that I address the meeting. I did so, and closed with prayer. All wept, and it broke up like a revival meeting."

In 1886, when Mr. Beecher was seventy-three years of age, he consented to go a third time to England, to see his friends and lecture. Mrs. Beecher accompanied him, with his friend and lecture agent,

149

Major J. B. Pond. Three thousand Plymouth Church people came to see him set sail in the early morning of June 19. Dodworth's band played "Hail to the Chief;" and then, as the vessel moved away, the great crowd sang, "Praise God from whom all blessings flow." One friend had sent a basket of twenty homing pigeons; and these in the afternoon carried back messages to the loved ones.

Everywhere in England Henry Ward Beecher was received with a royal welcome. There were no more meetings like those at Manchester and Liverpool in the days of the Civil War. So vast were the crowds to hear him preach, that the congregations had to be admitted by ticket. Thousands were necessarily turned away. His first lecture was at Exeter Hall, London.

"Between July 4 and Oct. 21, fifteen and one-half weeks," says Mr. Pond in his book, "A Summer in England with Henry Ward Beecher," "Mr. Beecher preached seven times, gave nine public addresses, and delivered fifty-eight lectures. For the fifty-eight lectures he cleared the sum of $11,600, net of all expenses for himself and Mrs. Beecher from the day they sailed from New York."

It is estimated that Mr. Beecher earned by his pen and voice during forty years in Brooklyn nearly a million and a half dollars, most of which he gave away.

But much as he enjoyed England, the brave man was growing weary with the work of life. He wrote, "I want to come home.... I long every year to lay down my tasks and depart.... It is simply a quiet longing of the spirit, a brooding desire to be through with my work, although I am willing to go on, if need be."

He came home Oct. 31, 1886, and soon promised to complete the second volume of the "Life of Christ." He also made a contract with a publishing firm to have his autobiography ready before July 1, 1888.

He wrote some on each book during the winter. March 3 he went to New York with his wife, who said, "I never knew my husband so lively, tender, or joyous before, or not in a long time." That night he retired early, feeling weary. The next day, Friday, he slept nearly all day, and, being aroused to go to a prayer-meeting, said he did not feel like getting up. A physician came in the afternoon and in the evening, and asked Mr. Beecher to raise his hand. He could not. The left side showed signs of paralysis. It was apoplexy.

The great man watched the faces of his wife and the doctor, seemed to divine the result, closed his eyes, gave the hand of his wife "a long, strong, loving, and earnest pressure. It was the realization of the inevitable. It was farewell. He never opened his eyes again. His sleep, thereafter, was constant.... From Saturday morning until the end were silence, sleep, heavy but regular breathing, and unconsciousness.... Mrs. Beecher held his hand in hers continually. When the end approached all the household were gathered.... Not one of them shed a tear or gave expression to a sob—then and there. The supreme self-control was in obedience to Mr. Beecher's often expressed hope and wish that around his bed of release no tears should fall, but the feeling should prevail as those who think of a soul gone to its crowning."

At half-past nine, Tuesday morning, March 8, 1887, the end came. He had often said, "Provide flowers for me, not crape, when I am gone;" so at once a wreath of pink and white roses were hung upon the door-knob.

Private funeral services were held at the house on Thursday, conducted by the Rev. Charles H. Hall, Rector of Trinity Church, Brooklyn, who in Mr. Beecher's time of trial, seeing him in his congregation, went down the aisle, took him by the hand, and led him to a seat within the chancel. Mr. Beecher never forgot a kind act, and wished Dr. Hall to attend at his burial.

"There was no man whom I ever heard," said Dr. Hall, "or whose works I have ever read, who inspired me so deeply with the inspiration of the Holy Spirit. He was a man of men, the most manly man I ever met; but he was also a man of God in the pre-eminent sense of the word."

The body was escorted to the church by Company G of the Thirteenth Regiment—"My boys," Mr. Beecher called them, as many were of Plymouth Church.

The coffin was laid in a perfect bower of flowers, lilies of the valley, maidenhair fern, and smilax entirely covering it. The organ, platform, and pulpit chair were a mass of bloom,—roses and pinks and graceful plants.

All day long, until ten at night, the throng of people, half or three-quarters of a mile in extent, passed by to look at the beloved face. On Friday, only those were admitted who had tickets. Four churches were open for services, and all were crowded. All public offices and schools were closed, and business was suspended.

Dr. Hall made the address at the funeral. Very tenderly he said of the dead preacher, "On his last Sunday evening in this place, two weeks ago, after the congregation had retired from it, the organist and one or two others were practising the hymn,—

> "'I heard the voice of Jesus say,
> Come unto me and rest.'

"Mr Beecher, doubtless with that tire that follows a pastor's Sunday work, remained and listened. Two street urchins were prompted to wander into the building; and one of them was standing in the position of the boy whom Raphael has immortalized, gazing up at the organ. The old man, laying his hands on the boy's head, turned his face upward and kissed him; and with his arms about the two, left the scene of his triumphs, his trials, and his successes forever.

151

"It was a fitting close to a grand life, the old man of genius and fame shielding the little wanderers, great in breasting traditional ways and prejudices, great also in the gesture, so like him, that recognized, as did the Master, that the humblest and poorest were his brethren, the great preacher led out into the night by the little nameless waifs."

After the services the doors were opened, and one hundred thousand people passed through the church by the coffin.

On Saturday, March 12, the body was taken to Greenwood Cemetery, and temporarily placed in a receiving vault filled with abundant flowers. Later it was buried on Dawn Path, near Hillside Avenue, on the south-easterly slope of Ocean Hill, with a simple headstone.

"When I fall," said the great preacher, "and am buried in Greenwood, let no man dare to stand over the turf and say, 'Here lies Henry Ward Beecher;' for God knows that I will not lie there. Look up! if you love me, and if you feel that I have helped you on your way home, stand with your feet on my turf and look up; for I will not hear anybody that does not speak with his mouth toward heaven."

CHARLES KINGSLEY

On a white marble cross in Eversley churchyard, England, under a spray of the passion-flower, are the Latin words, "Amavimus, Amamus, Amabimus" (we have loved, we love, we shall love); and above them, around the cross, "God is love." Those were the words chosen by the famous preacher and author; and they were the key-note of the life of one who lived for his people.

Charles Kingsley, the son of a minister, was born at Holne Vicarage, Devonshire, England, June 12, 1819. Of his father, he wrote in 1865, "He was a magnificent man in body and mind, and was said to possess every talent except that of using his talents. My mother, on the contrary, had a quite extraordinary practical and administrative power; and she combines with it, even at her advanced age (seventy-nine), my father's passion for knowledge, and the sentiment and fancy of a young girl."

From his father, Charles seems to have inherited his love of art, natural history, and athletic sports; from his mother, his love of poetry and romance, and the force and originality which made him a marked character in his town and nation.

When four years of age, he used to make a pulpit in his nursery, arrange the chairs for a congregation, and preach as follows, his mother taking down the words unobserved: "It is not right to fight. Honesty has no chance against stealing. We must follow God, and not follow the Devil; for if we follow the Devil, we shall go into that everlasting fire, and if we follow God, we shall go to heaven." His poems at this time were remarkable for a child.

He studied and loved nature, and delighted in sunsets, rocks, flowers, and the wonders of the sea. At Clovelly, whither the rector had moved his family, Charles found great delight in the study of shells, and in the company of the warm-hearted fishermen. But for this early association, it is probable that the beautiful song of the "Three Fishers" would never have been written.

When the lad was twelve years old he was sent, with his brother Herbert, to a preparatory school at Clifton, under the Rev. John Knight. Here he showed an affectionate and gentle nature, only excited to anger when the servant swept away the precious shells and grasses collected in his walks on the Downs.

Afterwards he and Herbert were sent to the grammar school at Helston, which was in charge of the Rev. Derwent Coleridge, son of Samuel Taylor Coleridge. Here he became the intimate friend of Richard Cowley Powles, afterwards fellow and tutor of Exeter College, Oxford.

Mr. Powles wrote of his friend later, "Of him, more than of most men who have become famous, it may be said, 'The boy was father of the man.' The vehement spirit, the adventurous courage, the love of truth, the impatience of injustice, the quick and tender sympathy, that distinguished the man's entrance on public life, were all in the boy.... For botany and geology he had an absolute enthusiasm.... He liked nothing better than to sally out, hammer in hand and his botanical tin slung round his neck, on some long expedition in quest of new plants, and to investigate the cliffs within a few miles of Helston, dear to every geologist."

"In manner," says the Rev. Mr. Coleridge, "he was strikingly courteous, and thus, with his wide and ready sympathies and bright intelligence, was popular alike with tutor, schoolfellows, and servants."

Kingsley always regretted that he did not go to school at Rugby, as he thought nothing "but a public school education would have overcome his constitutional shyness."

The Kingsley family removed to Chelsea when Charles was seventeen, and he became a day student at King's College. Two years later, in 1838, he went to Magdalene College, Cambridge, where he stood first in classics and mathematics at the examinations. For his prize he selected a fine edition of Plato in eleven volumes.

In the summer of 1839, July 6, when he was twenty, he met Fanny, daughter of Pascoe Grenfell, whom he afterwards married. "That was my real wedding-day," he said years later. At that time his mind was full of religious doubt, and he was far from happy. The young lady proved a most valuable intellectual and spiritual helper; and after two months of companionship, when he returned to Cambridge, she loaned him many books and wrote him letters which proved a life-long blessing. Carlyle's "French Revolution" had a great effect upon his mind, in establishing his belief in God's righteous government of the world; also Maurice's "Kingdom of Christ," to which he said he owed more than to any book he had ever read.

Young Kingsley was at this time robust in health, able to walk from Cambridge to London, fifty-two miles, starting early and reaching the latter city at nine P.M. For many years he delighted in a country walk of twenty or twenty-five miles.

In 1841, after the struggle through which most persons pass before deciding upon a life-work, he gave himself to the ministry, rather than to the law, for which his name had been entered at Lincoln's Inn. He wrote to Fanny, June 12,—

"My birth-night. I have been for the last hour on the seashore, not dreaming, but thinking deeply and strongly, and forming determinations which are to affect my destiny through time and through eternity. Before the sleeping earth, and the sleepless sea and stars, I have devoted myself to God; a vow never (if He gives me the faith I pray for) to be recalled."

After taking honors at Cambridge, and reading for Holy Orders, he began to write the life of his ideal saint, St. Elizabeth of Hungary, for his intended wife, if, indeed, he should ever win her.

The curacy of Eversley was offered him, and he accepted it at twenty-three. The fir-trees on the rectory lawn were a great comfort. He wrote to Fanny, "Those delicious self-sown firs! Every step I wander they whisper to me of you, the delicious past melting into the more delicious future."

But from the opposition of friends the correspondence was broken, and for a year the hard parish work was carried on alone. In his parting letter to her he says, urging her to practise music, "Music is such a vent for the feelings.... Study medicine.... I am studying it.... Make yourself thoroughly acquainted with the wages, wants, and habits and prevalent diseases of the poor, wherever you go....

"I have since nine this morning cut wood for an hour; spent an hour and more in prayer and humiliation ... written six or seven pages of a difficult part of my essay; taught in the school; thought over many things while walking; gone round two-thirds of the parish visiting and doctoring, and written all this." ...

The young curate lived in a thatched cottage, and found a remedy for his loneliness in hard work. The church services had been neglected, and the ale-houses were preferred on Sunday to the house of worship. There were no schools for the children worthy of the name, and the minister had to be teacher as well as preacher.

Finally the long silence was broken, and Kingsley wrote again to his Fanny, "I have been making a fool of myself for the last ten minutes, according to the world's notion of folly; for there have been some strolling fiddlers under the window, and I have been listening and crying like a child. Some quick music is so inexpressively mournful. It seems just like one's own feelings,—exultation and action, with the remembrance of past sorrow wailing up.... Let us never despise the wandering minstrel!... And who knows what tender thoughts his own sweet music stirs within him, though he eat in pot-houses and sleep in barns!"

Again he wrote, looking forward to the home they would some time have together, "We will hunt out all the texts in the Bible about masters and servants, to form rules upon them.... Our work must be done by praying for our people, by preaching to them, ... and by setting them an example,—an example in every look, word, and motion; in the paying of a bill, the hiring of a servant, the reproving of a child."

He carried out his Christian principles in his relations with his employees. At his death all the servants in his house had lived with him from seventeen to twenty-six years.

Early in 1844 Kingsley, then twenty-five, was married to the woman he loved, and the curate became the rector at Eversley. The house was damp, from the rain flooding the rooms on the ground floor, and the land required much drainage. But the happy husband was full of energy, and set to work to make the place habitable and attractive.

At once the young preacher established among the laborers a shoe-club, coal-club, loan-fund, and lending-library. A school for adults was held at the rectory three nights a week all through the winter; a class in music; a Sunday-school met there every Sunday morning and afternoon; and in the outlying districts weekly lectures were held at the cottages for the aged and feeble. None of the grown-up men and women among the laborers could read or write, and the minister became their devoted teacher. He taught them to love the nature he loved,—the flowers, trees, birds, and ever-changing sky. He visited the poor, the sick, and the dying, and soon became the idol of his people. He fed their minds as well as their souls; he knew, as so few really know, the all-important work which the pastor has committed to his hands. No wonder that London and England, and America finally, heard of this model preacher, and came to love him.

The year after his marriage, 1845, was saddened by the death of his brother, Lieut. Gerald Kingsley, in Torres Straits, on board Her Majesty's ship Royalist. All the officers and half the crew died of fever. His brother Herbert had died of heart-disease in 1834, when they were boys together at school.

The drama of "St. Elizabeth" was now finished; and in 1847 the young preacher started for London, on a serious mission,—to find a publisher. He read the poem to his noble friend, Mr. Maurice, who wrote a preface for it; and to Coleridge, who gave him a commendatory letter to a publisher. The poem met the usual fate,—declined with thanks.

He wrote his wife, "I am now going to Parker's in the Strand. I am at once very happy, very lonely, and very anxious. How absence increases love! It is positively good sometimes to be parted, that one's affection may become conscious of itself, and proud and humble and thankful accordingly." ...

Later he wrote to Mr. Powles, "'St. Elizabeth' is in the press, having been taken off my hands by the heroic magnanimity of Mr. J. Parker, West Strand, who, though a burnt child, does not dread the fire. No one else would have it."

Having earned a little money by extra Sunday services at Pennington, he took his wife and his two small children, Rose and Maurice, for a six weeks' holiday to the seaside, near the edge of the New Forest. Here, revelling in the scenery, he wrote several ballads.

When the drama "The Saints' Tragedy" was published, it was fiercely attacked by the High Church party at Oxford. In Germany it was read and liked, and Chevalier Bunsen wrote heartily in praise of it.

When Kingsley, now twenty-nine, went for a few weeks to Oxford, to visit his friend, Mr. Powles, Fellow of Exeter, he received much attention on account of his book. He wrote to his wife, "They got up a meeting for me, and the club was crowded with men merely to see poor me, so I found out afterwards: very lucky that I did not know it during the process of being trotted out. It is very funny and new.... Froude gets more and more interesting. We had such a conversation this morning!—the crust is breaking, and the man coming through that cold, polished shell. My darling babies! kiss them very much for me."

The parish work at Eversley increased month by month. A writing-class for girls was held in the empty coach-house, and a cottage school for infants was begun. He wrote his first article for Fraser's Magazine on Popery. He preached to his congregation on the topics of the day,—emigration, and the political and social disturbances of the time. He was, in fact, what a preacher should be,—a leader of the people.

He accepted the professorship of English literature and composition at Queen's College, Harley Street, of which Mr. Maurice was president, and went up to London once a week to lecture. He became the devoted friend of Thomas Hughes, author of "School Days at Rugby;" of Bishop Stanley of Norwich and his distinguished son, Dean Stanley, and of many others.

During this year, 1847-48, on account of great distress among the people, there were riots in London and in other large cities. The troops were called out under Wellington to disperse the Chartists, who demanded a "People's Charter" from Parliament, with more rights for the laborers.

Kingsley threw himself heartily into the conflict. He wrote a conciliatory letter to the "Workmen of England," which was posted up in London.

"You say that you are wronged. Many of you are wronged, and many besides yourselves know it. Almost all men who have heads and hearts know it—above all, the working clergy know it. They go into your houses; they see the shameful filth and darkness in which you are forced to live crowded together; they see your children growing up in ignorance and temptation, for want of fit education; they see intelligent and well-read men among you, shut out from a freeman's just right of voting; and they see, too, the noble patience and self-control with which you have as yet borne these evils. They see it, and God sees it."

And then he urges them "to turn back from the precipice of riot, which ends in the gulf of universal distrust, stagnation, starvation.... Workers of England, be wise, and then you must be free; for you will be fit to be free."

For four years, 1848-52, he wrote for three periodicals, Politics for the People, The Christian Socialist, and the Journal of Association.

Many friends and relations begged him to desist from fighting the battles of the people, as such sympathy "was likely to spoil his prospects in life." But he wrote his wife in reference to this matter, "I will not be a liar. I will speak in season and out of season. I will not shun to declare the whole counsel of God.... My path is clear, and I will follow in it. He who died for me, and who gave me you, shall I not trust Him through whatsoever new and strange paths He may lead me?"

He always felt "that the party-walls of rank and fashion and money were but a paper prison of our own making, which we might break through any moment by a single hearty and kindly feeling."

In the autumn of 1848, while writing "Yeast," a novel which was first published in Fraser's Magazine, doing the work at night, when his other duties werefinished and the house was still, he broke down, and for months was unable to do more than walk along the seashore and gather shells, even conversation being too exhausting for him.

Friends came to show their sympathy and fondness for the great-hearted man—among them Mr. Froude, who met Charlotte, the sister of Mrs. Kingsley, and married her.

Returning to the work at Eversley, where a low fever had broken out among the people, and where it was almost impossible to obtain nurses, Kingsley cared for the sick, watching all night with a laborer's wife, the mother of a large family, that she might receive nourishment every half-hour, and soon broke down again, and was obliged to go to Devonshire.

On his return to Eversley, cholera had once more appeared in England, and early and late he carried on a crusade against dirt and bad drainage.

As his means were limited, he usually took two or more pupils to fit them for the ministry; and now began his "Alton Locke," the autobiography of a tailor and a poet, in the interest of workingmen. "God grant," he says in the preface, "that the workmen of the South of England may bestir themselves ere it be too late, and discover that the only defence against want is self-restraint." He urges that they "organize among themselves associations for buying and selling the necessaries of life, which may enable them to weather the dark season of high prices and stagnation, which is certain, sooner or later, to follow in the footsteps of war."

To write this book, he got up at five every morning and worked till breakfast, devoting the rest of the day to his sermons, his pupils, and the various schools and societies of his parish. "His habit," says his wife, in her life of Kingsley, "was thoroughly to master his subject, whether book or sermon, always out in the open air,—in his garden, on the moor, or by the side of a lonely trout stream; and never to put pen to paper till the ideas were clothed in words.... For many years his writing was all done by his wife, from his dictation, while he paced up and down the room."

When "Alton Locke" was finished, the old difficulty of finding a publisher began. Messrs. Parker, who had brought out "Yeast," which had caused much theological discussion, refused to take another book.

Finally, through the influence of Carlyle, Messrs. Chapman & Hall were induced to bring it out.

The press, as in the case of "Yeast," was severe on "Alton Locke;" but brave Thomas Carlyle wrote Kingsley to "pay no attention at all to the foolish clamor of reviewers, whether laudatory or condemnatory."

Kingsley's correspondence increased day by day. One person wrote about going over to the Romish Church; another about his atheistic doubts; another desired to reform his life; and others asked advice on almost numberless matters.

To an atheist, who was later converted under Kingsley, he wrote, "As for helping you to Christ, I do not believe I can one inch. I see no hope but in prayer, in going to Him yourself, in saying, Lord, if Thou art there, if Thou art at all, if this all be not a lie, fulfil Thy reputed promises, and give me peace and a sense of forgiveness."

Kingsley would say to his wife, as a letter was answered, or another chapter of a book finished, "Thank God, one more thing done!—and oh, how blessed it will be when it is all over, to lie down in that dear churchyard!" The work of the great world, with all its sorrows, had tired Kingsley at thirty-two.

"Hypatia," one of the novels which will last for centuries, was begun in 1851. He writes to the Rev. Mr. Maurice in January, "If I do not use my pen to the uttermost in earning my daily bread, I shall not get through this year.... My available income is less than £400. I cannot reduce my charities, and I am driven either to give up my curate or to write; and either of these alternatives, with the increased parish work, for I have got either lectures or night school every night in the week, and three services on Sunday, will demand my whole time."

As to "Hypatia," he writes, "My idea in the romance is to set forth Christianity as the only really democratic creed, and philosophy, above all, spiritualism, as the most exclusively aristocratic creed."

In October he writes to a friend, "'Hypatia' grows, little darling, and I am getting very fond of her."

When the book was published in 1853, two years after it was begun, it aroused most bitter criticism from a portion of the English Church. But no adverse criticism could prevent its being read and loved by the people of two continents. Thirty years later it had gone through thirteen editions.

Our own Whittier wrote Mrs. Kingsley, after her husband's death, "My copy of his 'Hypatia' is worn by frequent perusal, and the echoes of his rare and beautiful lyrics never die out of my memory. But since I have seen him, the man seems greater than the author.... His heart seemed overcharged with interest in the welfare, physical, moral, and spiritual, of his race. I was conscious in his presence of the bracing atmosphere of a noble nature. He seemed to me one of the manliest of men."

No man could have drawn that masterful picture of the beautiful

159

maid of Alexandria, philosopher, mathematician, teacher, and leader of her time, who had not the greatest reverence for woman, and a belief in her marvellous power. Such a man could never limit the sphere of woman by any human barriers. He said to a friend that his aim was, in every book he wrote, to set forth "woman as the teacher, the natural, and therefore divine, guide, purifier, inspirer of the man."

One learns to love the brilliant Hypatia, as did the monk, Philammon, and the Jew, Raphael Aben-Ezra, and shudders when she is torn in pieces about the age of forty by the mob.

The book holds one spell-bound from beginning to end, and many another copy besides that of Whittier "is worn by frequent perusal."

Mr. C. Kegan Paul, the London publisher, was staying at the home of the Kingsleys when much of "Hypatia" was written. "I was struck," he says, speaking of the author, "not only with his power of work, but with the extraordinary pains he took to be accurate in detail. We spent one whole day in searching the four folio volumes of Synesius for a fact he thought was there, and which was found there at last." "When I have done 'Hypatia,'" he writes Mr. Ludlow, "I will write no more novels. I will write poetry—not as a profession, but I will keep myself for it; and I do think I shall do something that will live. I feel my strong faculty is that sense of form, which, till I took to poetry, always came out in drawing, drawing; but poetry is the true sphere, combining painting and music and history all in one."

"At that time," says a friend, "in his books and pamphlets, and often in his daily, familiar speech, he was pouring out the whole force of his eager, passionate heart in wrath and indignation against starvation wages, stifling workshops, reeking alleys, careless landlords, roofless and crowded cottages.... No human being but was sure of a patient, interested hearer in him. I have seen him seat himself, hatless, beside a tramp on the grass outside of his gate in his eagerness to catch exactly what he had to say, searching him, as they sat, in his keen, kindly way with question and look."

About the time of the opening of the Great Exhibition, so dear to the heart of the noble Prince Albert, Kingsley was asked to preach a sermon to workingmen in a London church near by, which he did with great sympathy and tenderness. Just as the blessing was to be pronounced, the clergyman who had invited Kingsley rose and remarked that it was his painful duty to say that he believed much of what Mr. Kingsley had said "was dangerous and untrue."

Kingsley, wounded beyond expression, quietly left the church, and a riot of the workmen was with difficulty prevented. That night in his sadness and exhaustion he wrote that immortal song of the "Three Fishers," which seemed to soothe and rest him.

160

"Three fishers went sailing out into the west,
Out into the west as the sun went down:
Each thought of the woman who loved him the best,
And the children stood watching them out of the town;
For men must work and women must weep,
And there's little to earn, and many to keep,
Though the harbor bar be moaning.

Three wives sat up in the lighthouse tower,
And they trimmed the lamps as the sun went down;
They looked at the squall, and they looked at the shower,
And the night-rack came rolling up ragged and brown.
But men must work and women must weep,
Though storms be sudden and waters deep,
And the harbor bar be moaning.

Three corpses lay out on the shining sands,
In the morning gleam as the tide went down;
And the women are weeping and wringing their hands,
For those that will never come back to the town.
For men must work and women must weep,
And the sooner it's over, the sooner to sleep,
And good-by to the bar and its moaning."

The winter and spring of 1854 were spent at Torquay, Mrs. Kingsley having become ill from the damp rectory at Eversley. Mr. Kingsley also had become worn in mind and body from the constant attacks of the religious press against his supposed liberal views. He and his children passed happy days along the seashore, gathering specimens to send to the scientist, Mr. H. P. Gosse, in London, and collecting materials for his articles in the North British Review on "The Wonders of the Shore." Before leaving Torquay he made a list of about sixty species of Mollusks, Annelides, Crustacea, and Polypes found on the shore, nearly all new to him.

In February he made his first visit to Scotland, to deliver before the Philosophical Institute at Edinburgh four lectures on the "Schools of Alexandria." He writes to his wife, "The lecture went off well. I was dreadfully nervous, and actually cried with fear up in my room beforehand; but after praying I recovered myself, and got through it very well, being much cheered and clapped."

When his wife was saddened on account of debts incurred through illness, Mr. Kingsley cheered her with his brave heart. "To pay them," he said, "I have thought, I have written, I have won for us a name which, please God, may last among the names of English writers.... So out of evil God brings good; or, rather, out of necessity He

161

brings strength ... and the meanest actual want may be the means of calling into actual life the possible but sleeping embryo of the very noblest faculties."

In the winter of 1851 Kingsley wrote "Brave Words to Brave Soldiers," several thousand copies of which were distributed among the suffering soldiers before Sebastopol in the Crimea; also his novel, "Westward Ho!"

Many letters of appreciation came after the publication of this book. A naval officer wrote from Hong Kong, "Among the many blessings for which I have had to thank God this night, the most special has been for the impressions produced by your noble sermon of 'Westward Ho!' Some months ago I read it for the first time, then sailed on a long cruise; and now on returning have read it again with prayer that has been answered, for God's blessing has gone with it."

Kingsley gave lectures in London before the Working Men's College, and a series to women interested in laborers. To the latter he said, "Instead of reproving and fault-finding, encourage. In God's name encourage! They scramble through life's rocks, bogs, and thorn-brakes clumsily enough, and have many a fall, poor things!"

As to teaching boys, he said, "It will be a boon to your own sex, as well as to ours, to teach them courtesy, self-restraint, reverence for physical weakness, admiration of tenderness and gentleness; and it is one which only a lady can bestow.... There is a latent chivalry, doubt it not, in the heart of every untutored clod."

In the summer of 1856, when he was thirty-seven, Kingsley spent a happy vacation with Mr. Thomas Hughes and Mr. Tom Taylor at Snowdon, Wales, which resulted in the writing of "Two Years Ago."

In June, 1857, Kingsley writes to his friend Thomas Hughes, "Eight and thirty years old am I this day, Thomas, whereof twenty-two were spent in pain, in woe, and vanities, and sixteen in very great happiness, such as few men deserve, and I don't deserve at all.... Well, Tom, God has been very good to me.... The best work ever I've done has been my plain parish work."

Diphtheria, then a new disease in England, appeared at Eversley. "Some might have smiled," says Mrs. Kingsley, at seeing her husband "going in and out of the cottages with great bottles of gargle under his arm."

The earnest preaching, the lectures, the books and correspondence, continued. Many guests came now to Eversley,— Harriet Beecher Stowe and others from America, where his literary work seemed at first more appreciated than at home; Miss Bremer, the Swedish novelist, who after she went home sent him Tegnèr's "Frithiof's Saga," with this inscription: "To the Viking of the New Age, Charles Kingsley, this story of the Vikings of the Old, from a daughter of the Vikings, his friend and admirer, Fredrika Bremer."

Dean Stanley came; Max Müller also, and spent the first week of his married life at the rectory—he had married a beloved niece of Kingsley's, the G. to whom he wrote the poem,—

"A hasty jest I once let fall."

When Kingsley was forty, he preached for the first time before the Queen and Prince Albert at Buckingham Palace, and was soon made one of Her Majesty's chaplains. He preached at the Chapel Royal, St. James's, and before the Court in the private chapel at Windsor Castle. From this time onward he received the utmost consideration and appreciation from the royal household. Having been made Professor of Modern History at Cambridge, which position he filled admirably for nine years, he was requested by the Prince Consort to give private lectures to the Prince of Wales, who had just left Oxford. The Prince came to Mr. Kingsley's house three times a week, twice with the class, and every Saturday to go over the week's work alone.

Every now and then Mr. Kingsley, from his ardent nature, broke down from overwork. Then he would go with his wife to the Isle of Wight to see Tennyson and his wife, or with James Anthony Froude to Ireland.

Death was beginning to enter the family circle. His father died in the winter of 1860. He wrote Mr. Maurice, "How every wrong word and deed toward that good old man, and every sorrow I caused him, rise up in judgment against one; and how one feels that right-doing does not atone for wrong-doing."

In the spring Charlotte, Mrs. Kingsley's sister, the wife of Froude, was laid under the fir-trees in Eversley churchyard. "Her grave," says Mrs. Kingsley, "was to him during the remainder of his own life a sacred spot, where he would go almost daily to commune in spirit with the dead, where flowers were always kept blooming, and where on the Sunday morning he would himself superintend the decorations,—the cross and wreaths of choice flowers placed by loving hands upon it." Prince Albert died in 1861, a great personal loss to Kingsley, as to all England.

In the spring of 1862 "The Water-babies" was written, and dedicated to his youngest son, Grenville Arthur, then four years old, named after his godfather, Dean Stanley, and Sir Richard Grenvil, one of the heroes of "Westward Ho!" from whom Mrs. Kingsley's family claimed descent.

The strange experiences of poor little Tom, the chimney-sweep, after he left the hard work in the chimneys, under his brutal master, Grimes, to enjoy the wonders of the sea, as a water-baby, are most amusing and graphic. The book has always had a great circulation.

Three years after this, Queen Emma of the Hawaiian Islands spent two days at the Eversley Rectory. She said to Mrs. Kingsley, "It is so strange to me to be staying with you and to see Mr. Kingsley. My husband read your husband's 'Water-babies' to our little prince." On her return she sent to Mr. Kingsley the Prayer Book in Hawaiian, translated by her husband, King Kamehameha IV.

Kingsley did not forget how hard it had been for an unknown author to find a publisher. Mr. Charles Henry Bennett, a man of genius, but struggling with poverty, had illustrated "Pilgrim's Progress," but could get no one to take it. Kingsley wrote a preface, and Messrs. Longman at once undertook to bring it out. Thus did the noble man help artist and author, tramp and sick laborer, seeker after knowledge or after the comfort of the gospel.

In 1863 Kingsley was made a Fellow of the Geological Society, proposed by his friend Sir Charles Bunbury, and seconded by Sir Charles Lyell. He was already a Fellow of the Linnean Society. His name was proposed for the degree of D.C.L. at Oxford by the Prince of Wales, but was withdrawn on account of opposition from the extreme High Church party.

He now gave lectures to the boys at Wellington College, to which his son Maurice had gone, and assisted them in forming a museum; he brought out a volume of poems and one or two volumes of sermons. No wonder he failed in health, and was obliged to go to France with Froude, the latter going on into Spain for historical work.

The labors of the devoted preacher and author increased year after year. Impressed more than ever with the monotonous life of the English laborer and his hard-worked wife, Kingsley started Penny Readings for the people, and village concerts, in which friends from London helped.

He attended the national science meetings; he preached in Westminster Abbey; he brought out a series of papers for children on natural science, called "Madam How and Lady Why;" he read sixteen volumes of Comte's works in preparation for his Cambridge lectures— he had already given a course on the History of America.

In 1869 he was appointed Canon of Chester. Here he started a class in botany,—a walk and a field lecture were enjoyed once a week by a hundred or more persons,—which has resulted in the Chester Natural History Society, with about six hundred members. He also gave many geological lectures. "The Soil of the Field," "The Pebbles in the Street," "The Stones in the Wall," "The Coal in the Fire," "The Lime in the Mortar," "The Slates on the Roof," were published in a book called "Town Geology." How broadened would be the minds of many in our congregations, especially the minds of our young men and women, if more of our ministers would teach the wonders of the world in which we live!

Kingsley was made President of the Education Section of the Social Science Congress at Bristol, and one hundred thousand copies of his valuable inaugural address were distributed. At this Congress he met Dr. Elizabeth Blackwell from America, and she became a welcome guest at Eversley. He was an ardent advocate of medical education for women.

He wrote to John Stuart Mill that his "Subjection of Woman" seemed to him "unanswerable and exhaustive, and certain, from its moderation as well as from its boldness, to do good service in this good cause." ...

After a journey with his daughter to the West Indies, from which came his book, "At Last," he returned to his multifarious duties. As President of the Midland Institute at Birmingham, he spoke on the Science of Health. As a result, a manufacturer gave £2,500 to found classes and lectures on Human Physiology and the Science of Health, believing that physical improvement would be followed by mental and moral improvement.

In the spring of 1873 Mr. Gladstone, with the sanction of the Queen, asked Kingsley to become Canon of Westminster. His aged mother, now eighty-six, who had made her home at Eversley since the death of her husband, lived long enough to rejoice in his appointment to the Abbey, and died April 16.

The Archbishop of Canterbury welcomed him heartily. "It is a great sphere," he wrote, "for a man who, like you, knows how to use it."

But those who knew him best had grave fears that he would not long fill the place. He was urged to make a sea voyage, and with his daughter Rose started for America in January, 1874, taking with him a few lectures, to meet his expenses.

They landed Feb. 11, in New York. His daughter wrote home to the anxious mother, "Before my father set foot on American soil, he had a foretaste of the cordial welcome and generous hospitality which he experienced everywhere, without a single exception, throughout the six months he spent in the United States and Canada. The moment the ship warped into her dock, a deputation from a literary club came on board, took possession of us and our baggage."

Mr. Kingsley wrote home Feb. 12, "As for health, this air, as poor Thackeray said of it, is like champagne. Sea air and mountain air combined; days already an hour longer than in England, and a blazing hot sun and blue sky. It is a glorious country, and I don't wonder at the people being proud of it.... I dine with the Lotus Club on Saturday night, and then start for Boston with R., to stay with Fields next week."

He took great interest in Salem and Cambridge. He dined with Longfellow, whom he greatly admired. "Dear old Whittier called on me, and we had a most loving and like-minded talk about the other world," he writes home. "He is an old saint. This morning I have spent chiefly with Asa Gray and his plants, so that we are in good company."

In New York he met William Cullen Bryant; was entertained by that considerate and lovely friend toeverybody, the late Mrs. Botta; spoke in the Opera House at Philadelphia to nearly four thousand persons, the aisles crowded; received cordial welcome from President Grant, and from the scientific men at the Smithsonian Institute in Washington; talked with Charles Sumner an hour before he was seized with his fatal illness; visited Mark Twain at Hartford, Conn.; preached in Baltimore to a large congregation; stopped on his way West at Niagara, where he longed for his wife "to sit with him, and simply look on in silence whole days at the exquisite beauty of form and color."

Then with a party of several English and Americans, in a Pullman car, Kingsley and his daughter journeyed to California. He preached at Salt Lake City to a crowded congregation. The scenery everywhere delighted him. "The flowers," he wrote, "are exquisite, yellow ribs over all the cliffs, etc., and make one long to jump off the train every five minutes, while the geology makes one stand aghast; geologizing in England is child's play to this."

Again he preached in the Yosemite. The Dean of Westminster in the old Abbey said that Kingsley, "who is able to combine the religious and scientific aspects of nature better than any man living, is on this very day, and perhaps at this very hour, preaching in the most beautiful spot on the face of the earth, where the glories of nature are revealed on the most gigantic scale,—in that wonderful Californian Valley, to whose trees the cedars of Lebanon are but as the hyssop that groweth out of the wall,—where water and forest and sky conjoin to make up, if anywhere on the globe, an earthly paradise."

Mr. Kingsley was ill of pleurisy for some time in California. He began to long for home. "I am veryhomesick," he writes to his wife, "and counting the days till I can get back to you."

He returned to Eversley in August, and, as there was much sickness, began at once his self-sacrificing ministrations. He preached his last sermon in the Abbey Nov. 29, with great fervor. Dec. 3 he and his wife went to Eversley, where she was taken very ill. When told that there was no hope for her, he said, "My own death-warrant was signed with those words."

He cared for her tenderly, and on Dec. 28 was stricken with pneumonia. He had been warned that he must not leave his room, as a change of temperature would prove fatal; but one day he sprang out of bed, came to his wife's room for a few moments, and, taking her hand in his, said, "This is heaven, don't speak;" but soon a severe fit of coughing came on: he went back to his bed, and they never met again.

A correspondence was kept up for a few days in pencil, but this became too painful. Towards the last he said, "No more fighting—no more fighting," and then he prayed earnestly. Again he murmured, "How beautiful God is!"

For two days he sent no messages to his wife, thinking that she had gone before him. He said to the nurse who cared for them both, "I, too, am come to an end; it is all right—all as it should be."

His last words were the Burial Service, "Shut not Thy merciful

166

ears to our prayers ... suffer us not, at our last hour, from any pains of death, to fall from Thee." On Jan. 23, 1875, without a struggle, his life went out.

Dean Stanley telegraphed, "The Abbey is open to the Canon and the Poet;" but Kingsley had said, "Go where I will in this hard-working world, I shall take care to get my last sleep in Eversley churchyard;" and under the fir-trees he was buried.

A great crowd of all classes stood around that open grave, and later, little children who had loved the "Water-babies" came often and laid flowers upon the mound.

"Few eyes were dry," says Max Müller, "when he was laid in his own gravel bed, the old trees which he had planted and cared for waving their branches to him for the last time.... He will be mourned for, yearned for, in every place in which he passed some days of his busy life."

A Memorial Fund was at once raised by friends in England and America. Eversley church was enlarged and improved; at Chester a prize was founded in connection with the Natural History Society; a marble bust of him placed in the Cathedral Chapter-house, and a stall restored in the Cathedral, which bears his name. In Westminster Abbey a marble bust of Kingsley, by Mr. Woolner, was unveiled Sept. 23, 1875, with appropriate services.

Mrs. Kingsley survived her husband sixteen years, dying at Leamington, Dec. 12, 1891, at the age of seventy-seven.

His daughter Rose, and Mary who married the Rev. William Harrison, are both authors, the latter using the name "Lucas Malet." Kingsley, himself, wrote thirty-five volumes.

Charles Kingsley was as lovable in his home-life as he was brilliant and noble in his public career. Said an intimate friend of him, "To his wife—so he never shrank from affirming in deep and humble thankfulness—he owed the whole tenor of his life, all that he had worth living for. It was true. And his every word and look and gesture of chivalrous devotion for more than thirty years seemed to show that the sense of boundless gratitude had become part of his nature, was never out of the undercurrent of his thoughts."

His son-in-law, the Rev. Mr. Harrison, says, "Home was to him the sweetest, the fairest, the most romantic thing in life; and there all that was best and brightest in him shone with steady and purest lustre."

With his children he was like an elder brother. He built them a little house, where they kept books and toys and tea-things, and where he often joined them, bringing some rare flower or insect to show them. He was always cheerful with them and his aged mother. He used to say, "I wonder if there is so much laughing in any other home in England as in ours."

Corporal punishment was never allowed in his home. "More than half the lying of children," he said, "is, I believe, the result of fear, and the fear of punishment."

He was especially tender to animals. "His dog Dandy," says his wife, "a fine Scotch terrier, was his companion in all his parish walks, attended at the cottage lectures and school lessons, and was his and the children's friend for thirteen years. He lies buried under the great fir-trees on the rectory lawn, with this inscription on his gravestone, 'Fideli Fideles;' and close by, 'Sweep,' a magnificent black retriever, and 'Victor,' a favorite Teckel given to him by the Queen, with which he sat up during the two last suffering nights of the little creature's life."

Cats, too, were his especial delight, a white one and a black. "His love of animals," says Mrs. Kingsley, "was strengthened by his belief in their future state—a belief which he held in common with John Wesley and many other remarkable men. On the lawn dwelt a family of natter-jacks (running toads) who lived on from year to year in the same hole in the green bank, which the scythe was never allowed to approach. He had two little friends in a pair of sand-wasps, who lived in a crack of the window in his dressing-room, one of which he had saved from drowning in a hand-basin, taking it tenderly out into the sunshine to dry; and every spring he would look out eagerly for them or their children, who came out of, or returned to, the same crack."

His guests were one day amused when his little girl opened her hand and begged him to "look at this delightful worm."

Mr. Harrison tells this characteristic incident. One Sunday morning, in passing from the altar to the pulpit, he disappeared, and was searching for something on the ground, which he carried into the vestry. It was found later that he had discovered a beautiful butterfly, which, being lame, he feared would be trodden upon. Thus great in all little humanities was the great preacher of Eversley and Westminster Abbey.

> His life was like his own poem,—
> "Be good, sweet maid, and let who will be clever;
> Do noble things, not dream them, all day long:
> And so make life, death, and that vast forever,
> One grand, sweet song."

GENERAL WILLIAM TECUMSEH SHERMAN

Like Grant, Sherman was born in Ohio; the former in a log house at Mt. Pleasant, 1822, the latter at Lancaster, Feb. 8, 1820.

His ancestor, Edmund Sherman, came from Dedham, England, to Massachusetts, with his three sons, in 1634. From his son Samuel, who was one of the original proprietors of Woodbury, Conn., came the noted general, through a line of ministers and lawyers.

The grandfather, Taylor Sherman, was a judge in Norwalk, Conn., and one of the commissioners appointed by the State to go to Huron and Erie Counties, Ohio, to settle some land matters with regard to the Indians. He received two sections of land for his services.

His wife, Betsey, was a woman, says E. V. Smalley, in the Century for January, 1884, "of uncommon strength of character, who was always called on to give advice in times of trouble to her whole circle of relatives and descendants—a strong-willed, intelligent, managing woman.... To Grandmother Betsey might be attributed the talent of the later members of the family."

Her son Charles, admitted to the bar at twenty, married Mary Hoyt, and soon went to Lancaster, Ohio. He returned in a year, and took his young wife and baby over six hundred miles on horseback to the new home in the West, where ten other children were born, the eleven comprising six boys and five girls.

The third son, William, was named Tecumseh after the famous Indian chief, who died at the battle of Tippecanoe. When the child was four years old, the father was appointed a judge of the supreme court of Ohio, but died suddenly in Lebanon while on the bench, after he had held the position for five years.

Mrs. Sherman found her home full of children, with an annual income of only two hundred and fifty dollars with which to support them. Her husband had been loved for his genial nature and his generous heart, so that friends were not wanting to help the young mother bear her burdens.

John, the now well-known senator, was sent to an uncle in Mount Vernon, another to a friend in Cincinnati, and Tecumseh to the home of the Hon. Thomas Ewing, a prominent United States Senator from Ohio.

The lad of nine attended the village schools till he was sixteen, when, through the influence of Mr. Ewing, he entered the Military Academy at West Point. He had no love for warlike pursuits, but looked forward to becoming a civil engineer in the far West.

He had all along cared for history, travel, and fiction, but never

169

especially for battles. He enjoyed out-door sports, and long rambles with rod and gun. He studied well while at West Point, standing high in drawing, chemistry, mathematics, and philosophy, reaching the sixth place in a class of forty-three at his graduation in 1840.

He was never fond of display, and had no relish for the minutiæ of dress and drill. "Men who havesuccessfully conducted great campaigns, and fought great battles, have not," says Mr. Smalley, "as a rule, taken much interest in the polishing of buttons, or the exact alignment of a company of troops."

Soon after graduating, young Sherman, tall, slender, with auburn hair and hazel eyes, a second lieutenant in the Third Artillery, was sent to Florida to keep in check the Seminole Indians. After two winters he was transferred to Fort Moultrie, near Charleston, South Carolina, as first lieutenant, where he remained for four years. Here he enjoyed Southern hospitality, and learned the character of the people and the topography of the country, both here and in Georgia. More than twenty years later, this knowledge was invaluable when he fought his battles at Atlanta and made his immortal March to the Sea.

War with Mexico was threatening; and in 1846 Sherman was sent to New York, and afterwards to Ohio, as a recruiting officer. When he heard of the battles of Palo Alto and Resaca de la Palma, May 8 and 9, he was eager to be at the front: recruiting, as he says in his memoirs, while "his comrades were actually fighting, was intolerable."

He was soon ordered to California, which his company reached, after a voyage of nearly two hundred days, by way of Cape Horn. At Rio Janeiro, "the beauty of whose perfect harbor words will not describe," they remained for a week, and the young Ohio officer enjoyed the delights of travel. He saw Dom Pedro and his Empress, the daughter of Louis Philippe of France, the Palace, the Botanic Gardens, the Emperor's coffee plantation, where the coffee-tree reminded him of "the red haw-tree of Ohio; and the berries were somewhat like those of the same tree, two grains of coffee being enclosed in one berry."

At Cape Horn, "an island rounded like an oven, after which it takes its name (ornos, oven)," they were followed by Cape-pigeons and albatrosses of every color. At Valparaiso they remained ten days, and enjoyed large strawberries in November. The last of January, 1847, they entered Monterey Bay, and saw live-oaks and low adobe houses, with red-tiled roofs, amid dark pine-trees.

The camp was soon established, and some of their six months' provisions hauled up the hillside in the old Mexican carts with wooden wheels, "drawn by two or three pairs of oxen yoked by the horns."

They brought a saw-mill and a grist-mill with them to the new country. Living was cheap, as cattle cost but eight dollars and fifty cents for the best, or about two cents a pound.

Sherman soon met Colonel Frémont, afterwards a candidate for the Presidency, General Kearney, and other officers noted in those early days of California. San Francisco was called Yerba Buena, and Sherman felt almost insulted when asked if he wished to invest money in land "in such a horrid place as Yerba Buena."

The best houses were single-story adobes; the population was about four hundred, mostly Kanakas, natives of the Hawaiian Islands.

Sherman spent much time in hunting deer and bear in the mountains back of the Carmel Mission, and could often in a single day load a pack-mule with the geese and ducks which he had shot. These geese would appear in profusion as soon as the fall rains caused the young oats to come up.

"The seasons in California," he writes, "are well marked. About October and November the rains begin, and the whole country, plains and mountains, becomes covered with a bright green grass, with endless flowers. The intervals between the rains give the finest weather possible. These rains are less frequent in March, and cease altogether in April and May, when gradually the grass dies and the whole aspect of things changes, first to yellow, then to brown, and by midsummer all is burnt up, and dry as an ash-leaf."

The "gold-fever" broke out in the spring of 1848. Thomas Marshall found some placer-gold fifteen miles above Mormon Island, in the bed of the American Fork of the Sacramento River. He had worked for Captain Sutter in his saw-mills, and seeing this gold in the tailrace of the saw-mill, tried at first to keep it a secret, after telling Sutter; but others soon found the yellow metal, and not only California, but the whole civilized world, was excited over the discovery.

Sutter's saw and grist mills soon went to decay. Men earned fifty, a hundred, and sometimes thousands of dollars a day, if they found a "pocket" of gold. Prices became fabulous. Flour and bacon and other eatables sold for a dollar a pound. A meal usually cost three dollars. Miners slept at night on the ground. All day they worked in cold water in the river-beds, their clothes wet; but no complaints were heard.

Soldiers deserted from the coast to join the gold-diggers. At one time six hundred ships were anchored at San Francisco, and could not get away for lack of crews. Sherman and his officers were obliged to pay three hundred dollars a month for a servant, or go without, as their own pay was but seventy dollars a month. Often they did their own work. Sherman cooked, and Lieutenant Ord cleaned the dishes, but "was deposed as a scullion because he would only wipe the tin plates with a tuft of grass, according to the custom of the country," says Sherman; "whereas, Warner insisted on having them washed after each meal with hot water. Warner was, in consequence, promoted to scullion, and Ord become the hostler."

Twice Sherman and some other officers visited the mines, being obliged to cross the Sacramento River in an Indian dug-out canoe. The unwilling horses and mules were driven into the water, following the one led by the man in the canoe. When across, several of the frightened

171

creatures escaped into the woods, where they were recovered and brought back by the Indians.

The winter of 1848-49 was a serious one to the thousands of homeless men and women who had come to seek their fortunes in the mountains. The president had made the gold-finding the subject of a special message to Congress, and emigrants were pouring into California by land and by sea. Of course there was much hardship, much disregard of law, and extremes of poverty and wealth.

The winter of 1849-50 only deepened the distress. In crossing the plains and mountains many animals of the emigrants perished, and they themselves lacked food. One hundred thousand dollars were used to buy flour, bacon, etc., for these people, and men and mules were sent out by General Persifer F. Smith to meet and relieve them. In San Francisco, after the long rains, Sherman says: "I have seen mules stumble in the streets and drown in the liquid mud. Montgomery Street had been filled up with brush and clay, and I always dreaded to ride on horseback along it, because the mud was so deep that a horse's legs would become entangled in the brushesbelow, and the rider was likely to be thrown, and drown in the mud."

A room twenty by sixty feet for a store or gambling-saloon rented for a thousand dollars a month. Sherman took a share in a store, and thereby made fifteen hundred dollars, which helped him to live with these exorbitant prices. Later he made about six thousand dollars in three lots in Sacramento.

He returned East in January, 1850, on a leave of absence for six months. His comrades had fought great battles in Mexico, which he had not been able to share. "I thought it the last and only chance in my day," he writes, "and that my career as a soldier was at an end."

He visited his mother, then living at Mansfield, Ohio, and on the 1st of May, 1850, married, after an engagement of some years, Miss Ellen Boyle Ewing, daughter of the man who had adopted him in his childhood. Mr. Ewing was then Secretary of the Interior, and, of course, the wedding, on Pennsylvania Avenue in Washington, was a brilliant one. President Taylor and his cabinet, Daniel Webster, Henry Clay, and other leaders were present. In the fall of 1851 Sherman was made a captain in the Commissary Department, and ordered to St. Louis. The following year he was sent to New Orleans, to which city Mrs. Sherman went with her two children.

Seeing little prospect of advancement in the army, in 1853 Captain Sherman resigned his position, and became manager of a bank in San Francisco, a branch of a house in St. Louis.

On his way to California, when near the Pacific coast, the ship Lewis struck on a reef, and all came near losing their lives. Sherman, with his usual mastery over circumstances, sat on the hurricane deck with thecaptain, and while others prayed, or called for help, waited calmly, and was among the last to leave the ship. When all were safely on the beach, he scrambled up the bluff, and finally saw a schooner loaded with lumber, on which he asked a passage to the city of San Francisco, that he might send help to the wrecked.

This schooner capsized, and Sherman found himself in the water, mixed up with planks and ropes, steadily drifting out to sea. He was finally picked up by a boat, and as soon as possible he sent two steamers to the relief of the passengers of the Lewis, which went to pieces the night after they got off.

In the unsettled state of the country, the bank did not prove a success, and was closed May 1, 1857. Mrs. Sherman and her three children, Minnie, Lizzie, and Willie, returned to Lancaster, Ohio.

For a time Sherman became agent in New York for the St. Louis house; but the latter failing in the financial disturbances of the country, his business ventures seemed at an end, and Sherman returned to Lancaster, July 28, 1858.

"I was then perfectly unhampered," he says, "but the serious and greater question remained, what was I to do to support my family, consisting of a wife and four children, all accustomed to more than the average comforts of life?"

Like General Grant, he had resigned from the regular army that he might earn enough to support his family. Banking had been no more successful than Grant's leather business.

Two sons of Mr. Ewing had gone to Leavenworth, Kansas, where they had bought some land, and opened a law office. They offered Sherman a partnership, as he had read law considerably. He accepted the position, but soon found that he did not earn money enough, so began to manage a farm, forty miles west of Leavenworth, for his father-in-law.

This not proving more remunerative than Grant's farming, he offered himself to the army again in 1859, feeling, that a sure, though small, amount was better for his family than the uncertainties of business. He was soon appointed the superintendent of a military college about to be organized at Alexandria, Louisiana.

This position did not prove an easy one. The building was a large and handsome one in the midst of four hundred acres of pine-land, but there was not a table, chair, or black-board ready for beginning. Sherman immediately engaged some carpenters, and went to work with his usual energy.

Meantime, the slavery question bade fair to rend the Union asunder. South Carolina seceded Dec. 20, 1860, and Mississippi soon after. In the middle of January, 1861, Sherman wrote to the Governor of the State: "If Louisiana withdraw from the Federal Union, I prefer to maintain my allegiance to the Constitution as long as a fragment of it survives.... I beg you to take immediate steps to relieve me as superintendent, the moment the State determines to secede, for on no

173

earthly account will I do any act or think any thought hostile to, or in defiance of, the old Government of the United States."

Sherman soon came North and visited his brother, Senator John Sherman. Both called upon Lincoln, and the President asked the soldier "how the people of the South were getting along." "They think," was the reply of Sherman, "they are getting along swimmingly—they are preparing for war."

"Oh, well!" said Lincoln, "I guess we'll manage to keep house."

April 1, through the influence of friends, Sherman was made President of the Fifth Street Railroad, in St. Louis, at a salary of twenty-five hundred dollars a year, and moved his family thither. Five days later, and six days before the attack on Sumter, April 12, 1861, he was asked to accept the chief clerkship of the War Department, with the promise that, when Congress met, he should be made Assistant Secretary of War. This offer he declined, as he had already moved his family to St. Louis, and did not feel at liberty to change his position.

He wrote later to Simon Cameron, Secretary of War, that he would not volunteer for three months, "Because," said he, "I cannot throw my family on the cold charity of the world," but for a three-years' call, good service might be done. He was appointed Colonel of the Thirteenth Regular Infantry, May 14, 1861, and again his family returned to Lancaster, Ohio.

The war feeling had been greatly intensified at the North by the death of Colonel E. Elmer Ellsworth, a young man of twenty-four, who had organized a body of Zouaves in Chicago, and had escorted President Lincoln to Washington. On May 24, when the Union forces crossed into Virginia, Ellsworth's Zouaves occupied Alexandria. A part of the troops were proceeding towards the centre of the town, when they saw a secession flag flying from the Marshall House.

Ellsworth ascended to the roof and pulled it down. The hotel keeper, James T. Jackson, shot him through the heart, and attempted to shoot Private Francis E. Brownell, who was with Ellsworth. Brownell at once shot Jackson through the head.

Brownell died at Washington, D.C., March 15, 1894.

The body of Colonel Ellsworth lay in state in the East Room of the White House for several hours. President Lincoln, and indeed the whole North, were deeply affected by his death.

Mr. Lincoln soon called for four hundred thousand men and four hundred million dollars, to carry on the war. Two Confederate armies were already before Washington; one at Manassas Junction under General Beauregard, the other at Winchester under General Joseph E. Johnston.

General Irvin S. McDowell, aged forty-three, of the Mexican War soldiers, had command of the Union forces, and Sherman held a brigade under him. The battle of Bull Run, or Manassas, was fought

Sunday, July 21, with a loss on our side of 2,896, and on the Confederate of 1,982. Over thirty thousand men were in each army.

General John D. Imboden, in vol. 1 of that most interesting and valuable series, "Battles and Leaders of the Civil War," edited by Messrs. Johnson and Buel, tells the following incident of "Stonewall" Jackson in this battle. He had been wounded in the hand, but paid no attention to it, binding it up with his handkerchief, saying, "Only a scratch, a mere scratch," and galloped along his line. Three days later General Imboden found him at a little farm-house near Centreville. Jackson was bathing his hand at sunrise, in spring water. It was swollen and very painful. Mrs. Jackson had already come to him. "General," said Imboden, "how is it that you can keep so cool, and appear so utterly insensible to danger, in such a storm of shell and bullets as rained about you when your hand was hit?" referring to the Bull Run battle.

"Captain," he said, "my religious belief teaches me to feel as safe in battle as in bed. God has fixed the time for my death. I do not concern myself about that, but to be always ready, no matter when it may overtake me." After a pause, he said, "Captain, that is the one way all men should live, and then all would be equally brave."

Imboden apologized for the use of profanity on the battle-field, and Jackson simply remarked, "Nothing can justify profanity."

The men idolized Jackson, in part because he almost always succeeded. They trusted him without questioning. "Where are you going?" was once asked of some of his troops.

"We don't know," was the reply, "but old Jack does."

"It is now generally admitted," says Sherman, "that it the Battle of Bull Bun was one of the best planned battles of the war, but one of the worst fought.... Nearly all of us for the first time then heard the sound of cannon and muskets in anger, and saw the bloody scenes common to all battles, with which we were soon familiar. We had good organization, good men, but no cohesion, no real discipline, no respect for authority, no real knowledge of war. Both armies were fairly defeated, and whichever had stood fast, the other would have run."

Though the Union army retreated in great disorder, and the North was saddened thereby, Sherman and some others were made brigadier-generals for their bravery.

President Lincoln and Seward came to the Union camps soon after the battle. Lincoln said, in his homely fashion, "We heard that you had got over the big scare, and we thought we would come over and see the 'boys.'"

He stood up in the carriage and made a most feeling address, telling them how much devolved upon them, and how all looked for brighter days. When they began too cheer, he said, "Don't cheer, boys. I confess, I rather like it myself; but Colonel Sherman here says it is not military, and I guess we had better defer to his opinion."

A little later an officer who had attempted to go to New York without leave, and whom Sherman had threatened to shoot if he deserted at that critical time, approached the President, saying that he had a grievance, and that Colonel Sherman had threatened to shoot him.

With that rare good sense for which Lincoln was famous, and knowing that his leaders must be supported in authority, he bent over toward the aggrieved officer, and said in a loud whisper, "Well, if I were you, and he threatened to shoot, I would not trust him, for I believe he would do it." Sherman afterwards thanked the President for his confidence.

Soon after this General Sherman was assigned to the department of the Cumberland, under General Robert Anderson, formerly at Fort Sumter. Anderson's health failing, Sherman soon took his place. Mr. Cameron, Secretary of War, having a consultation with Sherman, the latter complained that he had only eighteen thousand men, whereas two hundred thousand men were needed to destroy all the opposition in the Mississippi Valley.

It soon came out in the papers that Sherman was "crazy," as at that time the North seemed to have no adequate idea of the immensity of the work in hand. The succeeding years proved that Sherman was right in his estimate of the power and purpose of the South in its war against the Union.

Sherman was relieved by General Buell, and the "insane" general was ordered to take charge of a Camp of Instruction. Hurt by the cruel charge, he still performed his duties "for a country and government," as he said, "worth fighting for, and dying for if need be."

Early in 1862 Grant had won some great victories at Forts Henry and Donelson, on the Tennessee and Cumberland Rivers. The latter fort, under General Buckner, surrendered Feb. 16, with sixty-five guns, seventeen thousand six hundred small arms, and nearly fifteen thousand troops.

Major-General Grant was now commanding the Army of the Tennessee under Halleck, and Sherman was assigned to a division under Grant. The latter held about the same "crazy" idea that Sherman held,—that the Southerners were hard and brave fighters, and would never surrender till forced to it through exhaustion of men and money.

The next great battle was at Shiloh, or Pittsburg Landing, begun by the Confederates Sunday, April 6, 1862, and lasting two days. The first day our men were driven back a mile with heavy loss. General Albert Sidney Johnston, the commander-in-chief of the Confederates, was struck about 2 P.M. by a minie-ball in the calf of the leg, which penetrated the boot and severed the main artery. His horse was shot in four places. He would not leave the field till compelled by loss of blood, and died soon after.

Dr. D. W. Yandell, who had been with Johnston, left him to

establish a hospital for the wounded, among them many Federals. "These men were our enemies a moment ago," said Johnston; "they are our prisoners now. Take care of them." Had Yandell remained with him, his life would probably have been saved, as the wound would have been attended to.

"During the whole of Sunday," says Grant, "I was continually engaged in passing from one part of the field to another, giving directions to division commanders. In thus moving along the line, I never deemed it important to stay long with Sherman. Although his troops were then under fire for the first time, their commander, by his constant presence with them, inspired a confidence in officers and men that enabled them to render services on that bloody battle-field worthy of the best of veterans.

"A casualty to Sherman that would have taken him from the field that day would have been a sad one for the troops engaged at Shiloh. And how near we came to this! On the 6th, Sherman was shot twice— once in the hand, once in the shoulder, the ball cutting his coat and making a slight wound, and a third ball passed through his hat. In addition to this, he had several horses shot during the day."

Later, Colonel James B. McPherson's horse was shot quite through, just back of the saddle, but the poor creature carried his rider out of danger before he dropped dead.

Both armies slept on their arms that night in a pouring rain, and the next morning, April 7, renewed the fight, with a hard won victory for the Union forces. So dreadful was the conflict that Grant writes, "I saw an open field, in our possession on the second day, over which the Confederates had made repeated charges the day before, so covered with dead that it would have been possible to walk across the clearing in any direction, stepping on dead bodies, without a foot touching the ground.... On one part, which had evidently not been ploughed for several years, probably because the land was poor, bushes had grown up, some to the height of eight or ten feet. There was not one of these left standing unpierced by bullets. The smaller ones were all cut down."

Our loss in killed, wounded, and missing was 13,573; the Confederates reported their loss as 10,699, but General Grant thinks it was much greater.

The battle had been bravely and desperately fought on both sides. About five hundred yards east of Shiloh meeting-house there had been a deadly combat. Several times cartridges gave out; but Sherman appealed to the regiments to "stand fast," as their retiring would have a bad effect on others, and the men heroically kept their posts. Sherman's division lost over two thousand men.

Grant said, in his official report, "I feel it a duty to a gallant and able officer, Brigadier-General W. T. Sherman, to make mention that he was not only with his command during the entire two days of action, but displayed great judgment and skill in the management of his men."

177

Halleck said, "Sherman saved the fortunes of the day on the 6th, and contributed largely to the glorious victory on the 7th."

When on the 8th it was found that the enemy had retreated, "leaving killed, wounded, and much property by the way," says Sherman, "we all experienced a feeling of relief. The struggle had been so long, so desperate and bloody, that the survivors seemed exhausted and nerveless. We appreciated the value of the victory, but realized also its great cost of life."

Sherman was promoted to the position of major-general May 1. During June and July he was "building railroad-trestles and bridges, fighting off cavalry detachments coming from the South, and waging an everlasting quarrel with planters about the negroes and fences, they trying, in the midst of moving armies, to raise a crop of corn."

The desire now was to get complete possession of the Mississippi River. Admiral Farragut had taken New Orleans, after the dreadful passage of Forts Jackson and St. Philip. The brave old admiral had said, "If I die in the attempt, it will only be what every officer has to expect. He who dies in doing his duty to his country, and at peace with his God, has played the drama of life to the best advantage."

With his six sloops-of-war, sixteen gunboats, twenty-one schooners, and five other vessels, forty-eight in all, carrying two hundred guns, all led by the Hartford, Farragut pushed his way through a sea of fire. Five fire-rafts—flat boats, filled with dry wood smeared with tar and turpentine—blazed among his ships, while shot and shell strewed his decks with the dead; but he cut his way to victory, and won immortal honor.

Memphis had been captured by our gunboats and rams, under Admiral Davis, June 6. Of the eight Confederate gunboats in the flotilla, three, the Lovell, Beauregard, and Thompson, were destroyed by our vessels; four were captured and repaired for our use; while one, the Van Dorn, escaped. Five transports and some cotton were taken, and a large ram and two tugs on the stocks were destroyed.

Sherman was ordered to go to Memphis to take command of the district of West Tennessee. When he entered the city, the stores, churches, and schools were closed. He caused these and the places of amusement to be opened, and put the fugitive slaves to work on the fortifications, and gave them food and clothing.

The story is told of an Episcopal clergyman who came to Sherman, saying that he was embarrassed about his prayer for the President.

"Whom do you regard as President?" said Sherman.

"Mr. Davis," was his reply.

"Very well; pray for Jeff Davis if you wish. He needs your prayers badly. It will take a great deal of praying to save him."

"Then I will not be compelled to pray for Mr. Lincoln?"

"Oh, no. He is a good man, and don't need your prayers. You may pray for him if you feel like it, but there's no compulsion."

To some of the editors in Memphis, Sherman said, "If I find the press of Memphis actuated by high principle and a sole devotion to their country, I will be their best friend; but if I find them personal, abusive, dealing in innuendoes and hints at a blind venture, and looking to their own selfish aggrandizement and fame, then they had better look out; for I regard such persons as greater enemies to their country and to mankind than the men who, from a mistaken sense of State pride, have taken up muskets, and fight us about as hard as we care about."

Sherman went to the Argus office one day, and, in his familiar manner, said to the young editors, as he sat down and rested his feet on the table: "Boys, I have been ordered to suppress your paper, but I don't like to do that. I just dropped in to warn you not to be so free with your pencils. If you don't ease up, you'll get into trouble."

When some complained of the acts of the soldiers, Sherman replied that he knew of several instances where their conduct had been provoked by sneering remarks about "Northern barbarians" and "Lincoln's hirelings." "People who use such language," he said, "must seek redress through some one else, for I will not tolerate insults to our country or cause."

All sorts of ruses were adopted by the Southern army to obtain things from Memphis. While General Van Dorn was at Holly Springs, he desired supplies for his men. Some of our soldiers found, in a farmer's barn, a large hearse with pall and plumes, which had been used at a big funeral. It was filled with medicines for Van Dorn's army! "It was a good trick," said Sherman, "but diminished our respect for such pageants afterward."

In December there was a concerted movement by Grant and Sherman to capture Vicksburg. The latter was to move down the river, and with Admiral Porter's gunboats, "proceed," said Grant, "to the reduction of that place in such manner as circumstances and your own judgment may dictate." Sherman was to make the attack by land, in the rear, while Porter attacked by river front. Three divisions of Sherman's army were landed in the low, marshy lands, cut by the Chickasaw Bayou and other creeks, where a slight rise in the Mississippi River would drown them all. The bluffs of Walnut Hills, on which Vicksburg stands, are two hundred feet high, and impregnable.

Against these the fearless troops were led Dec. 29, with great slaughter. De Courcy's brigade of Morgan's division, and Frank Blair's brigade of Steele's division, with the Fourth Iowa, were under the hottest fire. De Courcy lost 700, Blair 743, and the Fourth Iowa 111 men; the Confederate loss was only about 187.

Sherman says, "The men of the Sixth Missouri actually scooped out with their hands caves in the bank, which sheltered them against

179

the fire of the enemy, who, right over their heads, held their muskets outside the parapet vertically, and fired down. So critical was the position, that we could not recall the men till after dark, and then one at a time. Our loss had been pretty heavy, and we had accomplished nothing."

It was evident that Vicksburg must be taken in some other manner. Grant decided to cut a canal across the peninsula opposite Vicksburg, that he might get below the city. All through January and February, Sherman's men were digging the canal, planned to be sixty feet wide and nine feet deep, and fighting off the Mississippi, which continued to rise, and threatened to drown them. When the men were not digging canals, they were clearing bayous, which were filled with cypress and cottonwood trees. Sometimes they marched at night through canebrakes, carrying lighted candles, Sherman walking with them, the water above his hips. The drummer-boys carried their drums on their heads, and the men slung their cartridge-boxes around their necks.

Admiral Porter, from his gunboats, used to send Sherman messages, written on tissue paper, concealed in a piece of tobacco. A negro carried them through the swamps.

Many weeks were spent on other canals, but all proved useless. Finally it was decided to move all the troops down the west bank of the river, cross over below Vicksburg, and attack it on the land side.

A series of battles followed at Port Gibson, Raymond, Jackson, Champion Hills, and Big Black. Grant had inflicted a loss upon the enemy during a few days of eight thousand in killed, wounded, and missing; had captured eighty-eight pieces of their artillery, and driven them into their defences at Vicksburg. "We must go back to the campaigns of Napoleon," says Francis Vinton Greene, lieutenant of engineers, "to find equally brilliant results accompanied in the same space of time with such small loss."

In these days of carnage, incidents even amusing happened. While Sherman and his troops were at Jackson, a fat man came to him and hoped that his hotel would not be burned, as he was a law-abiding Union man. Sherman said that this fact was manifest from the sign on his hotel, where the words "United States" had been faintly painted out and "Confederate Hotel" painted over it!

On May 22 the last assault was made on Vicksburg; and, though severe and bloody, it was unsuccessful, on account of the strength of the position, and the earnest fighting of the garrison.

"I have since seen the position at Sevastopol," writes Sherman, "and without hesitation I declare that at Vicksburg to have been the more difficult of the two."

It was during this dreadful assault that the drummer boy, Orion P. Howe, came to Sherman, calling out in a childish voice that one of the regiments was out of ammunition, and must abandon its position unless relief was sent. The general looked down from his horse upon the lad, and saw the blood running from a wound in the leg.

"All right, my boy," said Sherman, "I'll send them all they need; but as you seem to be badly hurt, you had better go to the rear and find a surgeon and let him fix you up."

The boy saluted and started for the rear; but again he came running back, shouting, "General, calibrefifty-eight, calibre fifty-eight!" fearing that the wrong size might be sent, and prove useless. He was afterwards, through Sherman, appointed a cadet at the Naval Academy, Annapolis.

The siege of Vicksburg was begun at once. Mines were dug by both sides and exploded. Chief Engineer S. H. Lockett, of the Confederates, tells how a private suggested the firing of a wicker case filled with cotton, which protected the Federals in their sapping. He took a piece of port-fire, put it into cotton soaked with turpentine and fired it from an old-fashioned bore musket. The wicker case took fire and burned up. Barrels of powder, lighted by a time-fuse, were thrown into the ranks of the besiegers.

As the weeks went by, the provisions for the soldiers and citizens of Vicksburg were well-nigh consumed. They ate rats and mules. Flour was five dollars a pound. Some of the people built rooms in the yellow clay banks, and thus escaped the shells.

The soldiers grew desperate. General Pemberton hoped they could cut their way out, and caused boats to be made out of some of the houses,—they planned to make two thousand,—which they could use in their escape down the river.

Finally, when all became hopeless, Pemberton said, "Far better would it be for me to die at the head of my army, even in a vain effort to force the enemy's lines, than to surrender it and live and meet the obloquy which I know will be heaped upon me. But my duty is to sacrifice myself to save the army which has so nobly done its duty to defend Vicksburg."

July 4, 1863, Pemberton surrendered his garrison of over thirty-one thousand men, sixty thousand muskets, and over one hundred and seventy cannon.

Grant said of Sherman, "His untiring energy and great efficiency during the campaign entitled him to a full share of all the credit due for its success. He could not have done more if the plan had been his own."

Before sunset of July 4, Sherman, with fifty thousand men, was in pursuit of Johnston, who had been trying to aid Pemberton. Johnston marched rapidly, driving all cattle, hogs, and sheep into the ponds, and shooting them, so that they should not furnish food for the Federals, and also to spoil the water. Johnston made a stand at Jackson, but soon evacuated the place.

For bravery and success in this campaign, Grant was made major-general in the regular army, the highest grade then allowed by law, and Sherman and McPherson brigadier-generals in the regular army.

After the fall of Vicksburg, Sherman's family, Mrs. Sherman, Minnie, Lizzie, Willie, and Tom, came from Ohio to visit him. Willie was nine years old, fond of the parade of war, and was made a "sergeant" in the regular battalion. He became ill in the low marshy country, and died of typhoid fever, just after the family reached the Gayoso Hotel in Memphis.

This death was a great blow to Sherman, as he showed in a letter which he wrote to Captain C. C. Smith, commanding Battalion Thirteenth United States Regulars: "I cannot sleep to-night till I record an expression of the deep feelings of my heart to you, and to the officers and soldiers of the battalion, for their kind behavior to my poor child.... The child that bore my name, and in whose future I reposed with more confidence than I did in my own plan of life, now being carried by steamer a mere corpse, seeking a grave in a distant land, with a weeping mother, brother, and sisters clustered about him. For myself I ask no sympathy. On, on I must go, to meet a soldier's fate, or live to see our country rise superior to all factions, till its flag is adored and respected by ourselves and by all the powers of the earth....

"Child as he was, he had the enthusiasm, the pure love of truth, honor, and love of country, which should animate all soldiers.... Assure each and all, if in after years they call on me or mine, and mention that they were of the Thirteenth Regulars when Willie was a sergeant, they will have a key to the affections of my family that will open all it has; that we will share with them our last blanket, our last crust!"

In the spring of 1867, Willie's body was removed from Lancaster, Ohio, to St. Louis, and buried by the side of another child, Charles, born in 1864. Sherman's officers and men erected a beautiful monument to Willie, and had inscribed on it, "Our little Sergeant Willie, from the First Battalion Thirteenth United States Infantry."

After the dreadful battle of Chickamauga, Ga., Sept. 20, 1863, in which we lost 15,851 men, and the Confederates 17,804, Grant went to Chattanooga to retrieve that disaster. In this battle Thomas, "who," says General Fullerton, "never retreated and had never been defeated," so wonderfully held his ground that he was ever afterwards called the "Rock of Chickamauga."

"With but twenty-five thousand men," said General Garfield, "formed in a semicircle, of which he himself was the centre and soul, he successfully resisted for more than five hours the repeated assaults of an army of sixty-five thousand men, flushed with victory and bent on his annihilation.

"Towards the close of the day his ammunition began to fail. One by one of his division commanders reported but ten rounds, five rounds, and two rounds left. The calm, quiet answer was returned,

182

'Save your fire for close quarters, and when your last shot is fired give them the bayonet.

"On a portion of this line the last assault was repelled by the bayonet, and several hundred rebels were captured. When night had closed over the combatants, the last sound of battle was the booming of Thomas's shells bursting among his baffled and retreating assailants."

Grant telegraphed to Thomas to hold Chattanooga at all hazards; and Thomas, with his troops on less than half rations for the past month, replied, "We will hold the town till we starve." He urged Sherman to come at once. Then followed those memorable battles of Lookout Mountain, when Hooker fought his "Battle above the clouds," and Missionary Ridge, when Wood's and Sheridan's divisions under Thomas lost in one hour's storming 2,287 men.

"Sherman was fighting the heavy column of the enemy on our left," said General Henry M. Cist, "and the main part of the battle had been his share." He lost about two thousand men.

At three o'clock the first rifle-pits on the ridge were to be carried, and there they were to halt to await orders. There was some delay, so that the order was not given till half-past three, when the guns sounded, one, two, up to six, for the charge.

The enemy had four lines of breastworks, but one had been captured by Thomas the day before. Three rifle-pits remained. As our men approached, cheering, and breaking into a double-quick, the enemy poured upon them shot and shell from their batteries, changing it soon to grape and canister, with a terrific fire of musketry.

"Dashing through this over the open plain," says General Cist, "the soldiers of the army of the Cumberland swept on, driving the enemy's skirmishers, charging down on the line of works at the foot of the ridge, capturing it at the point of the bayonet, and routing the rebels, sending them at full speed up the ridge, killing and capturing them in large numbers. These rifle-pits were reached simultaneously by the several commands, when the troops, in compliance with their instructions, lay down at the foot of the ridge awaiting further orders."

Here they waited under a hot fire. The orders did not come; and then without orders, first one regiment and then another, with their colors raised, pushed up the mountain covered with rocks and fallen timber.

The centre of Sheridan's division reached the crest first, and almost at the same time the ridge was carried in six places. Almost entire regiments were taken from the enemy, and batteries, the Confederates often bayoneted at their guns. In an hour the work had been accomplished, and the storming of Missionary Ridge had passed into history as a memorable instance of bravery. "After it was over," says General Fullerton, "some madly shouted, some wept from very excess of joy, some grotesquely danced out their delight,—even our wounded forgot their pain to join in the general hurrah."

Grant and Thomas were watching the battle through their glasses. Grant asked, "By whose orders are those troops going up the hill?"

"I don't know," said Thomas, "I did not."

"I didn't order them up," said Sheridan, "but we are going to take the ridge."

Grant remarked that "it was all right if it turned out all right, but, if not, some one would suffer."

By the capture of the ridge, Sherman was enabled to take the tunnel as he had been ordered. Captain S. H. M. Byers, who was captured at the tunnel with sixty of his regiment and put in Libby prison for seven months—the sixty were soon reduced to sixteen by death—thus describes the scene. "As the column came out upon the ground, and in sight of the rebel batteries, their renewed and concentrated fire knocked the limbs from the trees above our heads.... In front of us was a rail-fence. 'Jump the fence, boys,' was the order, and never was a fence scaled more quickly. It was nearly half a mile to the rebel position, and we started on the charge, running across the open fields. I had heard the roaring of heavy battle before, but never such shrieking of cannon balls and bursting of shells as met us on that run."

Sherman, in his official report, gave his officers and men due credit for their "patience, cheerfulness, and courage." "For long periods," he said, "without regular rations or supplies of any kind, they have marched through mud and over rocks, sometimes barefooted, without a murmur. Without a moment's rest after a march of over four hundred miles, without sleep for three successive nights, we crossed the Tennessee, fought our part of the battle of Chattanooga, pursued the enemy out of Tennessee, and then turned more than a hundred and twenty miles north, and compelled Longstreet to raise the siege of Knoxville."

Congress soon passed a resolution of thanks toSherman and his army for their "gallant and arduous services in marching to the relief of the Army of the Cumberland, and for their gallantry and heroism in the battle of Chattanooga, which contributed in a great degree to the success of our arms in that glorious victory."

The grade of lieutenant-general was now revived in the army, and bestowed upon Grant. He wrote Sherman at once to "express my thanks to you and McPherson, as the men to whom, above all others, I feel indebted for whatever I have had of success. How far your advice and suggestions have been of assistance, you know. How far your execution of whatever has been given you to do entitles you to the reward I am receiving, you cannot know as well as I do."

And Sherman wrote back: "I believe you as brave, patriotic, and just as the great prototype Washington; as unselfish, kind-hearted, and honest as a man should be; but the chief characteristic in your nature is the simple faith in success you have always manifested, which I can liken to nothing else than the faith a Christian has in his Saviour.

"This faith gave you victory at Shiloh and Vicksburg. Also, when you have completed your best preparations, you go into battle without hesitation, as at Chattanooga—no doubts, no reserve; and I tell you that it was this that made us act with confidence. I knew, wherever I was, that you thought of me, and if I got in a tight place you would come—if alive."

Sherman at this time was put in command of the military division of the Mississippi, with Schofield, Thomas, McPherson, and Steele under him. Grant was to conquer Robert E. Lee and his large army at the East; and Sherman, Joseph E. Johnston's army at the West and South.

Supplies were at once gathered by Sherman at Chattanooga for one hundred thousand men, which would necessitate one hundred and thirty cars, of ten tons each, to reach that city daily. Confederate raids under Forrest and others were frequent; but, as in the case of Grant, nothing could deter Sherman.

On May 5, 1864, the great army started for Atlanta, Ga., prepared to fight its way. The men fought bravely at Resaca, at Allatoona Pass, and elsewhere.

During the month of May, Sherman had advanced his army, as he says, "nearly a hundred miles of as difficult a country as was ever fought over by civilized armies. The fighting was continuous, almost daily, among trees and bushes, on ground where we could rarely see a hundred yards ahead." Sherman had lost 9,299 men; nearly two thousand in killed and missing, and over seven thousand wounded. The enemy's loss was a little over half that number.

From June 10 to July 3 an almost constant battle was waged about Kenesaw Mountain, with a loss on our side of nearly eight thousand, and the Confederate loss considerably less.

An amusing remark came to Sherman's ear at Kenesaw. One of the Confederate soldiers said to another, "Well, the Yanks will have to git up and git now, for I heard General Johnston himself say that General Wheeler had blown up the tunnel near Dalton, and that the Yanks would have to retreat, because they could get no more rations."

"Oh," said the listener, "don't you know that old Sherman carries a duplicate tunnel along?"

The enemy were constantly driven back towards Atlanta. On July 22 a bloody battle was fought near Atlanta, usually called the Battle of Atlanta, in which the brave General McPherson was killed in the hottest of the fight when passing from one column to another. He rode into a wood, and soon his horse returned, wounded, bleeding, and riderless. His body was recovered, with his gauntlets on and boots outside his pantaloons, but his pocket-book with his papers was gone. The spot where he fell was soon retaken by our men, and the pocket-

185

book and its contents were found in the haversack of a prisoner of war, captured at the time.

McPherson was only thirty-four years old, over six feet high, universally beloved, and apparently destined for a great future. Sherman could not look long upon the body. "Better start at once, and drive carefully," said the bluff but tender-hearted general to McPherson's staff, as he covered the body with the flag. It was taken home to Clyde, Ohio, where it was received with great honor, and buried near his mother's house in a small cemetery, part of which is the family orchard where he played when a boy.

General John A. Logan took the command after the death of McPherson, and fought bravely. The attack was made upon his line seven times, and seven times repulsed.

Sherman was often in extreme danger. Once, when he, Logan, and a few others were talking together, a minie-ball passed through Logan's coat-sleeve, scratching the skin, and struck Colonel Taylor in the breast. A memorandum-book saved his life. At another time a cannon-ball passed over Sherman's shoulder and killed the horse of an orderly behind. Another ball took off the head of a negro close by Sherman.

The month of July was an extremely hot one, but the soldiers had been in almost constant conflict. Our loss in that month was about ten thousand men, and that of the enemy perhaps greater by a few hundreds.

Sherman's men tore up railroad-tracks, made bonfires of the ties, wrapped the heated rails round trees and telegraph poles, and left them to cool,—such rails could not be used again,—and filled up deep cuts with trees, brush, and earth, commingled with loaded shells, so arranged that they would explode if disturbed. Thus the devastation of war went on.

Atlanta was full of foundries, arsenals, and machine-shops, and was called the "Gate City of the South." "I knew that its capture," says Sherman, "would be the death-knell of the Southern Confederacy."

Sept. 2 Atlanta could bear the Federal guns no longer, was evacuated by the enemy, and our troops marched into the city with great rejoicing. The losses during these four months had been over thirty thousand on each side.

President Lincoln wrote to Sherman: "The marches, battles, sieges, and other military operations, that have signalized the campaign, must render it famous in the annals of the war, and have entitled those who have participated therein to the applause and thanks of the nation."

Grant wrote from City Point, Va., "In honor of your great victory, I have ordered a salute to be fired with shotted guns from every battery bearing on the enemy.... I feel that you have accomplished the most gigantic undertaking given to any general in this war."

Sherman at once required all the citizens and families resident in Atlanta to leave the city and go North or South as they chose, with a reasonable amount offurniture and bedding. This order was denounced by Hood, who had relieved Johnston, as unprecedented and cruel. A bitter correspondence took place, in which Sherman said, "War is cruelty, and you cannot refine it.... You might as well appeal against the thunder-storms as against these terrible hardships of war. They are inevitable; and the only way the people of Atlanta can hope once more to live in peace and quiet at home, is to stop the war, which can only be done by admitting that it began in error and is perpetuated in pride....

"I want peace, and believe it can only be reached through union and war, and I will ever conduct war with a view to perfect and early success. When peace does come, you may call on me for anything. Then will I share with you the last cracker, and watch with you to shield your homes and families against danger from every quarter."

Hood then took his army into Tennessee, and much of the old battle ground was fought over. Allatoona Pass was wonderfully defended by General John M. Corse, who lost a cheek-bone and an ear by a ball cutting across his face, but still led his men, holding the pass and killing the enemy three to one. Mr. John C. Ropes regards this fight "as one of the most memorable occurrences of the war."

At Resaca, when General Hood demanded its surrender, Colonel Clark R. Weaver said, "In my opinion, I can hold this post. If you want it, come and take it." But Hood did not attempt it after his losses at Allatoona.

Sherman saw the impossibility of holding the country and defending the railroads without constant losses. He telegraphed Grant, "With twenty-five thousand infantry and the bold cavalry he has, Hood can constantly breako my road. I would infinitely prefer to make a wreck of the road and of the country from Chattanooga to Atlanta ... and with my effective army move through Georgia, smashing things to the sea."

On the morning of Nov. 15, 1864, this great army of about 65,000 men began its march from Atlanta to the sea. The depot, round-house, and machine-shops of the Georgia railroad had been burned. The fire destroyed the heart of the city, but did not reach the mass of the dwelling-houses. The army carried sixty-five guns, or one to each thousand men. Each gun, caisson, and forge was drawn by four teams of horses. There were twenty-five hundred wagons, with six mules each, and six hundred ambulances with two horses each. Every soldier carried on his person forty rounds of ammunition, and in the wagons were enough cartridges to make up two hundred rounds to a man. The procession occupied five miles or more of road.

Corps commanders alone were intrusted with the power of destroying mills, cotton-gins, etc. "Where the army is unmolested," said Sherman, "no destruction of such property should be permitted."

The cavalry and artillery were allowed to take horses, mules, and wagons, especially from the rich, who were not usually as friendly as the poor. Soldiers were not to enter the dwellings of the inhabitants, but might gather vegetables and stock. Regular foraging parties might gather provisions at any distance from the road travelled.

As the great company moved out of Atlanta, the black smoke of her buildings rising high in air, the men sang "John Brown's body lies a-mouldering in his grave." "Never before or since," says Sherman, "have I heard the chorus of 'Glory, glory, hallelujah!' done with more spirit, or in better harmony of time and place."

As Sherman moved past his men, some of them called out, "Uncle Billy,"—they usually called him this,—"I guess Grant is waiting for us at Richmond!"

The first night they camped by the roadside near Lithonia. All night long groups of men were tearing up railroads and bending the heated rails around trees or telegraph poles.

At the towns the white people came out to look upon the hated intruders, and the colored people were frantic with joy. Each day foraging parties, "Sherman's bummers" as they were called, usually about fifty men from a brigade, would go out to the plantations for food.

"The foragers," says Major-General Jacob D. Cox in his "March to the Sea," "turned into beasts of burden oxen and cows, as well as horses and mules. Here would be a silver-mounted family carriage drawn by a jackass and a cow, loaded inside and out with everything the country produced, vegetable and animal, dead and alive. There would be an ox-cart, similarly loaded, and drawn by a nondescript tandem team, equally incongruous. Perched upon the top would be a ragged forager, rigged out in a fur hat of a fashion worn by darkies of a century ago, or a dress-coat which had done service at stylish balls of a former generation." Many of the horses and mules collected were shot, as it produced a bad effect on the infantry when too many idlers were mounted.

The usual march for the army was about fifteen miles per day. The Southern press urged that the invading army be destroyed, starved, obstructed by gun, spade, and axe. But the great host swept on.

At Milledgeville the arsenal and such public buildings as could be used easily for hostile purposes were burned, while several mills and thousands of bales of cotton were spared. Other places shared the same fate.

As the army neared Savannah, they were assured by some prisoners whom they took, that it would be found strongly fortified. On one of the roads torpedoes had been planted, one of which exploded when touched by a horse's hoof, killing the animal and literally blowing off the flesh from the legs of the rider. This so angered General Sherman, that he made some rebel prisoners, much against their will, pass over the road to explode their own torpedoes, or to discover and dig them up.

Sherman demanded of General Hardee the surrender of Savannah. This Hardee declined to do; but he evacuated the city about the time the assault was to have been made, leaving behind his heavy guns, cotton, railway-cars, steamboats, and other property, but destroying his iron clads and navy-yards. The ground outside the forts was filled with torpedoes, as was also the Savannah River. Log piers were stretched across the channel below the city, and filled with the cobble-stones that formerly paved the streets. A heavy force at once set to work to remove the torpedoes and other obstructions from the river, and Savannah became the great depot of supply for the troops. Very many destitute Southern families were fed by Sherman.

Sherman telegraphed the President, Dec. 22, 1864: "I beg to present you, as a Christmas gift, the city of Savannah, with over one hundred and fifty heavy guns and plenty of ammunition, also about twenty-five thousand bales of cotton."

There was great rejoicing at the capture of the city, as now Sherman could march into the Carolinas and lay them waste, and then join his army to that of Grant, who was besieging Lee in Richmond. Thomas had conquered Hood at Nashville. The end of the war could be plainly seen.

Grant congratulated Sherman on his brilliant campaign. "I never had a doubt," he said, "of the result. When apprehensions for your safety were expressed by the President, I assured him, with the army you had, and you in command of it, there was no danger but you would strike bottom on salt water some place; that I would not feel the same security, in fact, would not have intrusted the expedition to any other living commander."

Lincoln wrote, "The undertaking being a success, the honor is all yours; for I believe none of us went further than to acquiesce.... But what next? I suppose it will be safer if I leave General Grant and yourself to decide."

Congress passed a vote of thanks to Sherman and his men for the great March to the Sea, of three hundred miles in twenty-four days. This march greatly interested Europe, though Sherman never considered it so important as the passage of the army afterwards through the Carolinas.

The London Times said: "Since the great Duke of Marlborough turned his back upon the Dutch, and plunged hurriedly into Germany to fight the famous battle of Blenheim, military history has recorded no stranger marvel than this mysterious expedition of General Sherman, on an unknown route, against an undiscovered enemy." Noted army men regard it as having "scarcely a parallel in the history of war."

In January the whole army left Savannah, Ga., for Columbia, S.C. Sometimes, in pouring rains, they waded up to their shoulders through swamps previously considered impassable, or made roads for miles through the mud by corduroying them with rails and split trees.

The Confederate General Johnston said later, in the hearing of General Cox, concerning this part of the march, "he had made up his mind that there had been no such army since the days of Julius Cæsar."

"Whoever will consider," says General Cox, "the effect of dragging the artillery and hundreds of loaded army wagons over mud roads, in such a country, and of the infinite labor required to pave these roads with logs, levelling the surface with smaller poles in the hollows between, adding to the structure as the mass sinks in the ooze, and continuing this till the miles of train have pulled through, will get a constantly increasing idea of the work, and a steadily increasing wonder that it was done at all."

On Feb. 16 Sherman camped near an old prison bivouac opposite Columbia, called Camp Sorghum, "where remained," he says, "the mud-hovels and holes in the ground which our prisoners had made to shelter themselves from the winter's cold and the summer's heat."

When the army entered Columbia, they found a long pile of burning cotton-bales, which Sherman was told had been fired by General Wade Hampton's men before their departure. At night a high wind fanned these flames; and though Sherman's men assisted in trying to put out the fire, the heart of the city was burned—several churches, the old State House, hotels, and dwellings. About half the city was in ashes. Sherman gave the mayor five hundred cattle to feed the people, and one hundred muskets to preserve order after the departure of his army.

One lady saved her home from pillage by showing to the troops a book which Sherman had given her years before. The boys knew Uncle Billy's writing. They guarded her house, and a young man from Iowa tended her baby while she was receiving a social call from Sherman.

While in Columbia, a poem was presented to Sherman by Adjutant S. H. M. Byers of the Fifth Iowa Infantry, written while a prisoner in that city, where it was arranged and sung by the prisoners. It was entitled "Sherman's March to the Sea," beginning,—

> "Our camp-fires shone bright on the mountains
> That frowned on the river below,
> As we stood by our guns in the morning,
> And eagerly watched for the foe;
> When a rider came out of the darkness
> That hung over mountain and tree,
> And shouted, 'Boys, up and be ready!
> For Sherman will march to the sea!'"

Sherman at once attached Byers to his staff.

Several foundries, the factory of Confederate money, and the state arsenal at Columbia, were destroyed by Sherman before leaving. Charleston was evacuated Feb. 18, for fear of its falling into Federal hands; and Wilmington was captured by General Terry Feb. 22. At Cheraw a large number of guns and thirty-six hundred barrels of powder were taken; at Fayetteville a magnificent United States arsenal was destroyed by our men.

Two battles were fought at Averysboro and at Bentonville, Johnston now commanding the Confederates, our loss being over two thousand men in both battles. March 23 Sherman's army entered Goldsborough, N.C., after a march from Savannah of four hundred and twenty-five miles, across five large rivers, and innumerable swamps, in fifty days, the army being almost as fresh as when they started from Atlanta.

General Sherman then left his army under Schofield, and started for City Point, Va., to meet Lincoln and Grant on March 28. "When I left Lincoln," says Sherman,—this proved to be their last meeting,—"I was more than ever impressed with his kindly nature, his deep and earnest sympathy with the afflictions of the whole people, resulting from the war, and by the march of hostile armies through the South." He wanted no more blood shed, and was anxious for the men on both sides to return to their homes.

"Of all the men I ever met," said Sherman, "he seemed to possess more of the elements of greatness, combined with goodness, than any other."

Sherman returned to his army, and made ready for one more march, to meet Grant. He was to start April 10. However, April 6 Richmond fell, and Lee and his whole army surrendered to Grant at Appomattox Court House, Va., April 9, 1865.

Sherman's army were resting, April 11, at the end of the hour's march, when a staff-officer galloped along the lines, shouting, "Lee has surrendered!" The soldiers were wild with delight, and flung their caps at him, as they shouted, "You're the man we've been looking for these three years!"

A Southern woman came to the gate with her children as the columns passed, and, learning the reason of the commotion, looked at her little ones, while the tears fell down her cheeks, and said tenderly, "Now father will come home."

April 13 Johnston asked for a suspension of hostilities; on the evening of April 14 Lincoln was assassinated, to the great grief of the nation; April 18 a basis of agreement was effected between Sherman and Johnston, which was modified at Washington, so as to correspond with the terms made between Grant and Lee. On April 26 Johnston surrendered to Sherman his whole force, 36,817 men, and the troops in Georgia and Florida, 52,453, making 89,270 men. The march to the sea and through the Carolinas had helped, as Sherman believed it would, to end the Civil War.

There remained only for the closing scene the grand review of the Army of the West for six hours and a half along Pennsylvania Avenue, Washington, May 24, the day following the review of the Army of the Potomac. Some of the division commanders, by way of variety, had added goats, cows, and mules, loaded with poultry, hams, etc. There were also families of freed slaves in the procession, the women leading the children. Each division was preceded by its corps of black helpers, with picks and spades.

In Sherman's farewell to his army he urged those who remained in the service to continue the same hard work and discipline which they had had in the past, and those who went to their homes "not to yield to the natural impatience sure to result from our past life of excitement and adventure," but to make a home and occupation in our grand, extensive, diversified country.

"Your general," he said, "now bids you farewell, with the full belief that, as in war you have been good soldiers, so in peace you will make good citizens; and if, unfortunately, new war should arise in our country, 'Sherman's Army' will be the first to buckle on its old armor, and come forth to defend and maintain the Government of our inheritance."

After the war Sherman was in command of the military division of the Mississippi, with headquarters at St. Louis. He took especial interest in the development of the Northern and Southern Pacific railroads. When Grant was made General, July 25, 1866, Sherman was made Lieutenant-General. In 1869 when Grant became President, Sherman was made General, with the provision that the office should go to no other person. Sheridan was made Lieutenant-General with the same provision.

From Nov. 10, 1871, to Sept. 17, 1872, General Sherman travelled abroad in Turkey, Russia, Austria, and Western Europe, and received distinguished honors. He kept full notes. After his return he published his memoirs in two volumes, which the Nation characterises as "one of the most noteworthy examples of self-revealing in the whole range of autobiography."

He received degrees from Harvard, Yale, Dartmouth, and Princeton colleges. To Harvard college he sent a large picture of himself, which now hangs in the library. He was much sought after in social circles, and was an interesting speaker and writer. Once when speaking on the American flag to the pupils of the Packer and Polytechnic Institutes in Brooklyn, he said of the "Stars and Bars," the Confederate flag, "They cut out the blue. They left heaven out of their flag, and so were destined to defeat."

To the cadets at West Point he said: "When war comes you can have but one purpose—your country—and by your country I mean the whole country, not part of it." Everywhere he was outspoken, of simplemanners, humorous, brave, unselfish, and comprehensive in mind and actions.

"The two or three great captains in any age," says the Nation, "are alike in the supreme qualities which make a general. They have the unruffled presence of mind which makes their intellectual operations most sure and true in the greatest and most sudden peril, and the true greatness which makes the most momentous decision and unhesitating action under vast responsibility, as if these were the every day work of their lives. The present generation has in our army seen two such, Grant and Sherman. It is doubtful if it has seen a third."

General Oliver O. Howard, who lost an arm under Sherman, writes, "Take him all in all, General Sherman was not only one of the greatest military geniuses in history, but a model of a kindly, generous, and faithful man in every position in life."

Sherman's soldiers idolized him. To them he was always "Old Tecums" or "Uncle Billy." He believed in fighting at the front. He said in his Memoirs: "No man can properly command an army from the rear. He must be at its front.... Some men think that modern armies may be so regulated that a general can sit in an office and play on his several columns as on the keys of a piano. This is a fearful mistake. The directing mind must be at the very head of the army—must be seen there, and the effect of his mind and personal energy must be felt by every officer and man present with it, to secure the best results."

General Sherman was strongly urged to become a candidate for the Presidency. He declined absolutely, as he did not wish its cares and duties; knowing also thato the religion of his wife and children, Roman Catholicism, though he was not a Romanist, would cause opposition. His son, Thomas Ewing Sherman, though educated for the law, became a Catholic priest.

After retiring from the army, as the law requires at sixty-four years of age, though allowed full pay, thirteen thousand five hundred dollars yearly to the end of his life, Sherman removed to New York, living at 75 West Seventy-first Street. Here, in the midst of his children and grandchildren, he passed his last days happily. Of his four sons, Willie, Charles, Thomas, and Philemon Tecumseh, the first two died. Of his four daughters, Minnie, Lizzie, Ella, and Rachel, Minnie was married to Lieutenant Fitch, Ella to Lieutenant Thackara, and Rachel to Dr. Thorndike.

General Sherman was always partial to the West, and believed in its great future.

Mrs. Sherman died Nov. 27, 1888, and was buried in Calvary Cemetery, St. Louis, in a plot selected by herself and husband over twenty years before. Here their two sons and three grandchildren were also buried.

Early in February, 1891, General Sherman took cold, which resulted in his death from bronchial trouble and asthma, Saturday afternoon at 1.50, Feb. 14. He died without apparent pain, all his family about him, except the Rev. Thomas E. Sherman, his son, who was on his way home from Europe.

Though requesting that his body should not lie in state, the family were finally persuaded to allow the thousands of the General's friends to pass by the coffin in his own parlors from ten to four o'clock. There was deep and unfeigned sorrow. The funeral was one never to be forgotten. New York City was draped withmourning. All the shipping bore the emblems of grief, with flags at half-mast. Business was practically suspended and the streets crowded.

For two hours and a half, while bells were tolling, the great procession moved past, with inverted muskets, muffled drums, torn battle-flags, cavalry and artillery, all following the caisson with its heroic dead wrapped in the flag. The caisson in its funereal trappings was drawn by five black horses, three of these abreast. Two of the horses were ridden by artillerymen in blue uniforms, with black helmets and red plumes. Behind the caisson was a soldier leading a handsome black riderless horse, covered with black velvet, on whose back were Sherman's saddle and his riding boots reversed.

The great of the nation were present to do Sherman honor. Among the distinguished generals was Joseph E. Johnston from the South, who was also at the funeral of Grant, and for whom both the Northern generals had great respect and admiration.

As the funeral cortège passed along, appropriate selections were played by the bands. Gilmore's band electrified all hearts by the song turned into a dirge, composed for Sherman by Henry C. Work.

"Bring the good old bugle, boys, we'll have another song,
Sing it with a spirit that will start the world along,
Sing it as we used to sing it, fifty thousand strong,
While we were marching through Georgia.

Chorus

'Hurrah! Hurrah! we bring the jubilee!
Hurrah! Hurrah! the flag that makes you free!'
So we sang the chorus from Atlanta to the sea,
While we were marching through Georgia.

****

"So we made a thoroughfare for Freedom and her train,
Sixty miles in latitude—three hundred to the main;
Treason fled before us, for resistance was in vain,
While we were marching through Georgia."

194

As the body was taken on board the ferry-boat, for the west, the Marine Band played the hymn:—

> "Here bring your bleeding hearts,
> Here tell your anguish;
> Earth has no sorrow
> That Heaven cannot heal."

All along the route to St. Louis great crowds gathered at the stations, the old soldiers weeping like children. At Coshocton, Ohio, five hundred school-children stood near the train, and sang "Nearer, my God, to Thee." At Columbus, Ohio, at the depot, was a large picture of Sherman surmounted by an eagle, and underneath the words, "Ohio's son, the nation's hero."

At St. Louis in the midst of thousands, after a brief service by his son, General Sherman was laid to rest in Calvary Cemetery by the side of his wife, who had died a little more than two years previously. Richard Watson Gilder voiced the sentiment of the nation:

> "But better than martial awe, and the pageant of civic sorrow;
> Better than praise of to-day, or the statue we build to-morrow;
> Better than honor and glory, and history's iron pen,
> Is the thought of duty done, and the love of his fellowmen."

CHARLES HADDON SPURGEON

No one who has sat in the great London Tabernacle, with its six thousand or more eager listeners, and heard Spurgeon preach, natural, brotherly, earnest, and eloquent, can ever forget it. I have seen a whole congregation moved to tears, as he talked of the relationship between God and His children, from the words, "Abba, Father." To hear a man like this, is always to ask the secret of his power. What was the childhood and youth that ushered in this rare manhood? Did he have more talent, more grace, more learning, than other men? He had no wealth, no superior education, no fortuitous circumstances, yet his career has been a remarkable one.

"He is a wonderful man," said Lord Shaftesbury, "full of zeal, affection, faith; abounding in reputation and authority, and, yet— perfectly humble, with the openness and simplicity of a child."

The London Speaker calls him "one of those born orators of whom this generation has seen only two,—himself and John Bright. Gifted with splendid common-sense, with a genuine humor, with a large-hearted love for his fellow-creatures." ...

Charles Haddon Spurgeon was born at Kelvedon, Essex, England, June 19, 1834, the eldest of seventeen children. His father, the Rev. John Spurgeon, was a pastor of the Independent or Congregational Church, a genial, warm-hearted man, and of fine presence. His mother, a Miss Jarvis, was a devoted Christian woman, esteemed for her good works wherever she resided. The Rev. John Spurgeon tells this story of his wife: "I had been from home a great deal, trying to build up weak congregations, and felt that I was neglecting the religious training of my own children while I toiled for the good of others. I returned home with these feelings.

"I opened the door, and was surprised to find none of the children about the hall. Going quietly up the stairs, I heard my wife's voice. She was engaged in prayer with the children. I heard her pray for them, one by one, by name. She came to Charles, and specially prayed for him, for he was of high spirit and daring temper. I listened till she had ended her prayer, and I felt and said, 'Lord, I will go on with Thy work. The children will be cared for.'"

It is related of her, after her brilliant son Charles had become a Baptist; that she said to him, "I have often prayed that you might be saved, but never that you should become a Baptist;" to which he answered, with his accustomed humor, "The Lord has answered your prayer with His usual bounty, and given you more than you asked."

Mrs. Spurgeon died May 18, 1888, having lived to see the wonderful success of her son, and be thankful for it. Mr. Spurgeon was much devoted to his mother, and her death brought on a severe attack of illness.

When Charles was quite young he was carried to the house of his grandfather, the Rev. James Spurgeon, who preached for fifty-four years in the Independent Church in Stambourne. When more than eighty years old he said, "I have not had one hour's unhappiness with my church since I have been over it.... I will never give up so long as God inclines people to come, and souls are saved."

He possessed the not unusual combination, a large family and a small income, and therefore cultivated a few acres of ground, and kept a cow. The latter died suddenly, and Mrs. Spurgeon was much worried over the matter.

"James," she said, "how will God provide for the dear children now? What shall we do for milk?"

"Mother, God has said that He will provide, and I believe that He could send us fifty cows if He pleased," was the reply.

That very day in London, a committee were distributing funds to poor ministers. The Rev. James Spurgeon had never asked aid, but all must have known how meagre was the salary of a village pastor.

One of the committee remarked, "There is a Mr. Spurgeon down at Stambourne, in Essex, who needs some help."

One person said he would give five pounds. Another said, "I will put five pounds to it; I know him: he is a worthy man." Others added, till there were twenty pounds subscribed and sent by letter.

When the letter reached the preacher's house, Mrs. Spurgeon hated to pay the postage, ninepence. When it was opened she was greatly astonished to find twenty pounds, about one hundred dollars. Her husband said, "Now can't you trust God about a cow?"

The Rev. Mr. Spurgeon, dressed in his knee-breeches, buckled shoes, silk stockings, and frilled shirts, must have been an interesting figure. He died when he was eighty-eight years old.

At the home of this grandfather in his early years, Charles found especial delight in reading Bunyan's "Pilgrim's Progress," Foxe's "Book of Martyrs," and De Foe's "Robinson Crusoe."

He read the Scriptures at family prayer, and on one occasion persisted in knowing what the "bottomless pit" in the Book of Revelation meant. If it had no bottom, where did the people go to who dropped into it? These were inconvenient questions to answer.

The Rev. Richard Knill visited the family, and was shown about the garden by the young Charles. In the great yew-tree arbor the good man knelt with the lad, and, with his arm about his neck, prayed for his conversion. In the house, taking him on his knee, Mr. Knill said, "I do not know how it is, but I feel a solemn presentiment that this child will preach the gospel to thousands, and God will bless him to many souls.

"So sure am I of this, that when my little man preaches in Rowland Hill's chapel, as he will do one day, I should like him to promise me that he will give out the hymn commencing,—

"God moves in a mysterious way
His wonders to perform!"

Years later the famous Charles Spurgeon preached in the pulpit of Rowland Hill, in the largest Non-conformist Church in London, before the Metropolitan Tabernacle was built, and read the hymn desired by Mr. Knill.

Charles attended school in Colchester, to which town his family had moved, and became well versed in Latin and mathematics. At an Agricultural College at Maidstone he spent a year, and then went to Newmarket, as an assistant in the school. After a year at the latter place, he removed to Cambridge, to assist a former teacher, Mr. Henry Leeding, in a school for young men. Here he taught, and carried on his own studies as well.

In January, 1850, at the age of sixteen, young Spurgeon was converted in Colchester. He had been for some time troubled at heart, and determined to visit every place of worship in the town, to see if he could not find help. "What I wanted to know," he says, "was, 'How can I get my sins forgiven?' and they never told me that. I wanted to hear how a poor sinner, under a sense of sin, might find peace with God; and when I went I heard a sermon on, 'Be not deceived; God is not mocked,' which cut me up worse, but did not say how I might escape. I went again another day, and the text was something about the glories of the righteous; nothing for poor me!...

"At last one snowy day—it snowed so much I could not go to the place I had determined to go to, and I was obliged to stop on the road; and it was a blessed stop to me—I found rather an obscure street, and turned down a court, and there was a little chapel. I wanted to go somewhere, but I did not know this place. It was the Primitive Methodist Chapel."

Spurgeon went in and sat down, waiting for the service to begin. "At last," he says, "a very thin-looking man came into the pulpit, and opened his Bible, and read these words, 'Look unto Me, and be ye saved, all the ends of the earth.' Just setting his eyes upon me, as if he knew all my heart, he said, 'Young man, you are in trouble.' Well, I was, sure enough. Says he, 'You will never get out of it unless you look to Christ.' And then, lifting up his hands, he cried out, as only aPrimitive Methodist could do, 'Look, look, look! It is only look,' said he. I saw at once the way to salvation. Oh, how I did leap for joy at that moment! I know not what else he said. I did not take much notice of it; I was so possessed with that one thought."

While at Newmarket, young Spurgeon was immersed in the River Lark, at Isleham Ferry, May 3, 1850, on his mother's birthday. He had read the Scriptures for himself, and believed that they favored this method of Baptism, rather than sprinkling. At first the youth of sixteen, in his round jacket and broad white turn-down collar, felt timid at

198

seeing the crowds on either side of the river; but once in the water, his fears left him, and he enjoyed great peace at heart.

Some years later, Spurgeon related a most suggestive incident. "I was a member of the church at Newmarket," he said, "when I first joined the church, and was afterwards transferred to the church at Cambridge, one of the best in England. I attended for three Lord's Days at the communion, and nobody spoke to me. I sat in a pew with a gentleman, and when I got outside I said, 'My dear friend, how are you?'

"He said, 'You have the advantage of me; I don't know you.'

"I said, 'I don't think I have, for I don't know you. But when I came to the Lord's table, and partook of the memories of His death, I thought you were my brother, and I thought I would speak to you.'

"I was only sixteen years of age, and he said, 'Sweet simplicity!'

"Oh, is it true, sir?' I said. 'Is it true?'

"He said, 'It is; but I am glad you did not say this to any of the deacons.'"

The stranger asked the lad home to supper, and they become good friends.

At once young Spurgeon began the Christian work for which he has ever been renowned. He revived a society for tract distribution. He talked in the Sunday-school, and in the vestry of the Independent Chapel, where many gathered to hear him.

Removing to the school in Cambridge, he joined the "Lay Preachers' Association." He was asked to go to the village of Teversham, four miles from Cambridge, to accompany a friend, for an evening service. On the way, Spurgeon said, "I trust God will bless your labors to-night."

"My labors?" said the friend; "I never preached in my life; I never thought of doing such a thing. I was asked to walk with you, and I sincerely hope God will bless you in your preaching."

Spurgeon was astonished; as he says, "My inmost soul being all in a tremble, as to what would happen." The youth of sixteen preached his first sermon from the words, "Unto you, therefore, which believe he is precious," and spoke to the edification of all present.

He was soon asked to go to Waterbeach, a small village, to supply the pulpit. The chapel was a rude one, made out of a barn. In a few months the membership rose from forty to nearly one hundred. The Rev. Mr. Peters had been their pastor for twenty-two years, receiving five pounds for each quarter of the year.

At this time, says one of the deacons, speaking of the young teacher. "He looked so white, and I thought to myself, he'll never be able to preach. "What a boy he is!... I could not make him out: and one day I asked him wherever he got all the knowledge from that he put into his sermons."

"'Oh,' said Spurgeon, 'I take a book, and I pull the good things out of it by the hair of their heads.'"

The mayor of Cambridge one day asked Spurgeon if he had really told the people at Waterbeach "that if a thief got into heaven, he would pick the angels' pockets."

"Yes," replied Spurgeon, "I told them that if it were possible for an ungodly man to go to heaven without having his nature changed, he would be none the better for being there; and then, by way of illustration, I said that were a thief to get in he would remain a thief still, and go round the place picking the angels' pockets."

"But, my dear young friend, don't you know that the angels have no pockets?"

"No, sir," answered the youthful preacher; but added, with ready wit, "but I am glad to be assured of the fact from a gentleman who does know. I will set it all right."

Being urged by his father and some others to take a college course, he agreed to meet Dr. Angus, the tutor of Stepney College, now Regents Park, at the house of Macmillan, the publisher, at Cambridge. Spurgeon went at the time appointed, and was shown into a room, where he waited for two hours for the tutor. Meantime, Dr. Angus had waited in another room, each not having been informed of the presence of the other by the servant; and, unable to wait longer, had taken the train for London. The result was that Spurgeon never went to College. At Cambridge, on the anniversary of the Sunday-school Union in 1853, Spurgeon, then nineteen, was asked to make an address. Mr. Gould, a Baptist deacon, liked the address so much, that he spoke of it to Mr.1 Thomas Olney, one of the deacons in New Park Street Chapel, Southwark, which had been one of the largest and richest of the Baptist churches in London. Mr. Gould thought the Waterbeach youth might put new life into the deteriorating church.

Spurgeon was invited to London to preach a sermon in December, 1853. Scarcely two hundred were in the chapel, which would seat twelve hundred. He preached earnestly from the words, "Every good gift, and every perfect gift, is from above." He was invited to come again for three Sundays in January, and soon asked to preach six months on probation.

He would not promise for more than three months. At the end of that time the church had filled so rapidly, that he was called to the pastorate; and before he was twenty, in 1854, was installed over the Baptist Church, with a salary of £150 a year. He came, as he says, to the great city of London, "a country lad," "wondering, praying, fearing, hoping, believing, ... all alone, and yet not alone; expectant of Divine help, and inwardly borne down by our sense of the need of it."

The church building soon became too small for the crowds which gathered to hear him. He was caricatured in the newspapers, standing beside a "polished" preacher, with his sermon on a velvet cushion. Spurgeon being called "Brimstone and Treacle." Again he was placarded as a man selling fly-paper, with judges, lords, and workingmen all sticking to his hat, or buzzing around him. This was called, "Catch-em-alive-O!" He was represented as "The Fast Train," his hair streaming in the wind, driving the engine. He was again pictured as a gorilla. But Mr. Spurgeon kept on preaching, and the interest deepened.

He has followed the dying words of the great Welsh Baptist minister, Christmas Evans, who used to drive from town to town in his evangelistic work, "Drive on! Drive on!"

"There is such a tendency," Spurgeon once said, "to pull up to refresh; such a tendency to get out of the gig and say, 'What a wonderful horse! Never saw a horse go over hill and down dale like this horse—the best horse that ever was; real sound Methodist or Baptist horse.' Now, brother, admire your horse as much as ever you like, but drive on!"

He worked day and night among his people when the cholera scourge came in the first year of his London pastorate. Neither praise nor blame deterred him in his work. His constant question of his deacons was, both there and at Waterbeach, "Have you heard of anybody finding the Lord?" One said, "I am sure there has been." "Oh," said Spurgeon, "I want to know it, I want to see it;" and he would at once seek out the inquirer.

"I have had nothing else to preach," said Mr. Spurgeon, "but Christ crucified. How many souls there are in heaven who have found their way there through that preaching, how many there are still on earth, serving the Master, it is not for me to tell; but whatever there has been of success has been through the preaching of Christ in the sinner's stead."

The church building soon became too cramped; and while it was being enlarged, from February to May, 1855, the congregation met in Exeter Hall. As the Strand became blocked with people, a Music Hall in Surrey Gardens was used, where ten thousand people gathered to hear him.

A serious accident soon occurred here through the cry of "Fire!" by some malicious person; and in the eagerness to rush out, seven persons were killed and twenty-eight removed to hospitals, badly injured. For days Mr. Spurgeon was prostrated on account of the accident, and unable to preach.

After this, services were held only in the morning, attended by the Prime Minister, the nobility, and the poor. Large numbers were converted. Thirty-five years after this time a Surrey Gardens Memorial Hall was erected near this spot, at a cost of £3,000, as one of the many mission-homes in connection with the Tabernacle work. This commemorates the many conversions in these early days, before the Tabernacle was built.

The "Greville Memoirs" thus describes the minister of twenty-three, preaching to nine thousand people in the Music Hall. "He is certainly very remarkable, and undeniably a fine character,—not remarkable in person; in face resembling a smaller Macaulay; a very clear and powerful voice, which was heard through the hall; a manner natural, impassioned, and without affectation or extravagance; wonderful fluency and command of language, abounding in illustration, and very often of a very familiar kind, but without anything ridiculous or irreverent. He gave me an impression of his earnestness and sincerity; speaking without book or notes, yet his discourse was evidently very carefully prepared.... He preached for about three-quarters of an hour, and, to judge by the use of the handkerchiefs and the audible sobs, with great effect."

The corner-stone of the new Tabernacle was laid Aug. 16, 1859, by Sir Samuel Morton Peto. The building was ready for occupancy in 1861. The opening services lasted a month, the first service being a prayer-meeting, held at seven o'clock on Monday morning, March 18. One thousand persons were present.

The Tabernacle is one hundred and forty-six feet in length, and eighty-one in width. There are five thousand five hundred sittings, and many more can be accommodated. Besides the audience-room, there are rooms for Sunday-schools, working-meetings, and the like. The cost was a little over £31,000, all raised by voluntary effort. All denominations gave, and all parts of the country responded. Mr. Spurgeon spoke in Scotland, giving half the receipts to some needy pastorate, and reserving half for his new church. The church building has always been crowded, so that pewholders were admitted at the side doors by ticket. For many years there have been over five thousand members in the church.

Mr. Spurgeon once said, "Somebody asked me how I got my congregation. I never got it at all.... Why, my congregation got my congregation! I had eighty, or scarcely a hundred, when I first preached. The next time I had two hundred—every one who had heard me was saying to his neighbor, 'You must go and hear this young man.' Next meeting we had four hundred, and in six weeks, eight hundred."

It was not enough for Mr. Spurgeon that crowds were flocking to hear him preach; that in Scotland twenty thousand gathered at a time to listen to him; that at the Crystal Palace, when he was but twenty-three, more than twenty-three thousand people came together to hear him preach, Oct. 7, 1857, the day of national humiliation on account of the Indian mutiny.

Others had been converted, and he wanted them to preach the gospel. They were for the most part poor, and could provide neither clothing nor books for their term of study. He needed a Pastor's College.

It began with one student, and increased to several, cared for in a minister's home, and supported by Mr. Spurgeon.

This incident is related by the Rev. James J. Ellis, of the first student, Mr. T. W. Medhurst. He called upon Spurgeon, and said that he feared he had made a mistake in entering the ministry.

"What do you mean?" asked Spurgeon.

"Well, I've been preaching for five or six months, and have not heard of any conversions."

"You don't expect conversions every time you preach, do you?"

"No, I don't expect them every time," said Mr. Medhurst.

"Then be it unto you according to your faith," was the reply. "If you expect great things from God, you'll get them; if you don't, you won't."

"The large sale of my sermons in America, together with my dear wife's economy," writes Mr. Spurgeon, "enabled me to spend from £600 to £800 a year in my own favorite work; but on a sudden—owing to my denunciations of the then existing slavery in the States—my entire resources from that 'Brook Cherith' were dried up. I paid as large sums as I could from my own income, and resolved to spend all I had, and then take the cessation of my means as a voice from the Lord to stay the effort; as I am firmly persuaded that we ought, under no pretence, to go into debt."

This was Mr. Spurgeon's life-long rule. He once related this story of his childhood. He wanted a slate-pencil, and had no money to buy it. So he went to the shop of a Mrs. Dearson, who kept nuts, cakes, and tops, and got trusted for one, the amount of debt being one farthing. His father heard of it, and reprimanded him severely; told the young Charles, "how a boy who would owe a farthing, might one day owe a hundred pounds, and get into prison, and bring his family into disgrace." The child cried bitterly, and hastened to pay the farthing.

Mr. Spurgeon said in later life, "Debt is so degrading, that if I owed a man a penny, I would walk twenty miles, in the depth of winter, to pay him, sooner than to feel that I was under an obligation.... Poverty is hard, but debt is horrible.... Without debt, without care; out of debt, out of danger; but owing and borrowing are bramble-bushes full of thorns. If ever I borrow a spade of my neighbor, I never feel safe with it for fear I should break it."

"I was reduced to the last pound," says Mr. Spurgeon, "when a letter came from a banker in the city, informing me that a lady, whose name I have never been able to discover, had deposited a sum of £200, to be used for the education of young men for the ministry.... Some weeks after, another £100 came in from the same bank, as I was informed, from another hand.... A supper was given by my liberal publishers, Messrs. Passmore & Alabaster, to celebrate the publishing of my five-hundredth weekly sermon, at which £500 were raised and presented to the funds. The college grew every month, and the number of the students rapidly increased from one to forty."

A "weekly offering" was soon taken at the church for the Pastor's College. This in the year 1869 amounted to £1,869. When "seasons of straitness" came, as Spurgeon says, the "Lord always interposed." On one occasion, £1,000 came from an unknown source.

Mr. G. Holden Pike says of these weekly offerings, "How high a figure the total reached nobody knew; for, as Sunday is a day of rest, the money would not be counted until the following morning. Gold, silver, and copper pieces, together with little packets neatly tied with thread, made up the motley heap. One miniature parcel enclosed fifteen shillings from 'A workingman.' When the whole mass was placed in a strong black bag, I ventured to raise it for the sake of testing its weight.... It was certainly the 'heaviest' collection I had ever set eyes upon, for it was as much as one could conveniently raise from the table with one arm."

A yearly supper was provided by Mr. Spurgeon, at which guests gave as they were able or inclined. At this supper in 1891, £3,000 were subscribed.

After a time the College buildings were erected near the Tabernacle property. A lady gave £3,000 as a memorial to her husband; £2,000 were left as a legacy by a reader of the sermons. The cost of the buildings, £15,000, was paid as soon as the work was done.

The whole number added to the churches by these men educated at the Pastor's College is, as nearly as can be ascertained, considerably over one hundred thousand. Some of these men have gone to India, China, the West Indies, Africa, Australia, among the Jews, and elsewhere.

The annual address of the President, Mr. Spurgeon, was eagerly looked for. That given in 1891, "The Greatest Fight in the World," in defence of the Inspiration of the Bible, has been translated into French, German, Danish, and other languages.

In 1866 another important work was laid upon the busy preacher, whose hands seemed already full. The widow of an Episcopal clergyman, Mrs. Hillyard, was desirous of giving £20,000 to found an orphanage for boys. She was personally unknown to Mr. Spurgeon, but had read his sermons, and had great faith in his spirituality and sense.

Another lady, her husband having given her £500 on the twenty-fifth anniversary of their marriage, made a present of it to the Orphanage. One house was built with it, called "The Silver Wedding House." A gentleman gave £600 for another house; an unknown donor £1,000 for two other houses, and soon after £2,000 more.

In 1868 the Baptist churches of England gave Mr. Spurgeon £1,765 for the Orphanage. One building is called "The Merchant's House;" another, "The Workmen's House."

At the close of 1869, all the buildings or houses for the orphan boys were completed in Stockwell, on the Clapham Road, free from debt, at a cost of £10,200, Mrs. Hillyard's funds being used for endowment.

When the funds were low,—for Mr. Spurgeon says, "Our boys

persist in eating, and wearing out their clothes,"—money was raised by a bazaar, by a fête on his birthday, or in some other way.

The long row of attractive houses for boys did not fill Mr. Spurgeon's heart; there must be similar homes for girls.

In September, 1879, Mr. Spurgeon writes, "Our friends know that we bought a house and grounds called 'The Hawthorns,' for £4,000. This we needed to pay for. For various reasons the payment of the purchase-money for 'The Hawthorns' was delayed until July 30; andon that very morning we received a letter telling us that a gentleman had died, and left £1,500 for the Girls' Orphanage, thus bringing up our total to within a very small sum of the amount required. The whole £4,000 is now secured, including this legacy, and the property is our own."

Not long after, the £11,000 necessary for the first block of buildings was obtained.

In January, 1882, a great bazaar was held, which in three days netted the sum of £2,000 for the Girls' Orphanage. In his opening speech at this bazaar Mr. Spurgeon said, "We don't want to sell anything that is not worth the money paid for it; for we think that such should not be the case when the object is to benefit orphan children. When you leave here, you need not be in the plight of the gentleman who was met by footpads on his way home. 'Your money or your life!' demanded one of them.

"'My dear fellow, I have not a farthing about me. Do you know where I have been? I have been to a bazaar.'

"'Oh, if you've been to a bazaar, we should not think of taking any money from you. We'll make a subscription all round, and give you something to help you home.' That is a bazaar as it ought not to be."

About one thousand boys and girls are now in the Stockwell Orphanage, the larger number of the children coming from Church of England families. Some are also from Roman Catholic, Presbyterian, and Methodist families, as well as Baptist.

Mr. Spurgeon tells this story: "Sitting down in the Orphanage grounds, upon one of the seats, we were talking with a brother trustee, when a funny little fellow, weo should think about eight years of age, left the other boys who were playing around us, and came deliberately up to us. He opened fire in this fashion, 'Please, Mister Spurgeon, I wants to come and sit down on the seat between you two gentlemen.'

"'Come along, Bob and tell us what you want.'

"'Please, Mister Spurgeon, suppose there was a little boy who had no father, who lived in an orphanage with a lot of other little boys who had no fathers; and suppose those little boys had mothers and aunts who comed once a month and brought them apples and oranges, and gave them pennies; and suppose this little boy had no mother and no aunt, and so never came to bring him nice things; don't you think somebody ought to give him a penny? 'Cause, Mister Spurgeon, that's me!'"

Bob received a sixpence from Mr. Spurgeon, and went away with face all aglow.

The Orphanage covers four acres. Each house is complete in itself, and has its own "mother." The boys dine in a common hall; the girls in their respective houses. Both boys and girls assist in domestic duties. "The children are not dressed in a uniform," says Mr. Spurgeon, "to mark them as the recipients of charity."

In 1876 the Redpath Lecture Bureau of Boston asked Mr. Spurgeon to come to America and lecture, they offering to pay him $1,000 in gold for each lecture, and all expenses from England to America and return; but he declined the offer. He did not care to lecture, and would not preach for money.

On Wednesday evening, June 18, 1884, a remarkable jubilee service was held in the Tabernacle on Mr. Spurgeon's fiftieth birthday. Among the speakers was Mr. Spurgeon's father, the Rev. John Spurgeon; his brother,1 the Rev. James A. Spurgeon, of whom Charles said, "If there is a good man on the earth, I think it is my brother;" and the son of the great preacher, young Charles Spurgeon, one of the twins, affectionately called by the people, Charlie and Tommy. Both are ministers of the gospel. D. L. Moody from America also made an earnest address.

On the following evening the good Earl of Shaftesbury presided, and spoke with his wonted power. "Whatever Mr. Spurgeon is in private he is in the pulpit," said the earl; "and what he is in the pulpit he is in private. He is one and the same man in every aspect; and a kinder, better, honester, nobler man never existed on the face of the earth."

Canon Basil Wilberforce, the son of the Bishop, the Rev. Dr. Newman Hall, and others spoke. The Rev. Dr. O. P. Gifford presented an address from the Baptist ministers of Boston and vicinity.

A Spurgeon Jubilee Fund of £45,000 was given at this time. Five years previously a larger sum was given him, £3,000 of it being raised by a bazaar; and a large part of this money was used for seventeen almshouses, in which are the aged members of the Tabernacle. These are near the Elephant and Castle Station.

Another important agency for Christian work in connection with the Tabernacle is the Colportage Association, founded in 1866. The colporteurs sell religious books, conduct temperance and open-air meetings, distribute tracts, visit the sick, and are really home missionaries. The yearly distribution is about a half million Bibles, and as many, or more, books and periodicals.

Mr. Spurgeon loved to give away the Bible. He once said before the British and Foreign Bible Society, "Somebody may say it is of very little use to give away Bibles and Testaments. That is a very great mistake. I have very seldom found it to be a labor in vain to give a present of a Testament. I was greatly astonished about a month ago. A

206

cabman drove me home, and when I paid him his fare, he said, 'It is a long time since I drove you last, sir.'

"'But,' said I, 'I do not recollect you!'

"'Well,' he said, 'I think it is fourteen years ago; but,' he added, 'perhaps you will know this Testament?' pulling one out of his pocket.

"'What,' I said, 'did I give you that?'

"'Oh, yes!' he said; 'and you spoke to me about my soul, and nobody had done that before, and I have never forgotten it.'

"'What,' said I, 'haven't you worn it out?'

"'No,' he said, 'I would not wear it out; I have had it bound.'"

Besides this society, there are ten Bible classes in the Tabernacle; a Loan Tract Society, for the distribution of Mr. Spurgeon's sermons in the neighborhood, and another to spread them in country districts; a Flower Mission, Maternal Society, Mothers' Meetings, Training Class for workers, and the like. There are twenty-three mission stations in connection with the Tabernacle, and twenty-seven Sunday-schools, with over eight thousand scholars.

With all this work, Mr. Spurgeon was a voluminous writer, as well as speaker. He published thirty-seven volumes of sermons, all of which have had an immense circulation. These were regularly printed in many papers. In Australia some of these were published and paid for as advertisements, at a fabulous price, by a gentleman deeply interested in doing good.

The Rev. Thomas Spurgeon wrote home to his father, from Australia, "I received a visit, in Geelong, from a man who produced from his pocket a torn and discolored copy of The Australasian, dated June, 1868, which contained a sermon by C. H. Spurgeon, entitled, 'The Approachableness of Jesus' (No. 809). To this sermon my visitor attributed his conversion.

"He lived alone, about twenty miles from Geelong, and had not entered a place of worship more than four or five times in twenty years, and had taken to drink, until delirium tremens seized upon him. When partially recovered, with not a human being near, his eye lighted on the sermon in the newspaper, which brought him to Jesus."

Mr. Pike says an admirer of Mr. Spurgeon gave away a quarter of a million copies of these sermons. Many were elegantly bound, and presented to the crowned heads of Europe. Others were sent to every member of Parliament, and to all the students of Oxford and Cambridge. Many of these sermons have been translated into German, French, Welsh, Italian, Swedish, Danish, Russian, Spanish, Gaelic, Hungarian, Arabic, Telegu, Hindustani, Syriac, and other languages.

These sermons have been scattered all over the world. At Bryher, one of the Scilly Isles, with a population of one hundred and twenty persons, Spurgeon's sermons are often read in the chapel. In Silesia and Russian Poland, many asked about "Brother Spurgeon," and read his sermons. On the Labrador coast they were read in a mission church Sunday after Sunday.

In 1880 a Red Kaffir, living at Port Elizabeth, South Africa, wrote to Mr. Spurgeon:—

"Dear Sir,—I don't know how to describe my joy and my feelings in this present moment. We never did see each other face to face, but still there is something between you and me which guided me to make these few lines for you. One day, as I was going to my daily work, I met a friend of mine in the street. We spoke about the word of God, and he asked me whether I had ever seen one of Mr. Spurgeon's books....

"He said he bought it from a bookseller. I asked the name of the book, and he said it was 'The Metropolitan Tabernacle Pulpit;' and I went straight to the shop and bought one. I have read a good bit of it. On my reading it, I arrived on a place where Job said, 'Though he slay me, yet will I trust in Him.'

"I am sure I can't tell how to describe the goodness you have done to us, we black people of South Africa. We are black not only outside, even inside; I wouldn't mind to be a black man only in color. It is a terrible thing to be a black man from the soul to the skin; but still I am very glad to say your sermons have done something good to me." ...

David Livingstone carried one of these sermons with him, No. 408, entitled "Accidents not Punishments," in his last sad journey to Africa. Yellow and travel-stained it was found by his daughter Mrs. Bruce in his boxes after his death. He had written across the top, "Very good. D. L."

His son Thomas writes his mother from Auckland, New Zealand, concerning sermon No. 735, "Loving Advice for Anxious Seekers," copied into the Melbourne Argus, "This scrap of newspaper has been given to me by a town missionary here, who regards it as a very precious relic. It came to him from a man who died in the hospital, and bequeathed it to his visitor as a great treasure. The man found it on the floor of a hut in Australia, and was brought by its perusal to a knowledge of the truth as it is in Jesus. He kept it carefully while he lived (for it was discolored and torn when he found it), and on his death-bed gave it to the missionary as the only treasure he had to leave behind him."

In writing "The Treasury of David," seven volumes, Mr. Spurgeon spent a considerable part of twenty years. "During the whole of that period," says the Rev. Robert Shindler, in his valuable life of Spurgeon, "Mr. J. L. Keys, one of Mr. Spurgeon's secretaries, continued to search the library of the British Museum, and other libraries, and to cull from every available source everything worthy of quotation upon the book of Psalms." Over one hundred and twenty thousand volumes have been sold. Dr. Philip Schaff thought it "the most important homiletical and practical work of the age on the Psalter."

Of Spurgeon's "Morning by Morning" and "Evening by Evening," for home reading and devotions, over two hundred thousand copies have been sold.

"Commenting and Commentaries" was a work of great labor, showing his students and others what to use. "If I can save a poor man," he wrote, "from spending his money for that which is not bread, or, by directing a brother to a good book, may enable him to dig deeper into the mines of truth, I shall be well repaid. For this purpose I have toiled, and read much, and passed under review some three or four thousand volumes."

Twenty-seven volumes of the Sword and Trowel, Mr. Spurgeon's magazine, have had an enormous circulation. This is also true of "Lectures to My Students," abounding in sensible suggestions. To those about to become ministers he says:—

"Avoid little debts, unpunctuality, gossiping, nicknaming, petty quarrels, and all other of those little vices which fill the ointment with flies....

"Even in your recreations, remember that you are ministers.... His private life must ever keep good tune with his ministry, or his day will soon set with him, and the sooner he retires the better; for his continuance in his office will only dishonor the cause of God and ruin himself."

Spurgeon urged private prayer upon his young men, and related this incident from Father Faber: "A certain preacher, whose sermons converted men by the scores, received a revelation from heaven that not one of the conversions was owing to his talents or eloquence, but all to the prayers of an illiterate lay brother, who sat on the pulpit steps, pleading all the time for the success of the sermon."

The great John Knox used to say he "wondered how a Christian could lie in his bed all night and not rise to pray."

Of public prayer, Spurgeon said, "Do not let your prayer be long.... 'He prayed me into a good frame of mind,' George Whitefield once said of a certain preacher, 'and if he had stopped there, it would have been very well; but he prayed me out of it again by keeping on.'"

Of the sermon he said, "Preach Christ always and evermore. He is the whole gospel.... Your pulpit preparations are your first business. A man great at tea-drinkings, evening parties, and Sunday-school excursions is generally little everywhere else.

"The sensible minister will be particularly gentle in argument," said Spurgeon. "He should take care not to engross all the conversation," and at the same time, "do not be a dummy."

"Have a good word to say to each and every member of the family,—the big boys and the young ladies and the little girls and everybody. No one knows what a smile and a hearty sentence may do. A man who is to do much with men must love them, and feel at home with them. An individual who has no geniality about him had better be an undertaker, and bury the dead, for he will never succeed in influencing the living."

"Be cool and confident. As Sydney Smith says, 'A great deal of talent is lost to the world for want of a little courage.' ... When a speaker feels, 'I am master of the situation,' he usually is so."

"If a man would speak without any present study, he must usually study much." This Mr. Spurgeon exemplified in his own life. Dr. Theodore Cuyler of New York wrote, after visiting Spurgeon at his home, "Westwood," Beulah Hill, Upper Norwood, "a rural paradise," as he says, "Saturday afternoon is his holiday. For an hour he conducted us over his delightful grounds, and through his garden and conservatory, and then to a rustic arbor, where he entertained us with one of his racy talks, which are as characteristic as his sermons....

"It was six o'clock on Saturday when we bade him 'Good-by,' and he assured us that he had not yet selected even the texts for next day's discourses. 'I shall go down in the garden presently,' said he, 'and arrange my morning discourse and choose a text for that in the evening; then to-morrow afternoon, before preaching, I will make an outline of the second one.' ... He never composes a sentence in advance, and rarely spends over half an hour in laying out the plan of a sermon. Constant study fills his mental cask, and he has only to turn the spigot and draw."

Again he says, "To acquire the art of impromptu speech, one must practise it. It was by slow degrees, as Burke says, that Charles Fox became the most brilliant and powerful debater that ever lived. He attributed his success to the resolution which he formed when very young of speaking well or ill at least once every night. 'During five whole seasons,' he used to say, 'I spoke every night but one, and I regret only that I did not speak on that night too.' At first he may do so with no other auditory than the chairs and books of his study."

Mr. Spurgeon's suggestions about voice, gesture, and throat are helpful. "Think nothing little," he says, "by which you may be even a little more useful. But, gentlemen, never degenerate in this business into pulpit fops, who think gesture and voice to be everything.... When you have done preaching, take care of your throat by never wrapping it up tightly.... If any brother wants to die of influenza, let him wear a warm scarf round his neck, and then one of these nights he will forget it, and catch such a cold as will last him the rest of his natural life. You seldom see a sailor wrap his neck up." Mr. Spurgeon used beef-tea, strong with pepper, for his throat, or a little glass of Chili vinegar and water.

"Beware of being actors! Never give earnest men the impression that you do not mean what you say, and are mere professionals. To be burning at the lips and freezing at the soul is a mark of reprobation....

"Away with gold rings and chains and jewellery! Why should the pulpit become a goldsmith's shop?"

To gain and keep the attention, he says, "The first golden rule is, always say something worth hearing.... Let the good matter which you give them be very clearly arranged.... Be sure, moreover, to speak plainly.... Do not make the introduction too long.... Be interested yourself, and you will interest others.... Many ministers are more than half asleep all through the sermon; indeed, they never were awake at any time, and probably never will be unless a cannon should be fired off near their ear.

"A very useful help in securing attention is a pause. Pull up short every now and then, and the passengers on your coach will wake up.... The next best thing to the grace of God for a preacher is oxygen. Pray that the windows of heaven may be opened, but begin by opening the windows of your meeting-house.

"Be masters of your Bibles, brethren.... Having given precedence to the inspired writings, neglect no field of knowledge.... Know nothing of parties and cliques, but be the pastor of all the flock, and care for all alike."

He urged them not to mind gossips, "who drink tea and talk vitriol;" and "to opinions and remarks about yourself turn also, as a general rule, the blind eye and the deaf ear."

Of Mr. Spurgeon's most popular books, "John Ploughman's Talk; or, Plain Advice for Plain People," and "John Ploughman's Pictures; or, More of His Plain Talk for Plain People," over four hundred and fifty thousand volumes have been sold. These are full of helpful words in homely garb, but most useful for rich and poor alike.

"Don't wait for helpers," he says. "Try those twoo old friends, your strong arms.... Don't be whining about not having a fair start.... The more you have to begin with, the less you will have at the end. Money you earn yourself is much brighter and sweeter than any you get out of dead men's bags.... As for the place you are cast in, don't find fault with that. You need not be a horse because you were born in a stable.... A fool may make money, but it needs a wise man to spend it. If you give all to back and board, there is nothing left for the savings bank. Fare hard and work hard while you are young, and you have a chance of rest when you are old.... No matter what comes in, if more goes out you will always be poor.... Plod is the word. Every one must row with such oars as he has.... Never be security for more than you are quite willing to lose."

Spurgeon was an untiring worker. He had no respect for idleness. "Many of our squires," he said, "have nothing to do but to part their hair in the middle; and many of the London grandees, ladies and gentlemen both alike, as I am told, have no better work than killing time.... The greater these people are, the more their idleness is noticed, and the more they ought to be ashamed of it.

"I don't say they ought to plough, but I do say that they ought to do something for the state, besides being like the caterpillars on the cabbage, eating up the good things; or like the butterflies, showing themselves off, but making no honey...."

"Let me drop on these Surrey Hills, worn out ... sooner than eat bread and cheese and never earn it; better die an honorable death, than live a good-for-nothing life.

"Rash vows are much better broken than kept. He who never changes, never mends.... Learn to say 'No,' and it will be of more use to you than to be able to read Latin.

"An open mouth shows an empty head. Still waters are the deepest, but the shallowest brook brawls the most.... Beware of every one who swears; he who would blaspheme his Maker would make no bones of lying or stealing.... Commit all your secrets to no man ... seeing that men are but men, and all men are frail."

In "John Ploughman's Pictures" he says, "He who cannot curb his temper carries gunpowder in his bosom, and he is neither safe for himself nor his neighbors.... Anger is a fire which cooks no victuals, and comforts no households; it cuts and curses and kills, and no one knows what it may lead to.... It takes a great deal out of a man to get in a towering rage; it is almost as unhealthy as having a fit.... Shun a furious man as you would a mad dog.... A man in a thorough passion is as sad a sight as to see a neighbor's house on fire, and no water handy to put out the flames." Mr. Spurgeon's books number about one hundred volumes.

Mr. Spurgeon was blest in his home-life. On Jan 8, 1856, he married Susannah Thompson, daughter of Mr. Robert Thompson, of Falcon Square. He was married in new Park Street Chapel, before the Tabernacle was built. The church was full at the ceremony, while two thousand persons outside were unable to enter.

Their twin sons, Charles and Thomas, their only children, have always been a comfort to them. The wife has long been an invalid, but has been enabled to do great good in her home and out of it.

Mr. Spurgeon once said of her, "My experience of my first wife, who will, I hope, live to be my last, is much as follows: Matrimony came from Paradise, and leads to it. I never was half so happy before I was a married man as I am now.... I have no doubt that where there is much love there will be much to love, and where love is scant, faults will be plentiful. If there is only one good wife in England, I am the man who put the ring on her finger, and long may she wear it. God bless the dear soul! if she can put up with me, she shall never be put down by me."

From Hull he once wrote her a poem, beginning,—

> "Over the space that parts us, my wife,
> I'll cast me a bridge of song:
> Our hearts shall meet, O joy of my life,
> On its arch unseen, but strong."

"Unkind and domineering husbands," he said, "ought not to

pretend to be Christians, for they act clean contrary to Christ's commands."

Mr. Spurgeon once said of home, "That word home always sounds like poetry to me. It sings like a peal of bells at a wedding, only more soft and sweet, and it chimes deeper into the ears of my heart."

Concerning beer-shops he wrote, "Beer-shops are the enemies of home, and therefore the sooner their licences are taken away the better.... Those beer-shops are the curse of this country; no good ever can come of them, and the evil they do no tongue can tell.... I wish the man who made the law to open them had to keep all the families that they have brought to ruin."

Again he writes, "Certain neighbors of mine laugh at me for being a teetotaller, and I might well laugh at them for being drunk, only I feel more inclined to cry that they should be such fools."

Mrs. Spurgeon's "Book Fund"[1] is well known. In the summer of 1875 Mr. Spurgeon published the first volume of "Lectures to My Students." His wife, feeling that they would do great good, desired to place them in the hands of ministers. Speaking to her husband about it, he said. "Why not do so? How much will you give?"

She had been keeping for years all the crown-pieces which came in her way; and on counting them, found that she had just enough to send away one hundred copies of the book. Others learned of this work, and were glad to aid it.

During the fifteen years since the Book Fund was started, up to 1890, there have been distributed by Mrs. Spurgeon to needy ministers of all denominations, a hundred and twenty-two thousand one hundred and twenty-nine volumes, largely Mr. Spurgeon's sermons, "The Treasury of David," and other works. The books of other authors have also been used.

Besides books, clothing and other needed things have been sent to ministers whose salary was the meager sum of sixty-five pounds per annum, or less. One village pastor for twenty years had received but sixty pounds yearly, and sometimes only forty-five pounds. Some had not purchased a new book in several years, and wrote back most thankful letters.

The money for this work has been furnished by the very poor as well as the rich. After the death of a woman who had had a struggle to support herself by her needle, more than two pounds, all in three-penny pieces, were found wrapped up in a drawer "dedicated to the Lord's work under the hand of Mrs. Spurgeon."

Mr. Spurgeon had suffered from rheumatism for many years, and had been obliged sometimes in winter to go to Mentone, in the South of France. In the middle of May, 1891, he had an attack of la

---

[1] An account of her work may be found in my book, "Social Studies in England."

grippe, from which, after a serious illness, he seemed to rally; but this was only temporary.

On all sides there was the greatest interest and sympathy. The Prince of Wales, Gladstone, the Archbishop of Canterbury, Chief Rabbi Hermann Adler, and scores of the highest in the land, all religious sects, all classes, sent letters or telegrams, to hear about the distinguished sufferer. Gladstone wrote of his "cordial admiration, not only of his splendid powers, but still more of his devoted and unfailing character."

And Spurgeon added to the letter sent back by his wife, July 18, 1891, these lines, "Yours is a word of love such as those only write who have been into the King's country, and have seen much of His face—My heart's love to you."

Mr. Spurgeon was always an admirer of Mr. Gladstone, which was heartily reciprocated. In the year 1880 the former took, for him, an unusually active part in politics. Having to preach for a friend, the Rev. John Offord, Mr. Spurgeon said to him, "I should have been here a quarter of an hour sooner, only I stopped to vote."

"My dear friend," said Offord, "I thought you were a citizen of the New Jerusalem, and not of this world."

"So I am," was the reply; "but I have an old man in me yet, and he is a citizen of the world."

"But you ought to mortify him."

"So I do; for he's an old Tory, and I make him vote Liberal," replied Spurgeon.

In the autumn of 1891, the month of October, the preacher started for Mentone, his friends singing the Doxology as he left Hearne Hill Station, London. "Baron Rothschild's private saloon-carriage was placed at Mr. Spurgeon's service to travel in throughout France to Mentone."

Mr. Spurgeon grew better in the warm climate for a time, and wrote back letters to his church. He soon failed, however; and on the last day of January, 1892, on Sunday, at five minutes past eleven at night, at Hotel Beau Rivage, he passed away. At half-past three he had been unable to recognize his wife, or other friends. He grew weaker, and the end was painless.

The next day the body was almost hidden from sight by the flowers sent by friends. It was embalmed, sealed up in a leaden case, and this was enclosed in a coffin of olive-wood. On it were the last Scripture words uttered by Mr. Spurgeon to his secretary, Mr. J. W. Harrald, before his death, "I have fought a good fight, I have finished my course, I have kept the faith."

After service, Thursday, Feb. 4, at the Scottish Church at Mentone, the body was taken to London, where an immense crowd awaited its coming.

Through all of Tuesday, Feb. 9, the body lay in state in his

214

beloved Tabernacle. Friends had been requested not to send flowers, but to use the money which they would have expended thus, for the Stockwell Orphanage. Yet the body was covered with flowers notwithstanding the request. Wednesday was spent in memorial services, the Tabernacle being crowded until after midnight.

At eleven o'clock Thursday, the 11th, the public funeral service was held. Deputations from sixty religious associations were present. Members of the House of Commons, the Baroness Burdett-Coutts, bishops and laity, all came to honor the distinguished preacher.

The boys of Stockwell Orphanage sang the last hymn announced by Mr. Spurgeon before he became ill,—

> "The sands of time are sinking,
> The dawn of heaven breaks,
> The summer morn I've sighed for,
> The fair sweet morn awakes."

Dr. A. T. Pierson of the United States delivered an earnest address, and the coffin was borne down the aisle, while the great congregation rose and sang,—

> "There is no night in Homeland."

Through four miles of streets, crowds lining the way, the large mourning procession passed,—forty coaches and a vast number of private carriages. Flags were at half-mast, bells were tolled, and houses were draped with black.

At Stockwell Orphanage, on a raised platform covered with the emblems of mourning, five hundred boys and girls, who had loved the great man, once as poor as they, saw the solemn procession pass to the grave. Norwood Cemetery, where none had been admitted save by ticket, was already thronged. After a brief service, the Bishop of Rochester pronounced the benediction, and the sorrowing crowd went back to their homes.

More than two years afterwards, March 21, 1894 the Rev. Thomas Spurgeon was called to succeed his father at the Metropolitan Tabernacle.

The manifold work of Charles Haddon Spurgeon will go on forever, through his books, and through those whose steps he has turned heavenward.

> Say not his work is done;
> No deed of love or goodness ever dies,
> But in the great hereafter multiplies:
> Say it is just begun.

215

PHILLIPS BROOKS

"I never met any man, or any ecclesiastic, half so natural, so manly, so large-hearted, so intensely Catholic in the only real sense, so loyally true in his friendships, so absolutely unselfish, so modest, so unartificial, so self-forgetful.... A blessing and a gracious presence has vanished out of many lives. With a very sad heart I bid him farewell ... the noblest, truest, and most stainless man I ever knew." Thus wrote Canon Farrar of London in The Review of Reviews for March, 1893, two months after the death of Phillips Brooks.

The various pulpits, the press, the millionnaires, the poor, and the lonely, all felt and said nearly the same thing. Canon Farrar wrote elsewhere, before Dr. Brooks's death, "I cannot recall the name of a single divine among us, of any rank, who either equals him as a preacher, or has the large sympathies and the rich endowments which distinguish him as a man."

The Nation said, "The death of Phillips Brooks strikes down the greatest figure left to the American church."

The Rev. Stopford W. Brooke, of the First Unitarian Church of Boston, said, "He was so vigorous, so noble, so persuasive, so ever welcome a guest of all our hearts, that we had almost forgotten he, too, was mortal.... We never once doubted his sincerity, or his large, pure, generous humanity. There was a power in his presence, his smile, the grasp of his hand, that deep and magnificent eye, which triumphed, unconsciously to himself, over all our haggling differences of temperament and opinion, and drew, by the same unconsciousness of itself, our best manhood to his side. I think this long consistent unconsciousness of himself was one of the great qualities that so endeared him to us all. Here was a man possessed of most remarkable gifts,—an extraordinary vitality, an astonishing 'volume velocity' and beauty of language, a rich and fertile imagination which idealized everything it touched, a power of feeling which rose and swept into his audience like the tides in the Bay of Fundy; and yet he never seemed aware that he was anything exceptional.... I believe that greatness is more common, goodness is far more common, than that unconsciousness with which he wore his greatness and goodness."

Stopford Brooke speaks of another remarkable characteristic of Phillips Brooks,—"His radiance and his joy. No one who has read at all carefully the literature of our time can have failed to remark how dominant in it is the note of sadness. The leaders of the past generation bore, with a certain sombre melancholy, the burden of the chaos, as Carlyle puts it, which they were endeavoring to fashion into cosmos."

Not so Phillips Brooks. "Goodness and happiness, duty and joy, were constant companions in his life. We looked at him, listened to

216

him, talked with him, and knew he had saved and kept through many long years the soul's best secret. Through all that he said and did there ran this river, fresh, clear, and abundant, of inner joy. What an inspiration that joy was to us!"

Dr. Samuel Eliot, a member of Phillips Brooks's church, and his life-long friend, says in the eulogy of him, delivered at the Boston Memorial Meeting, "He was blessed with a hopefulness of which most of us have but a comparatively scanty share. No trait of his was more conspicuous. No single source of his power over his generation was more abundant or more effective. Whatever the foreground might harbor in shadows, he looked beyond into the distance and saw it radiant....

"How he helped others to be hopeful also, how many shackles he thus loosed from the heavy-laden, how he thus encouraged his people to work their way forward to a future filled with promise, is a familiar story. His hopefulness gave him his strong hold upon young men. To them, always looking before and not behind, he stood beckoning, and the fire caught from him spread through them and out from them. Neither they, nor any others, may have known all the hope that was in him; indeed, he may not have known it all himself. It often seemed as if he were hoping for brighter days and holier lives than are consistent with human imperfections."

Dr. Eliot, after speaking of Phillips Brooks's affection, playfulness of conversation with his friends, his humor, which rendered his companionship charming, his delight in children, his unconsciousness of all his distinctions and successes, the unchangeable simplicity of his habits, his manners, his opinions, says, "These are pleasant recollections to all who loved him.... They linger like the soft glow of a summer twilight, now that his day on earth is over....

"This great man was never greater than he was in the sight of those who knew him best. 'I shall not change,' he said to a brother clergyman who seems to have been doubtful whether he would be the same after being a bishop,—'I shall not change, and you will always find me just as you have found me heretofore.'"

The Rev. Arthur Brooks, D.D., in a memorial sermon preached in the Church of the Incarnation, New York City, says that on the afternoon of the day of the consecration of his brother as a bishop, fearing that some of his friends might not come to see him as often as heretofore, he said earnestly, "Don't desert me."

Phillips Brooks was born Dec. 13, 1835, on High Street, Boston, the second in a family of six sons. His mother, Mary Ann Phillips, the granddaughter of Judge Phillips, the founder of Phillips Academy, Andover, was a woman of fine intellect and unusually earnest piety. His father, William Gray Brooks, a hardware merchant, whose ancestors, like the Phillipses, held high social position, and power in the State as well, was a man of refinement and scholarly tastes.

The son Phillips, says the Rev. Julius H. Ward in the New England Magazine for January, 1892, "seems to have inherited from his mother the deep and earnest piety and intellectual strength which have always been his characteristics, and from his father the robust physical constitution, the strong and resolute spirit, which he has shown in using them."

"Parents whose praise," says Dr. Arthur Brooks, "because of this great son, is in the churches to-day, earned it by self-denial and the subordination of all interests and ambitions to the training and education of a family of boys.... That love to Christ which glowed in his words and flashed in his eye, was caught from a mother's lips, and was read with boyish eyes as the central power of a mother's soul and life."

Mother-love was always a strong force in the heart of Phillips Brooks. It is related that when some one asked him if he was not afraid when he first preached before Queen Victoria, he replied, "Oh no; I have preached before my mother."

He said in one of his sermons, "The purest mingling of all elements into one character and nature which we ever see, is in the Christian mother, in whom the knowledge of all that she knows, and the love which she feels for her child, make not two natures, as they often do in men, in fathers, but perfectly and absolutely one."

He often spoke of "that self-sacrifice which is the very essence of her motherhood."

At eight years of age, Phillips and his brother William Gray, a year and a half older, were at the Adams School in Mason Street, and entered the Latin School, then on Bedford Street, in 1846, when Phillips was eleven years old. Here he was a quiet, good scholar, excelling in the languages, and all unconscious of his great future. His teacher, Francis Gardner, was a sad, earnest man, whom Phillips Brooks described nearly forty years later, when he spoke, April 23, 1885, at the two hundred and fiftieth anniversary of the Latin School, the oldest school in America.

"Tall, gaunt, muscular ... impressing every boy with the strong sense of vigor, now lovely and now hateful, but never for a moment tame or dull or false; indignant, passionate, an athlete both in body and mind.... He was not always easy for the boys to get along with. Probably it was not always easy for him to get along with himself. But it has left a strength of truth and honor and devoted manliness which will always be a treasure in the school he loved."

In this school young Brooks learned his fondness for and advocacy of the public school system. He said in his anniversary address, "The German statesman, if you talk with him, will tell you that, with every evil of his great military system, which makes every citizen a soldier for some portion of his life, it yet has one redeeming good. It brings each young man of the land once in his life directly into the country's service; lets him directly feel its touch of dignity and

218

power; makes him proud of it as his personal commander, and so insures a more definite and vivid loyalty through all his life.

"More graciously, more healthily, more Christianly, the American public school does what the barracks and the drill-room try to do. Would that its blessing might be made absolutely universal! Would that it might be so arranged that once in the life of every Boston boy, if only for three months, he might be a pupil of a public school; might see his city sitting in the teacher's chair; might find himself, along with boys of all degrees and classes, simply recognized by his community as one of her children! It would put an element into his character and life which he would never lose. It would insure the unity and public spirit of our citizens."

These words of Phillips Brooks. Mr. Edwin D. Mead thinks, should "be printed in letters of gold, and hung up in every home where parents are thinking of sending their children into private schools, thereby condemning them to a narrower and less sturdy education than that given by the State, while also thus withdrawing their own personal interest from the public schools, which need the personal interest and love of every earnest citizen to-day as they have never needed them before."

From the Boston Latin School young Brooks went to Harvard College when he was about fifteen and a half years old. "The college attracted him with its promises," writes the Rev. Dr. Alexander McKenzie, in the May, 1893, New England Magazine. "Even the Triennial Catalogue was stimulating as he read there of twenty-five men named Phillips and twenty named Brooks, who had graduated from this university. The place for his own name which should join the two lines was inviting."

And yet Phillips Brooks in no way distinguished himself in college, save, perhaps, in composition. His professors were such men as Agassiz, Longfellow, Asa Gray, Lowell, and others. During his junior year he roomed in Massachusetts Hall, and his senior year in Stoughton.

One of Brooks's class writes, "He was a general favorite, always hearty and kindly, with an abounding sense of humor, which he carried with him through life.... No one could have surmised what profession he would choose, and almost any calling would have seemed appropriate."

Mr. Robert Treat Paine, his classmate, says, "At college he cared little for sport, but preferred to read omniverously almost everything and anything that came in his way." Tennyson was an especial favorite.

After graduation Brooks returned to the Boston Latin School, and became a tutor. Here he failed. He could not or would not be a strict disciplinarian, and he left the position.

Francis Gardner, his former teacher, had said that he "never knew a man who had failed as a schoolmaster to succeed in any other occupation." In one case at least he was mistaken. The young man might and did fail as a schoolteacher; he was a great success as a preacher and a man.

He went back to his college president, James Walker, to advise about his future work in life, and decided to enter the ministry.

At the suggestion of his pastor, Dr. Alexander H. Vinton, of St. Paul's Church on Tremont Street, he went to a theological seminary at Alexandria, Va., in 1856. Here his piety seemed to deepen, as he gave himself to study and to mission work.

He preached his first sermon in a little hamlet called Sharon, two or three miles from the seminary, urged to go thither by a classmate. The people were mostly poor whites and negroes, who, being plain themselves, enjoyed the plain preaching. The schoolhouse was soon crowded, and more came than could be accommodated.

His classmate told, at his home in Philadelphia, of this good work. The Church of the Advent in that city needed a rector. A committee came to hear Brooks, of course without his knowledge, were delighted, and called him to their poor parish.

Fearful that he would not give satisfaction, young Brooks, now twenty-four years of age, consented to preach for three months, and at the end of that time accepted the call for a year, at a salary of one thousand dollars.

"The dissatisfaction with his work," says Dr. Arthur Brooks, "and the eagerness to press on to something better and more complete, while all the time men were praising what he had done, was always a recognized feature of his power."

Fortunately for young Brooks, Dr. Vinton had moved to Philadelphia, and had become rector of the Church of the Holy Trinity, in a wealthy part of the city.

Not forgetting his former parishioner, he invited the young preacher to occupy his pulpit Sunday afternoons. Both here and at the Advent, Phillips Brooks soon won a place in the hearts and lives of his hearers.

Dr. Vinton was called to St. Mark 's Church, in New York, and Phillips Brooks was asked to take his place at the Holy Trinity. He did not accept till invited the third time, and finally became rector Jan. 1, 1862, when he was twenty-seven.

During Phillips Brooks's ten years in Philadelphia, he took a fearless stand for the colored people, and in all that related to the Civil War.

When the three months' men were called out to defend Philadelphia from a feared attack of the Confederates, young Brooks, with a shovel on his shoulder, was in the van to help throw up earthworks.

In his Thanksgiving sermon, Nov. 26, 1863, he thanked God "that the institution of African slavery in our beloved land is one big

220

year nearer to its inevitable death than it was last Thanksgiving Day."

When Abraham Lincoln lay dead at Independence Hall, in the journey from Washington to Springfield, Ill., Phillips Brooks preached a noble sermon, April 23, 1865. Many have recalled these words, which might be written of himself, now that he has gone from us.

"In him," said Phillips Brooks, "was vindicated the greatness of real goodness and the goodness of real greatness.... How many ears will never lose the thrill of some kind word he spoke—he who could speak so kindly to promise a kindness that always matched his word. How often he surprised the land with a clemency which made even those who questioned his policy love him the more for what they called his weakness; seeing the man in whom God had most embodied the discipline of freedom not only could not be a slave, but could not be a tyrant....

"The gentlest, kindest, most indulgent man that ever ruled a state!... The shepherd of the people!... What ruler ever wore it like this dead President of ours? He fed us faithfully and truly. He fed us with counsel when we were in doubt, with inspiration when we sometimes faltered, with caution when we would be rash, with calm, clear, trustful cheerfulness through many an hour when our hearts were dark. He spread before the whole land feasts of great duty and devotion and patriotism, on which the land grew strong. He fed us with solemn, solid truths....

"He showed us how to love truth, and yet be charitable—how to hate wrong and all oppression, and yet not treasure one personal injury or insult. He fed all his people, from the highest to the lowest, from the most privileged to the most enslaved. Best of all, he fed us with a reverent and genuine religion."

When Harvard celebrated the close of the war, and Lowell gave his immortal "Commemoration Ode," Phillips Brooks offered the prayer, as only one with his great heart and eloquent lips could pray. Nobody ever forgot that prayer. Harvard from that day forward knew and honored her son.

A few years later, May 30, 1873, Phillips Brooks spoke at the dedication of Memorial Hall in Andover. He said, "They saw that their country was like a precious vase of rarest porcelain, priceless while it was whole, valueless if it was broken into fragments. What they died to keep whole may we in our several places live to keep holy!"

In 1869 Phillips Brooks was called to Trinity Church, Boston. He loved his native city, "the home of new ideas," as he called it, and accepted. At that time the church edifice of Quincy granite was on Summer Street. It was burned in the great fire of 1872, whereupon the wealthy congregation, idolizing their pastor, built on the Back Bay, at Copley Square, the present Trinity Church edifice, costing about one million dollars, one of the handsomest and most complete church buildings on this continent. It was designed by the famous architect, Mr. H. H. Richardson. It is in the form of a Latin Cross.

"The style of the church," says Mr. Richardson, "may be characterized as a free rendering of the French Romanesque, inclining particularly to the school that flourished in the eleventh century in Central France,—the ancient Aquitaine."

Four thousand five hundred piles were driven to support the building, the tower of which, resting on four piers, weighs nearly nineteen million pounds. Mr. John La Farge decorated the building with great skill and beauty. Dr. Vinton, the venerable pastor of Phillips Brooks's boyhood, preached the consecration sermon in the new church, Feb. 9, 1877.

Phillips Brooks did not wish that this grand church should be for the people of Trinity only. The galleries were made free, and the rented pews could be occupied by strangers after a stated hour. He said, "Such a church as this has no right to exist, or to think that it exists, for any limited company who own its pews. It would not be a Christian parish if it harbored such a thought. No, let the world come in. Let all men hear, if they will, the truths we love. Let no soul go unsaved through any selfishness of ours."

This year Mr. Brooks was made a Doctor of Divinity by Harvard University. He had already been one of her overseers for several years. In 1881 the beloved Dr. Andrew P. Peabody resigned his office as preacher at Harvard, and the President and Fellows naturally turned to Phillips Brooks as the one of all others who could win and hold the students to a higher spiritual life. He was chosen preacher to the university, and Plummer Professor of Christian Morals.

Dr. Brooks loved his Alma Mater, and hated to refuse, but Trinity Church and Boston could not spare him. When he gave his answer, President Eliot says, "He was very pale and grave, and he spoke like a man who had seen a beatific vision which he could not pursue."

More and more, however, Phillips Brooks became a part of the higher life of Harvard. The religious work at the college is divided among six preachers. In each half-year, for two or three weeks, a minister conducts morning prayers, preaches Sunday evenings, and each forenoon is at Wadsworth House, to talk with any students who may choose to come.

These were precious seasons to Phillips Brooks: for he loved young men, and they loved him. The Rev. Julius Ward tells of a letter written by Dr. Brooks to the father of a freshman, in which the warm heart of the preacher exclaims. "What dear, beautiful creatures these boys are!"

For twenty-two years Phillips Brooks did his grand work in Trinity Church, and, indeed, in the whole cityo and the whole land. He said, "No man has come to true greatness who has not felt in some degree that his life belongs to his race, and that what God gives him He gives him for mankind."

When the Rev. Dr. George A. Gordon of Boston remarked to Dr. Brooks, after hearing his twentieth anniversary sermon, that he had also heard him preach his ninth, he replied, "Twenty years is a long time in a man's life, and I cannot expect more than another twenty;" and then with a serious but eager look, added, "And then I hope something better will come."

He preached to overflowing congregations at Trinity, at the Young Men's Christian Union, the Moody Tabernacle, Appleton Chapel at Harvard, and elsewhere. He did not seem to realize that men crowded the house to hear him. To a brother minister in a Boston suburb, where he frequently preached, and where every inch of standing-room was utilized when he came, he remarked, "Grey, what a splendid congregation you have!"

He was extremely modest. When invited to furnish some data for his college class record, he wrote, "I have had no wife, no children, no particular honors, no serious misfortune, and no adventures worth speaking of. It is shameful at such times as these not to have a history, but I have not got one, and must come without."

Phillips Brooks was as great in pastoral work as in preaching. He said in his "Lectures on Preaching," delivered at the Yale Divinity School, in January and February, 1877, "The preacher needs to be pastor, that he may preach to real men. The pastor must be preacher, that he may keep the dignity of his work alive. The preacher who is not a pastor grows remote. The pastor who is not a preacher grows petty.... Be both; for you cannot really be one unless you also are the other."

He visited his people, both poor and rich. Two young men had attended Trinity Church for a time, and then ceased going. They roomed at the top of a high building in a plain quarter of the city. One day, answering a rap at their door, they beheld the majestic figure of Phillips Brooks. "Well, boys," he said, grasping them cordially by the hand, "you did not expect to see me here, did you?"

Indeed, they did not, for they supposed that the rector did not know them even by sight. They went regularly to Trinity after that friendly visit.

A physician tells this story, which has appeared in the press. He said to a poor woman whom he had visited, "You don't need any more medicine. What you need now is nourishment and fresh air. You need to get out."

"But I have nobody to leave with the children," was the reply.

"Well, you must manage to get out somehow," was the response.

The doctor dropped in a day or two later to see how the poor woman had "managed." She had told her troubles to the man who bore many burdens cheerfully, Phillips Brooks; and he was there caring for the children while the poor mother took the air.

Dr. Brooks loved mission work. Like Charles Kingsley, he was always very close in heart with the poor and the laborers. He said, "It is not wealth simply in itself,—it is the pride of wealth, the indifference of wealth, the cruelty of wealth, the vulgarity of wealth, in one great word, the selfishness of wealth, which really makes the poor man's heart ache and the poor man's blood boil, and constitutes the danger of a community where poor men and rich men live side by side." He was especially interested in St. Andrew's Church on Chambers Street, which was under the care of Trinity. Here one of the first, if not the first, girls' clubs in the country was organized, to which Dr. Brooks delighted to speak of his travels abroad. The Vincent Hospital, the Guild Hall of St. Andrew's, hung with pictures, gifts from him, the Kindergarten for the Blind,—all were dear to his heart.

Phillips Brooks was a generous man, with both money and time. He helped many a boy through college. On one occasion he received a check for one hundred dollars from a parish where he had preached, and immediately sent it to a poor clergyman. To a chapel in a suburban town he gave five hundred dollars towards paying its debt.

He did not like to have his photograph taken and sold; but when informed by those who were holding a fair for St. Andrew's Mission that they would probably make fifty dollars through such sale, he immediately sent a check for that amount.

He was finally prevailed upon to sit for his picture in 1887. In the following eight months more than three thousand photographs were sold. Four years later an arrangement was made whereby a royalty was paid on each picture, and the proceeds used in mission work.

A lady desired some instruments for a medical missionary about to start for Japan. She applied to Phillips Brooks, with the thought that some of his wealthy parishioners might provide them. "A good set will cost one hundred dollars," she said; "but an inferior one can be bought for fifty dollars."

"Would you send your son to the war with an old-fashioned musket," he said, "instead of a rifle? The man who goes to fight Satan in his strongholds must have the best appliances that can be obtained." And Dr. Brooks paid the money from his own pocket.

A printer, the husband of a woman attending Dr. Brooks's church, became ill, and the men in the office raised money to send their fellow-workman to California. The preacher heard of it, and called at the building. The cashier spoke through the tube to the foreman in the composing-room, saying that a gentleman wished to see him. "Send him up," was the reply. And up four flights walked Phillips Brooks, and quietly slipped twenty dollars into the foreman's hands, though refusing to allow his name to be put on the subscription paper.

He gave his time generously. When his private secretary, the Rev. William Henry Brooks, DD., said to him that in using so much time for others he had none left for himself, he replied, "I have plenty of time." Being asked "Where?" he answered, "In the railroad cars."

Soon after Phillips Brooks became bishop he was urged to have office hours, but refused. He said, writes his secretary, in a sketch of the great leader, "A clergyman may come from a distance to see me, and be compelled to return very soon. Not knowing my office hours (should there be such), he might fail of the accomplishment of his errand, and so have his journey to no purpose. Or a layman, leaving his business to consult with me, not knowing of the observance of office hours, might find his time wasted, and be disappointed of the desired interview. No, I am not willing to have office hours. If people wish to see me I ought to and will see them."

When some one expressed fear that these numberless calls would wear him out, he said, "God save the day when they won't come to me."

When I had occasion myself two or three times to consult him, he never seemed in a hurry, never cold or indifferent, never ostentatious,—only small souls are that,—and never exclusive. He had so mastered himself as not to be annoyed; and such mastery over self gives mastery over others.

He answered letters by the thousands; indeed, none ever went unanswered. He was like Longfellow in this respect,—a true gentleman.

He received letters from all countries, and upon all subjects. A lady wrote from the South, wishing a position in the house of one of the diocesan institutions, with her two children, and if that were not possible, asked that he would recommend a boarding-place. Phillips Brooks was abroad, but sent the letter to his secretary, asking that he send her the desired information. "Be sure," wrote Dr. Brooks, "and tell her that the answer was not delayed any longer than was absolutely necessary. Explain to her that I am in Europe."

A widow in Minnesota, whose husband, a Massachusetts man, had been killed in the war, could not prove that he was her husband, as she had lost her marriage certificate, and therefore could not obtain a pension. She knew the name of the minister who married her, but he was dead. Phillips Brooks took time to find evidence of her marriage, and she received her pension.

A letter came from New York City, asking that a list of all the papers and periodicals published by the several parishes in Dr. Brooks's diocese be sent. It was a work of many hours, but it was done.

The Girls' Friendly Magazine tells this incident. Phillips Brooks said to a friend in his study, "Who is this man who writes this letter? You ought to be able to tell me, for he comes from your town. He wants to know if I think it is right to play chess."

"That man," said the friend, "is a poor old crank. There is nothing for you to do but to throw his letter in the waste-basket."

"That I will not do," was the answer of Phillips Brooks. "He has

225

written me a courteous letter, and I am going to return him a courteous answer, like a gentleman."

Phillips Brooks was extremely fond of children, as one may see from his letters to his nieces, published in the August, 1893, Century Magazine, or from the beautiful picture in "The Child and the Bishop," where, in 1890, Dr. Brooks holds, as he says, "'Beautiful Blessing' in my happy arms."

In 1882-83 he spent over a year in Europe, sailing in the Servia about the middle of June, 1882, with his friend, the Rev. Dr. McVickar of Philadelphia, with other friends. Dr. Brooks visited England, France, Italy, India, and Spain.

From Venice he writes to his niece Gertie, the daughter of William Gray Brooks, in a Boston bank, "Do go into my house, when you get there, and see if the doll and her baby are well and happy, but do not carry them off; and make the music-box play a tune, and remember your affectionate uncle,

Phillips."

The people of Trinity Church had built for their pastor a beautiful home on Clarendon Street. In one of the closets were kept dolls for his nieces. This home was the scene of many merry-makings for the children of his brothers, and for other children.

From Jeypoor he writes to Gertie about the monkeys of India, and the nose-jewels of the women, and tells her he has got a nose-jewel for her. He rides on a great elephant, "almost as big as Jumbo."

To Josephine, the little daughter of the Rev. John Cotton Brooks, his brother, in Springfield, Mass., be sends an amusing poem of his own composition. From England he writes that he wished the strawberries grew on trees, as it was difficult for him to pick them, as one might imagine from his great size,—six feet four inches tall, and large frame in proportion.

At Badgastein he takes a bath for Gertie, who has rheumatism, back in America; and from Chamouni, he writes her that she must get well and strong, "to play with me."

He writes to his brother William interesting accounts of India. Bombay, with its great hospital for sick and wounded animals, where "they cure them if they can, or keep them till they die," is very curious. It is to be hoped that we, with our boasted civilization, will some time be as kind to animals as they are in India.

He preaches at Delhi. He is extremely interested in Benares, with its five thousand Hindoo temples, the "very Back Bay of Asia." He sees thousands of pilgrims bathing in the sacred Ganges to wash their sins away, or burn their dead upon its banks.

Phillips Brooks preached during his absence at St. Botolph's Church, Boston, Lincolnshire, England; at the Chapel Royal, Savoy, London; at St. Paul's Cathedral, the Temple Church, St. Margaret's, at Westminster Abbey, at Lincoln Cathedral, Oxford and Cambridge

Universities, and elsewhere, always to the great delight of his hearers. He met such men as Browning and Tennyson. He was the warm friend of the lamented Dean Stanley.

Of Browning he writes, in "Letters of Travel," "He was one of the men whom I wanted most to see here; a pleasant gentleman, full of talk about London and London people, with not a bit of the poet about him externally."

Again he writes, "I dined with Mr. Forster and Mr. Bright, and had our great English friend pretty much to myself for two hours. He is a great talker, especially when he gets onto America; and he knows what he is talking about. Both he and Forster are friends worth having. Bright, personally, wins you in a minute by his frankness and cordialness and manliness of his greeting."

He attended one of Mrs. Gladstone's receptions; met Mr. Gladstone at dinner at Mr. Bryce's; breakfasted with Matthew Arnold, "and liked him very much;" met Jean Ingelow, Mrs. Ritchie (Thackeray's daughter), Hughes, and many others.

Dr. Brooks returned to Boston Sept. 22, and the people received him with open arms.

Dr. Brooks was a Broad Churchman, and broad in every sense of the word. His secretary tells of a conversation he had with the rector, when, after differing in opinion, he said to Phillips Brooks, "I am very sorry that I have said what I have just said."

"Why?" was asked.

"Because it is not pleasant to me to differ with you in opinions," was the reply of the secretary. Dr. Brooks answered with much earnestness, "This is a free country, and every man has the right to express his own opinions."

Phillips Brooks was one of the most tolerant of men. In two lectures on "Tolerance," delivered before the students of several divinity schools of the Episcopal Church, he said, "Tolerance is the willing consent that other men should hold and express opinions with which we disagree, until they are convinced by reason that those opinions are untrue.

"I know some ministers," he said, "who want all their parishioners to think after their fashion, and are troubled when any of their people show signs of thinking for themselves, and holding ideas which the minister does not hold. Thank God, the human nature is too vital, especially when it is inspired with such a vital force as Christian faith, to yield itself to such unworthy slavery....

"Bidden to believe that souls would be punished for wrong-thinking, people have come to doubt whether souls would be punished for anything at all. The only possibility of any light upon the darkness, any order in the confusion, must lie in the clear and unqualified assertion that such as God is can punish such as men are for nothing except wickedness, and that honestly mistaken opinions are not wicked....

"The only ground for us to take is simply the broad ground that error is not punishable at all. Error is not guilt. The guilt of error is the fallacy and fiction which has haunted good men's minds."

Again he said, "Insincerity (whether it profess to hold what we think is false or what we think is true), cant, selfishness, deception of one's self or of other people, cruelty, prejudice,—these are the things with which the Church ought to be a great deal more angry than she is. The anger which she is ready to expend upon the misbeliever ought to be poured out on these."

"The noblest utterance of hopeful tolerance in all that noble century," said Dr. Brooks of the Pilgrims, "was in the famous speech in which John Robinson, their minister, bade loving farewell to his departing flock at Leyden, in which occur those memorable words, 'I am verily persuaded, I am very confident, that the Lord has more truth to break out of His holy word.'"

"At the consecration of Trinity Church," says the Rev. Julius H. Ward, "he invited prominent Unitarian clergymen, and at least one layman, to receive the communion." And yet Phillips Brooks's one gospel message, in which he believed and spoke, was the power of Christ unto salvation.

"Of the Episcopal Church," he said, "there are some of her children who love to call her in exclusive phrase The American Church. She is not that; and to call her that would be to give her a name to which she has no right. The American Church is the great total body of Christianity in America, in many divisions, under many names ... as a whole bearing perpetual testimony to the people of America of the authority and love of God, of the redemption of Christ, and of the sacred possibilities of man....

"The church which to-day effectively denounces intemperance and the licentiousness of social life, the cruelty or indifference of the rich to the poor, and the prostitution of public office, will become the real church of America. Our church has done some good service here. She ought to do more.... She ought to blow her trumpet in the ears of the young men of fortune, summoning them from their clubs and their frivolities to do the chivalrous work which their nobility obliges themo to do for their fellow-men. She ought to speak to Culture, and teach it its responsibility."

Five volumes of Dr. Brooks's sermons have been published and read widely: one in 1878; another in 1881, "The Candle of the Lord and Other Sermons,"—the first sermon was preached in London, and attracted wide attention; in 1883, "Sermons in the English Churches;" in 1886, "Twenty Sermons," dedicated to the memory of Frederick Brooks, his brother; and in 1890, "The Light of the World and Other

Sermons," dedicated to the memory of his "brother, George Brooks, who died in the great war."

The Rev. Frederick Brooks, who was the talented young pastor of St. Paul's Church in Cleveland, Ohio, was drowned by falling one dark evening through the Charlestown draw of the Boston and Lowell Railroad bridge. The last inspiring talk which he made was at one of the Temperance Friendly Inns in Cleveland, where he encouraged us with his words of sympathy and interest.

Phillips Brooks wrote two other books, "Lectures on Preaching," and the "Bohlen Lectures," on "The Influence of Jesus." Besides these he has written several Christmas carols of extreme beauty, and some pamphlets. All his books have gone through many editions, and, like Spurgeon's, have been read by thousands.

In an address on "Biography," delivered at Phillips Exeter Academy, he said that he would rather have written a great biography than any other great book.

The "Lectures on Preaching" abound, like all his work, in short, concise sentences full of meaning, and should be read especially by every one who intends to preach.

He tells young men that the talk about prevalent aversion to hearing the gospel is foolish. "The age," he says, "has no aversion to preaching as such. It may not listen to your preaching. If that prove to be the case, look for the fault first in your preaching, and not in the age. I wonder at the eagerness and patience of congregations.... Never fear, as you preach, to bring the sublimest motive to the smallest duty, and the most infinite comfort to the smallest trouble."

The necessary qualities in a preacher, Phillips Brooks thinks, are, "Personal piety,—nothing but fire kindles fire,"—hopefulness; such physical condition as comes from a due regard to health; enthusiasm; "the quality that kindles at the sight of men, that feels a keen joy at the meeting of truth and the human mind."

First among the elements of power, Phillips Brooks puts "personal uprightness and purity." "No man permanently succeeds in the ministry who cannot make men believe that he is pure and devoted; and the only sure and lasting way to make men believe in one's devotion and purity is to be what one wishes to be believed to be." He said. "No man can do much for others who is not much himself.... The priest must be the most manly of all men."

The second element of power is "freedom from self-consciousness." "No man ever yet thought whether he was preaching well without weakening his sermon."

The third element is "genuine respect for the people whom he preaches to." "There is no good preaching in the supercilious preacher."

The fourth is "gravity." Dr. Brooks thinks the "merely solemn ministers are very empty ... cheats and shams;" but thinks the "clerical jester" merits "the contempt of Christian people." "He is full of Bible

229

jokes.... There are passages in the Bible which are soiled forever by the touches which the hands of ministers who delight in cheap and easy jokes have left upon them.... Refrain from all joking about congregations, flocks, parish visits, sermons, the mishaps of the pulpit, or the makeshifts of the study. Such joking is always bad, and almost always stupid; but it is very common, and it takes the bloom off a young minister's life." Dr. Brooks was especially careful in remarks about any person.

The fifth element of power is "courage." "If you are afraid of men, and a slave to their opinion, go and do something else. Go and make shoes to fit them."

Phillips Brooks then turns to the dangers which beset young preachers. The first is self-conceit. "He who lives with God must be humble," he has said in his sermon, "How to Abound." Another danger is narrowness. Still another is self-indulgence. "We are apt to become men of moods, thinking we cannot work unless we feel like it.... The first business of the preacher is to conquer the tyranny of his moods, and to be always ready for his work. It can be done.... Resent indulgences which are not given to men of other professions. Learn to enjoy and be sober; learn to suffer and be strong. Never appeal for sympathy."

Again he said, "The clergy are largely what the laity make them.... It was not good that the minister should be worshipped and made an oracle. It is still worse that he should be flattered and made a pet. And there is such a tendency in these days among our weaker people.... It is possible for such a man, if he has popular gifts, to be petted all through his ministry, never once to come into strong contact with other men, or to receive one good hard knock of the sort that brings out manliness and character."

Dr. Brooks liked to have ministers share their knowledge; giving such lectures as Norman Macleod's on geology to the weavers at Newmilns. "Would that more of us were able to follow his example." This was what Charles Kingsley loved to do.

Of political preaching, Dr. Brooks said to the students, "I despise, and call upon you to despise, all the weak assertions that a minister must not preach politics because he will injure his influence if he does, or because it is unworthy of his sacred office.

"When some clear question of right and wrong presents itself, and men with some strong passion or sordid interest are going wrong, then your sermon is a poor, untimely thing if it deals only with the abstractions of eternity, and has no word to help the men who are dizzied with the whirl and blinded with the darkness of to-day."

He constantly urged men of all classes to do their best. "The primary fact of duty lies at the core of everything," he said.

He preached his own sermons with the single motive "of moving men's souls." He wrote rapidly, and spoke rapidly, over two hundred words a minute. Two stenographers were always necessary to record his sermons or addresses. His Lenten noonday sermons at Trinity Church, New York, or at St. Paul's Church, Boston, were crowded with the busiest business men of both cities. He could preach with or without notes. He could write a sermon in six hours, at two sittings of three hours each; but he had been studying and thinking all his life for it.

In 1886 Dr. Brooks was elected assistant-bishop of Pennsylvania, but declined.

In 1889 the freshmen of Wellesley College made him an honorary member of their class. He accepted the position, as had Dr. Holmes and others with former classes. He enjoyed meeting with the young women, for he always treated men and women alike, with no increased suavity for the latter. About a week before his death, says an article in the Feb. 15, 1894, Golden Rule, he went to Wellesley College to address the students, and afterwards received them in the large parlors. "I met my class here one Sunday afternoon," he said, "and they asked me questions, ten to the minute. It was very interesting. They did not differentiate at all between the questions that may be answered and the questions that may not."

In 1891 Phillips Brooks was chosen Bishop of Massachusetts, after a heated contest between the High and Broad Churchmen. Dr. Brooks wisely kept silent during the whole controversy.

He possessed, what he said impressed him most about Mr. Moody, "astonishing good sense."

He was consecrated with most impressive services, Oct. 14, 1891, in Trinity Church; Bishop Potter of New York preaching the consecration sermon.

It is said that the regular salary of the former Massachusetts bishop was six thousand dollars. As Phillips Brooks received eight thousand from Trinity, it was suggested that he be given eight as bishop, but this he would not permit.

Bishop Brooks took up his work with his wonted earnestness and zeal. "The amount of speaking that he did was appalling," says Bishop William Lawrence; "four to seven sermons and addresses on a Sunday, with sermons, addresses, and speeches in quick succession through the week."

"He was the most unselfish man I ever knew," says his secretary. "He was always sacrificing himself for others. Not only did he never speak of himself, but he never even thought of himself." He seemed never to waste a moment of time, and yet had time for everything. He was careful always to keep appointments promptly.

Bishop Brooks lived the frankness which he preached. "To keep clear of concealment," he said, "to keep clear of the need of concealment, to do nothing which he might not do out on the middle of Boston Common at noonday—I cannot say how more and more that seems to me to be the glory of a young man's life. It is an awful hour when the first necessity of hiding anything comes. The whole life is different thenceforth."

Phillips Brooks kept his warm heart through life. "Sentiment," he said, "is the finest essence of the human life. It is, like all the finest things, the easiest to spoil.... Let him glow with admiration, let him burn with indignation, let him believe with intensity, let him trust unquestioningly, let him sympathize with all his soul. The hard young man is the most terrible of all. To have a skin at twenty that does not tingle with indignation at the sight of wrong, and quiver with pity at the sight of pain, is monstrous." He thought a young man should "go responsive through the world, answering quickly to every touch, knowing the burdened man's burden just because of the unpressed lightness of his own shoulders, ... buoyant through all his unconquerable hope, overcoming the world with his exuberant faith.... Be not afraid of sentiment, but only of untruth. Trust your sentiments, and so be a man."

Phillips Brooks urged the joy which he always showed in his own life. "Joy, not sadness, is the characteristic fact of young humanity. To know this, to keep it as the truth to which the soul constantly returns,— that is the young man's salvation. Whatever young depression there is, there must be no young despair. In the morning, at least, it must seem a fine thing to live."

He loved his work better than all else on earth. He wrote a friend in England, "I have had a delightful life; and the last twenty years of it, which I have spent in Trinity Church, have been unbroken in their happiness."

Bishop Brooks was courageous. In his sermon, "The Man with Two Talents," he says, "To do great things in spite of difficulties, that is a very bugle-call to many men."

Again he says, in "Going up to Jerusalem," "Oh, do not pray for easy lives! Pray to be stronger men. Do not pray for tasks equal to your powers. Pray for powers equal to your tasks! Then the doing of your work shall be no miracle. But you shall be a miracle!"

He emphasizes this in his sermon, "The Choice Young Man," in his Fifth Series. "Sad is it when a community grows more and more to abound in young men who worship wealth, and think they cannot live without luxury and physical comfort. The choicest of its strength is gone."

Of gambling he said, "In social life, in club, in college, on the street, the willingness of young men to give or receive money on the mere turn of chances is a token of the decay of manliness and self-respect, which is more alarming than almost anything besides."

Bishop Brooks was grandly optimistic. Dr. Samuel Eliot says, "A mother wrote, asking him to baptize her little boy, and he wrote back, 'What a glorious future before a child born at the close of our century!'"

"I don't want to be old," he used to say, "but I should like to live on this earth five hundred years."

"Believe in man with all your childhood's confidence," he wrote in "Visions and Tasks," "while you work for man with all a man's prudence and circumspection. Such union of energy and wisdom makes the completest character, and the most powerful life."

He said, "I always like men who believe terribly in other men."

"Nothing was more remarkable in him," says Canon Farrar, "than his royal optimism. With him it was a matter of faith and temperament. I think he must have been born an optimist. Often, when I was inclined to despond, his conversation, his bright spirits, his friendliness, his illimitable hopes, came to me like a breath of vernal air."

The summer of 1892 was spent in Europe by Dr. Brooks. He wrote Archdeacon Farrar after his return, on his birthday, Dec. 13, "In the midst of a thousand useless things which I do every day, there is always coming up the recollection of last summer, and how good you were to me, and what enjoyment I had in those delightful idle days. Never shall I cease to thank you for taking me to Tennyson's, and letting me see the great dear man again. How good he was that day!... and how perfect his death was!... And Whittier, too, is gone.... How strange it seems, this writing against one friend's name after another that you will see his face no more!... I hope that you are well and happy. Do not let the great world trouble you."

While he enjoyed England, he was thoroughly American. He wrote from London, "I think that the more one travels here the more he feels that, while there is very much to admire and desire in these English ways, the simplicity and directness of our American fashions of doing things are far more satisfactory."

Two weeks later he preached a Christmas sermon at the Church of the Incarnation, New York, for his brother, Dr. Arthur Brooks. This was the day of all days which he loved. He enjoyed giving and receiving Christmas gifts.

He said in his sermon, "One of the very wonderful things about our human life is the perpetual freshness, the indestructible joy, that clings forever about the idea of birth. You cannot find the hovel so miserable, the circumstances and the prospects of life so wretched, that it is not a bright and glorious thing for a child to be born there.

"Hope flickers up for an instant from its embers at the first breathing of the baby's breath. No squalidness of the life into which it came can make the new life seem squalid at its coming. By and by it will grow dull and gray, perhaps, in sad harmony with its sad surroundings; but at the first there is some glory in it, and for a moment it burns bright upon the bosom of the dulness where it has fallen, and seems as if it ought to set it afire.

"And so there was nothing that could with such vividness

represent the newness of Christianity in the world as to have it forever associated with the birth of a child.

"It is a strange, a wonderful, birth.... I do not care to understand that story fully. It is enough for me that in it there is represented the full truth about the wondrous child of Christmas Day. He is the child of heaven and earth together. It is the spontaneous utterance of the celestial life. It is likewise the answer to the cry of need with which every hill and valley of the earth has rung, that lies here in the cradle....

"The humble birth of Jesus in the stable of the inn at Bethlehem was a proclamation of the insignificance of circumstances in the greatest moments and experiences of life."

A few days later, Jan. 14, 1893, Bishop Brooks took cold at the consecration of a church in East Boston, and a soreness of throat resulted. Five days later, Thursday, he seemed somewhat ill, and went to bed. A physician came, but no alarm was felt. Sunday night the throat grew diphtheretic, and the bishop became delirious. Monday morning, Jan. 23, at 6.30, Phillips Brooks ceased to breathe.

His last words, spoken to his brother William and the faithful servants and nurse who stood by the bedside, as he waved his hand, were, "Good-by; I am going home. I will see you in the morning."

The sad news could scarcely be believed. The great, strong man, bishop for only a year and three months, had fallen in his very prime. Men's faces were blanched, and women wept. The poor and the rich had a common sorrow. Even children felt the bereavement. A little five-year-old girl was told by her mother that "Bishop Brooks had gone to heaven."

The child knew and loved him, and had always delighted to meet him. "O mamma!" she replied, "how happy the angels will be!"

On Thursday, Jan. 26, Bishop Brooks was buried. No other funeral was ever like it in Boston. At 7.45 in the morning the coffin was borne from the bishop's residence, at the corner of Clarendon and Newbury Streets, to the vestibule of Trinity Church, accompanied by a guard of the Loyal Legion, of which Phillips Brooks was chaplain. The colors of the Loyal Legion covered the coffin, on which lay some Easter lilies among palms.

It is estimated that from eight to eleven o'clock twelve or fifteen thousand persons passed by the body as it lay in state, and looked once more upon the face of the man they loved and honored. A heavy plate glass was over the face, and the coffin was hermetically sealed.

Rich and poor, children and adults, sobbed as they passed on. A gray-haired and very poorly dressed woman drew a cluster of roses from her bosom, and, with tears flowing down her cheeks, laid them reverently upon the casket.

A pale-faced woman, with a little boy scantily dressed for the winter weather, who could not enter the church for the crowd, begged a policeman to let her in. He replied brusquely, telling her to get into line.

"Oh, but I must see him once more!" she sobbed; "he paid for the operation which gave sight to my boy, and I must see him again."

The people about her were moved by her entreaty, and an usher quietly told the officer to allow the mother and her child to come in.

Meantime Trinity Church had become filled with the various delegations,—from Harvard College, Boston University, the Governor and Committee of the Legislature, clergymen from a distance, theological schools, officers of the Young Men's Christian Association and Young Men's Christian Union, and various other organizations.

The church was beautifully decorated. At the back of the chancel was an arch of laurel, fifteen feet high and nine feet wide, with a spruce-tree eight feet high on each side. In front of this was a tall cross of Easter lilies, and the baptismal font was filled with the same flowers. Roses and lilies sent by friends were heaped everywhere, although a request had been made that no flowers should be sent.

Among the flowers was a cross with the words, "From Helen." This was the gift of the little blind girl, Helen Keller, at the South Boston Institute for the Blind, of whom the dead preacher was very fond.

Just before noon the body, borne on the shoulders of eight strong men, picked from the various athletic teams of Harvard, passed up the aisle of the church, headed by the bishops and honorary pall-bearers. The whole congregation joined in singing "Jesus, lover of my soul," the music broken by audible sobbing. After brief services, while the people remained standing, and the organ played its low, solemn notes, the body was borne out into Copley Square in front of Trinity, and placed on a draped platform, where an out-door service was held for the more than twenty thousand persons who could not get inside the church.

A memorial service was held at the same hour in the First Baptist Church, near by.

After the Lord's Prayer, in which all joined, the hymn beginning,—

> "O God, our help in ages past,
> Our hope for years to come,
> Our shelter from the stormy blast,
> And our eternal home;"

was sung. Copies of it had been distributed among the people. Three cornetists led the singing.

It was an hour never to be forgotten. Eyes unused to tears were wet that day.

The funeral procession of fifty carriages then moved towards Mount Auburn, across Harvard Bridge, through a line of thousands of people. Places of business throughout the city were closed, and the bells upon the churches and public buildings in Boston and other cities were tolled.

When the head of the procession reached Beck Hall, Cambridge, the university bell began tolling, with the old bell in Harvard Hall, and the bells of Christ Church, chiming,—

> "Heaven's morning breaks
> And earth's vain shadows flee."

Two thousand college students, standing several deep, with heads uncovered, were formed in two lines from the University building to the West Gate. Through their ranks, entering from Harvard Street, the body of their beloved preacher was borne. "Never in all our college life," writes Dr. McKenzie, "has there been a burial like his."

From the college grounds the procession moved to Mount Auburn, where the brothers, John and Arthur, conducted the services. Flowers, which the dead bishop loved, lay everywhere upon the pure, white snow,—lilies, roses, carnations, and sheaves of wheat. The fence about the family lot was hung with ivy and violets tied with purple ribbon.

The crowd drew aside to let three weeping women look into the open grave, before the dirt fell upon the coffin. They were three sisters,—servants who had long ministered in the bishop's home, and whose devotion had been repaid by constant appreciation and kindness.

The world went back to its work, but we are never the same after a great life has touched our own. Phillips Brooks said in his sermon on "Withheld Completion of Life," "The ideal life is in our blood, and never will be still. We feel the thing we ought to be beating beneath the thing we are. Every time we see a man who has attained our human ideal a little more fully than we have, it awakens our languid blood and fills us with new longings."

All who ever knew or heard Phillips Brooks will forever strive after his unselfishness, his courage, his thoughtfulness, his eagerness to make the world better.

Bishop William Lawrence, who succeeded Phillips Brooks, wrote of him in the March-April, 1893, Andover Review, "When all has been said about his eloquence, his mastery of language, and his tumult of thought, we are turned back to the thought that the sermons were great because the man was great. His was a great soul. He stood above us; he moved in higher realms of thought and life; he had a wider sweep of spiritual vision; he was gigantic. And yet he was so completely one of us, so sympathetic, childlike, and naturally simple, that it was often only by an effort of thought that we could realize that he was great. Kingly in character, we buried him like a king."

Memorial services were held in scores of churches; in Boston, in Lowell, in Worcester, in New York, in Maine, in Rhode Island, and elsewhere. At the old South Church in Boston, Protestants and Roman Catholics united in the service.

The Rev. Dr. Philip S. Moxom of the First Baptist Church well said of Phillips Brooks, "He was a loyal Episcopalian in the very best sense in which a man can be loyal to the church of his choice; but he was not and could not be confined in the Episcopal Church. He belonged to no church or party or sect; rather he belonged to all churches and parties and sects in so far as they represent elemental truths and express elemental sympathies. The Congregationalists claimed him, the Unitarians claimed him, the Baptists claimed him, the Methodists claimed him; and the claims of all were just, because beneath all these names and party badges is the common human heart and the one universal church of God; and to that human and that church of God, Phillips Brooks belonged." The next generation will not remember the rush of his voice in the pulpit, or the warm clasp of his hand, or his kindling eye, but his influence will go on forever.

As he himself said, "He whose life grows abundant grows into sympathy with the lives of fellow-men, as when one pool among the many on the seashore rocks fills itself full, it overflows, and becomes one with the other pools, making them also one with each other all over the broad expanse."

For such a life there are no seashore limits; no limits of time or space. His words will have fulfilment. We shall "see him in the morning."

www.ingramcontent.com/pod-product-compliance
Lightning Source LLC
LaVergne TN
LVHW030633080426
835509LV00022B/3453